DATE DUE

Brodart Co.   Cat. # 55 137 001   Printed in USA

SOUTHERN FUJIAN

Southern Fujian

Reproduction of Traditions in Post-Mao China

Edited by

Tan Chee-Beng

The Chinese University Press

Southern Fujian: Reproduction of Traditions in Post-Mao China
 Edited by Tan Chee-Beng

© **The Chinese University of Hong Kong,** 2006

ISBN 962–996–233–0

THE CHINESE UNIVERSITY PRESS
The Chinese University of Hong Kong
SHA TIN, N.T., HONG KONG
Fax: +852 2603 6692
    +852 2603 7355
E-mail: cup@cuhk.edu.hk
Web-site: www.chineseupress.com

Printed in Hong Kong

Contents

Map of Fujian showing the Minnan Region

List of Plates

Introduction

■ Tan Chee-Beng

This book has grown out of the research project "Tradition, Change and Identity: A Study of Minnan People in China and Southeast Asia."[1] Minnan, or southern Fujian, is an important region in China that is the ancestral homeland to many Chinese in diaspora. There have been a number of important sociocultural studies on this region in the context of larger south China. Chen Ta's work (1939) is an early comprehensive study of emigrant communities in south China. De Groot's famous study (1892–1910) of the religious system of China is based on his observation in southern Fujian. The best-known modern Western anthropologist on southern China is Freedman (1958, 1966), whose study of lineages has influenced many scholars. In post-Mao China since 1979, anthropologists have been able to do fieldwork again. The best-known anthropological publication in English on Fujian in this period is that of Huang (1989). Wang Mingming (1997) and Zhuang (1996) are pioneer post-Mao anthropologists from China. Wang, a contributor to this volume, is himself a Minnan person who has received anthropological training in both China and the West, and has published widely on his study in Minnan. Zhuang is known for his restudy of Lin Yueh-hwa's famous work (1947) on family and lineage in eastern Fujian. Some other Chinese anthropologists have also done fieldwork in southern China, and two of them, Fan Ke and Pan Hongli, have papers in this book. The post-Mao era has also seen "overseas" Chinese scholars doing research in China, and in the case of Minnan, we have the example of Kuah Khun Eng (2000). Both she (Chinese from Singapore) and Tan Chee-Beng (Chinese from Malaysia) are contributors of this book.

There have been many socioeconomic changes since 1979. Economic liberalization has led to tremendous economic and social transformation in China. The economic transformation of China has been studied and talked about, but there is less attention to the study of cultural traditions. On

Fujian, there are a number of studies on historical and economic aspects (see Tan and Zhang 1999). Some major studies in English include Lyons and Nee (1994) and Yeung and Chu (2000). Mention should be made of Szonyi's study (2002) of the history of kinship practices in the Fuzhou region. Recent historical studies that are useful for our understanding of southern Fujian include Vermeer (1990) and So (2000). Dean (1993) on popular religion in southeastern China is of anthropological interest. There are also Chinese historians writing in Chinese, such as Chen Zhiping, Zheng Zhenman, and Dai Yifeng (see Tan and Zhang 1999), who have contributed significantly to our understanding of lineage as well as to socioeconomic aspects of life in Fujian. In addition, there are some recent works on emigrant villages and Chinese overseas, such as Douw, Huang, and Godley (1999), and Douw and Dai (2000); the latter, however, is on western Fujian.

This book is an effort by Chinese scholars from Fujian and outside the mainland to examine the reproduction of traditions in post-Mao southern Fujian. The renovation of temples and "revival" of lineage activities, for example, provide good cases for studying not only social change but also for reflecting on past studies of lineage organizations and other cultural traditions. Ordinary people understand traditions, or *chuantong* in Chinese, as cultural institutions or those aspects of culture seen as persistent and having a long history and being meaningful to their cultural life. However, traditions are not static, and as Eric Hobsbawm (1983) has pointed out, they can in fact be "invented." Traditions may be understood as cultural reproduction as they are reinterpreted and used in local politics, and that at the same time are able to link people to their cultural past. Using data from southern Fujian, we shall see how traditions are used in local politics — the instrumental aspect of tradition — and the relevance of traditions to cultural identity — the identity aspect of tradition.

In the more liberal post-1978 atmosphere, traditions are reproduced by both officials and ordinary people. While government institutions selectively reproduce traditions and try to influence the ordinary people's choice of tradition, their combined actions of selection and reproduction bring about a dynamic cultural revival. Chapter One shows the official and non-official involvements in reproducing traditions in Quanzhou. Reproduction of traditions involves interpretations. Officials and ordinary people have different views. Even among the officials, there are differences. The local officials, for example, are more concerned about local traditions. They are more sympathetic to certain local practices. Wang Mingming's paper shows that the Bureau of Culture in Quanzhou, when preserving and promoting certain temples, focuses on those that its officials view as having "historical depth," — temples that can attract tourists or are relevant to contemporary politics. Thus the Temple of Tianhou in Quanzhou is greatly supported by the local officials. Tianhou, the Heavenly Queen, is a popular deity among the people in Fujian and Taiwan, and among Chinese overseas, so it is considered politically relevant. In fact, at the Temple of Tianhou, there is a Museum of Fujian and Taiwan Relations. Non-local officials, as Wang shows, are not so concerned about reproducing local traditions. They are more concerned with new cultural forms that are profitable, such as dance halls, sports centers, and cinemas. In spite of all these, the different views and actions have brought about a dynamic cultural revival.

Government officials are guided by the official ideology of seeing popular beliefs and practices as backward and superstitious. Thus, not only do they selectively reproduce tradition in relation to economic and political needs, they also try to control ordinary people's involvement in "superstitious" practices. Wang's paper illustrates this very well. The local government in Quanzhou promotes certain art festivals to counterbalance certain superstitious traditions. For example, a Grand Concert of Southern Music (Nanyin Dahuichang) is organized on the 15th day of the 1st lunar month to coincide with the traditional Lantern Festival, which celebrates the last day of the Chinese New Year. An Operatic Performances Festival is organized to coincide with the Ghost Festival (Universal Salvation Festival) on the 15th day of the 7th lunar month. An International Puppet Festival is organized around the Mid-Autumn Festival on the 15th day of the 8th lunar month. The Nanyin (Southern Music), operas, and puppet shows are all important cultural traditions in southern Fujian. Their promotions actually help reinforce these traditions while at the same time attract tourists. But ordinary people continue to have their own celebrations at local sites and in their own way. In fact, the differences between the officials and the masses are seen in these sites. The activities promoted by the local government are performed at the city courtyard and government-related venues. The ordinary people celebrate and worship at their own local temples.

Wang Mingming's paper shows how the official Bureau of Culture, which is in charge of museums and officially recognized temples, redefines culture to accommodate expressions of tradition. Elements of religious culture are reinterpreted or given another label so that they are not branded "superstitious" and thus official involvement is allowed. Relaxation of control and even promotion of "tradition" is necessary to link Fujian to the world, including "overseas" Chinese, and to accommodate local cultures. In other words, since the people cling to local traditions, which can also attract overseas Chinese and foreign tourists, such relaxation is necessary. Indeed, the official staging of "traditions," such as Minnan opera performance and Nanyin, partly serves to separate these from local religious celebrations, which are officially viewed as superstitions. However, such official sponsorship of "tradition" does not discourage people's own religious celebration; paradoxically, it adds to the thriving of local traditions.

In a way, the Bureau of Culture represents official and élite views of traditions and history. Ordinary people have their own perspective of tradition, which is meaningful to them and which links them to their cultural past. They are active in organizing their local lineage and religious activities, and they have means to secure official recognition and even gain financial assistance for them. Linking their religious activities to the interests shown by "overseas" Chinese, for instance, is a way to obtain official recognition and the resources required to underwrite them.

The masses' practice of "superstitions" can be tolerated and even accepted as long as they are put in the right political rhetoric that erases or rather masks that superstitious nature of events. This is further illustrated in Fan Ke's paper in Chapter Two. In his study of the Ding community in Chendai, Fujian, Fan Ke shows how the stigma of "superstitions" can be rhetorically erased to gain political legitimacy. For example, Party officials are invited to attend a function to celebrate the compilation of genealogy. The compilation may officially be described as the compilation of gazetteers, even though it in fact is the compilation of genealogy. In this way, Party officials would grace the occasion, and the people obtain official recognition.

The Ding trace their ethnic origin to Muslim pioneers, although today they are physically and culturally indistinguishable from other Han people, except for the reassertion of Muslim identity. Interestingly, Fan Ke shows how the Ding use lineage identity as a way to exert their minority status, which entitles them to some social and political benefits. The renovation of the ancestral hall, for example, provides a public display of local achievements. The compilation of the genealogy was partly legitimized and financially assisted by the participation of kin worldwide. The Ding now want to link up with other Hui communities in China and to identify with them rather than with the Han, as a *minzu*, one of the 56 meta-ethnic categories recognized by the state. Overall, Fan Ke illustrates how the Ding use traditions for their identity politics.

The Ding cling to their Muslim ancestry even though they have been sinicized. Their classification as Hui theoretically returns them to Muslim status. Yet instead of ridding themselves of un-Islamic traditions, such as the honoring of ancestors, they reproduce the focus on the ancestral hall to publicize their achievements. To enhance Hui status, they have adopted some Islamic symbols, and Ding business people have established business networks in Muslim countries. Chendai is today known for producing shoes, and there are many shoe factories owned by Ding families. There is a big export trade to Saudi Arabia and Muslim countries in the Middle East, as I gathered from my visit to Chendai in 1998. In a sense, the Ding use both Islamic symbols and the role of the ancestral hall to play out their unique Hui identity. The tradition of ancestral cult is practiced in ways that display their achievement and status in Chinese society, while new traditions are created to project their Hui status. As Fan Ke has described, the Ding ancestral graves were moved to the historical Muslim site called Lingshan (Holy Mountain), which today attracts many tourists, including Muslims from different parts of the world. The graves are made in the Muslim style, and instead of making offerings at the graves, the Ding today offer flowers, a new tradition promoted by the Committee of Chendai Hui Affairs.

Lineage organization had been important in south China, as Freedman illustrated. Lineage activities were revived in the post-1978 period. Scholars have noted the role of Chinese overseas in this revival. Locally, too, important agents have helped in this revival and in bridging lineage leaders with the local officials, who theoretically should not deal with "superstitious" organizations. In Chapter Three, Pan Hongli discusses the roles of Old Folks' Association (Laorenhui) in the revival of lineage organizations in southern Fujian. Established in the 1980s, these associations are encouraged by the state, for they provide a way for the government to simultaneously reach out to and more effectively control the people. However, since they are not considered official organizations, their leaders are able to carry out activities pertaining to Chinese popular religion and lineage organizations, activities deemed "superstitious." Thus the Old Folks' Associations play a double role: they act as a buffer for the government and as a link to the government for the people. They are recognized by the state, and their leaders are core members of local lineages. The associations are involved in lineage "revival." As Pan points out, the important roles played by the leaders of these associations have led to the revival of the Chinese tradition of leadership by elders.

Religious activities are important in cultural reproduction in southern

Fujian. We see this in ancestor halls and in lineage activities. Chapter Four uses the examples of such reproductions in Yongchun to highlight the religious traditions in a rural community in post-1978 Fujian. Chinese popular religion is seen through family-focused and community-focused worship. Family-focused worship is best seen in domestic worship during festivals as well as worship at temples, especially at the village temple. Here, religion is part of a people's social life, and its reproduction is necessary for a meaningful social life. Communal worship dramatizes communal life and publicizes a communal identity. For the people, religious performances express their symbolic values and wishes for a good life. Contemporary political and social realities reinforce certain religious symbols and rites. The wish for cash-earning opportunities is seen in religious worship, and the one-child policy reinforces religious symbolism in blessings for having children, sons in particular, as well as the dynamics in the reproduction of women worshipping the Bedroom Spirits. Although there are various theoretical approaches to the study of religion, Tan Chee-Beng emphasizes that the functional and symbolic approaches best reflect the people's religious attitudes and behavior as well as their own consciousness in religious participation.

In Chapter Five we see religious "revivalism" in another community, which has substantial "overseas" Chinese involvement. In this chapter, Kuah-Pearce Khun Eng shows the importance of "overseas" Chinese in sanctioning "superstitious" activities: ancestor worship and the worship of the popular local deity Qingshui Zushi (Clear Water Patriarch) in Anxi. Religious activities provide cultural capital for the local authorities and villagers to encourage "overseas" Chinese sponsorship not only for them but also for local infrastructure development. These religious activities provide opportunities for local and "overseas" kin to come together. Today, women play major public roles in organizing these activities. This is significant, as in the past (pre-1949) public worship was dominated by men. There is obviously a reinterpretation of tradition.

In the patriarchal culture of China, women are seen as oppressed by men. In Fujian, from where many Chinese emigrated overseas, the migration of men did not relieve women of their suffering; in fact, it brought much bitterness. In Chapter Six, Siumi Maria Tam describes the memories of Minnan women about their life as wives of emigrant husbands. Before 1949, and especially since the 19th century, many Fujian men migrated overseas, leaving the women behind to cope with a hard life. Tam's paper deals with the impact of emigration and migration on Minnan women.

Based on her research on Minnan women in Jinjiang in southern Fujian, Hong Kong, and the Philippines, she plays out the voice of such women. She also describes the contrasting fates of women who migrated to Hong Kong and the Philippines. The women who stayed in Hong Kong had originally intended to join their husbands in other destinations (especially the Philippines) but were not successful in obtaining the necessary papers to immigrate. Despite the women's grudges against husbands who left them, they did not question the patriarchal system. Instead, Tam remarks that they "justify inequality with traditionalism, and resign themselves to a female fate." This is in sharp contrast to the Xunpu women, as described by Ding Yuling, who use their economic achievement to reconstruct their gender status and exert their influence in the community.

In Chapter Seven, Ding Yuling shows that the Xunpu women were not oppressed, and after 1978, business opportunities and economic achievement have enabled them to have more influential domestic and public roles. Ding describes women taking care of their own interests in addition to managing family finances. They play an influential role in an otherwise patriarchal tradition. Not only do they work hard in their oyster farms, they also take charge of selling fish in urban wet markets, while the men concentrate on deep-sea fishing. Under the former collective system, the women were in charge of oyster farms. Indeed, the state-planned economy gave recognition to women's labor and allowed them to have more say and authority in the running of production brigades. This experience taught them collective power and gender equality. The market economy since 1979 provided the opportunity for the Xunpu women to prosper and take charge of the domestic economy. In other words, the Xunpu women have been able to exert their influence and control over their own fate through strategic use of resources and cultural rules. In the words of Ding Yuling, they have turned hard work into financial gain and personal freedom. The economic achievement and increase in social status have provided them with the opportunities to reconstruct their gender status and redefine gender relations. The Xunpu women did not challenge the patrilineal ideology but use their better economic positions and the changing political contexts to redefine the tradition of gender relations.

Overall, this book provides a timely contribution to our understanding of traditions and politics of identity in an important region of south China. It provides new perspectives on the study of lineages, on the roles of tradition and women's status, as well as on aspects of cultural life in Fujian today. The papers in this book show the dynamic nature of traditions that are reproduced by different agents. In post-1978 southern Fujian, the most important agents are cadres and bureaucrats representing the government, and ordinary people and non-governmental local leaders. Between them, various non-governmental and semi-governmental organizations play important roles in bridging the gap between the state and the ordinary people and in helping to reproduce and even reinvent local traditions. The state is officially against traditions that are "superstitious," but the changing economic and political situations after liberalization provide much scope for toleration and negotiation. The more liberal political situation allows local cadres to ignore small-scale religious activities, and the larger celebrations are tolerated because they have economic value, attracting tourists and Chinese from overseas. Furthermore, cadres from local areas share the local traditions and they are therefore more sympathetic than non-native cadres to activities involving local traditions. Paradoxically, official attempts to control "superstitious" traditions actually contribute to their revitalization.

The papers show that ordinary people are active agents in the practice of traditions. They are adept at adjusting to changing post-1978 situations. Adjusting to relevant political rhetoric and organizing "superstitious" activities in the name of attracting "overseas Chinese" are examples of such adjustments that contribute significantly to the revitalization of local traditions. In the case of the Ding, they also revive and reinvent traditions in the name of promoting *minzu* activities, which are sanctioned by the state. The reproduction of traditions is part of the reconstruction of people's cultural life as well as the projecting of local identities. The study of local traditions is very much the study of cultural politics and the politics of local space.

Underlying all this, as shown by the papers in this book, especially those of Fan Ke and Tan Chee-Beng, traditions as meaningful parts of cultural life are embedded in people's mind. They are not easily eliminated by political campaigns. Despite the many political campaigns and the oppression of the Cultural Revolution, post-1978 China has seen the quick revival and revitalization of local traditions, such as the renovation of temples, revival of lineage activities, and resumption of "superstitious" religious activities including ancestor worship and the practice of such private cults as the worship of Bedroom Spirits. It is the survival of traditions as meaningful culture in people's mind and the relevance of their political use in post-Mao China that explain the "revival" of traditions since 1979.

To ordinary people, traditions provide a sense of cultural continuity and remain important in their rhetoric. They thus form an important aspect of anthropological study. However, traditions are reproduced and practiced in context and are always changing, although ordinary people may see them as rather unchanging. The papers in this book discuss the politics of traditions and their relevance to local identities. They contribute to an understanding of the "revival" of traditions in post-Mao south China.

Note

1. I am grateful to Hong Kong Research Grants Council for sponsoring this project, RGC Ref. No. CUHK 4025/97H.

References

Chen, Ta. 1939. *Emigrant Communities in South China: A Study of Overseas Migration and Its Influence on Standards of Living and Social Change.* Shanghai: Kelly and Walsh.

de Groot, J. J. M. 1892–1910. *The Religious System of China: Its Ancient Forms, Evolution, History and Present Aspect, Manner, Customs and Social Institutions Connected Therewith.* New York: Paragon Book Gallery.

Dean, Kenneth. 1993. *Taoist Ritual and Popular Cults of Southeast China.* Princeton, NJ: Princeton University Press.

Douw, Leo and Dai Yifeng, eds. 2000. *West Fujian: Land and Migration.* Xiamen, China: Xiamen University Press.

Douw, Leo, Huang Cen, and Michael R. Godley, eds. 1999. *Qiaoxiang Ties: Interdisciplinary Approaches to "Cultural Capitalism" in South China.* International Institute for Asian Studies.

Freedman, Maurice. 1958. *Lineage Organization in Southeastern China.* London: Athlone Press.

———. 1966. *Chinese Lineage and Society: Fukien and Kwangtung.* London: Athlone Press.

Hobsbawm, Eric. 1983. Introduction: Inventing Traditions. In Eric Hobsbawm and Terence Ranger, eds., *The Invention of Tradition,* pp. 1–14. Cambridge: Cambridge University Press.

Huang, Shu-min. 1989. *The Spiral Road: Change in a Chinese Village through the Eyes of a Communist Party Leader.* Boulder, CO: Westview Press.

Kuah, Khun Eng. 2000. *Rebuilding the Ancestral Village: Singaporeans in China.* Aldershot, England: Ashgate Publishing.

Lin, Yueh-hwa. 1947. *The Golden Wing: A Sociological Study of Chinese Familism.* London: Kegan Paul, Trench, Trubner and Co.

Lyons, Thomas P. and Victor Nee, eds. 1994. *The Economic Transformation of South China: Reform and Development in the Post-Mao Era*. Ithaca, NY: East Asia Program, Cornell University.

So, Billy K. L. 2000. *Prosperity, Region, and Institutions in the Maritime China: The South Fukien Pattern, 946–1368*. Cambridge, MA: Harvard University Asia Center.

Szonyi, Michael. 2002. *Practicing Kinship: Lineage and Descent in Late Imperial China*. Stanford: Stanford University Press.

Tan, Chee-Beng and Zhang Xiaojun. 1999. *Bibliography of Studies on Fujian with Special Reference to Minnan*. Hong Kong: Hong Kong Institute of Asia-Pacific Studies.

Vermeer, Eduard B., ed. 1990. *Development and Decline of Fukien Province in the 17th and the 18th Centuries*. Leiden, The Netherlands: E. J. Brill.

Wang, Mingming. 1997. *Shequ de Licheng: Xicun Hanren Jiazu de Ge'an Yanjiu* (Historical Journey of a Community: A Case Study of a Chinese Lineage Community in Xicun). Tianjin, China: Tianjin Renmin Chubanshe.

Yeung, Y. M. and David K. Y. Chu, eds. 2000. *Fujian: A Coastal Province in Transition and Transformation*. Hong Kong: The Chinese University Press.

Zhuang, Kongshao. 1996. *Yinchi: Zhongguo de Difang Shehui yu Wenhua Bianqian* (Silver Wing: Local Society and Cultural Change in China). Beijing: Sanlian Shudian.

"Great Tradition" and Its Enemy: The Issue of "Chinese Culture" on the Southeastern Coast

■ Wang Mingming

Introduction

In this article, I examine some contesting ways in which "culture" is dealt with in the city of Quanzhou, Fujian province, in southeast China. In particular, I deal with, on the one hand, the work of the Bureau of Culture (Wenhua Ju) of the municipal government in the field of "tradition" (*chuantong*) and, on the other hand, the efforts made by ordinary residents to revive old small temples and their festivals. My discussion is derived from a period of fieldwork within and surrounding the spaces of the Bureau of Culture and those of small temples known as *pujing miao* (temples of wards and precincts) whose histories have been investigated elsewhere (Wang 1995).

Resurgent Traditions

First, I should explain why I have chosen to focus on the two "senses" of tradition that I have just indicated. Like many of my compatriots, I have lived in a nation that tried extremely hard to mediate between "the teleology of progress" and "the timeless discourse of irrationality" (Bhabha 1990: 294). In such a nation, I have strongly felt socially trapped into an ideal of homogenous modernity that has been pushed too far to "assume something resembling the archaic body of the despotic" (Bhabha 1990: 294). The problem of culture in relation and contrast to "superstition" (Feuchtwang 1989) is part and parcel of that "body" of ambivalence and power, and it has been what has deeply intrigued me as a native anthropologist.

From March 1990 to April 1991, I stayed in Quanzhou, conducting ethnographic fieldwork for my London-based doctoral degree research.[1] I was born and raised in Quanzhou. Before fieldwork, my memories of social life in the city carried with them the enduring tensions between what was designated as the "new" (*xin*) and the "old" (*jiu*), which later intrigued me as anthropologically significant in the course of my study. When preparing for my field trip, I decided to examine such tensions.

During fieldwork, the social networks that I gradually developed through my childhood and youth made it possible for me to enter government offices and people's homes easily. I was invited through a personal contact, a former middle school teacher of mine who had become a senior official in the city, to work in the Bureau of Culture as a consultant. Through working there, I gained certain "internal (*neibu*) knowledge" of the state and the local government agencies' politics with regard to culture. Through both official introduction letters and personal contacts, I also gained good access to local historians, temple managers, donors, and ordinary worshippers, from whom I learned a great deal about different views of local tradition.

I attended many banquets. The "festival reunions" of the new and old forms of mutual entertainment took me to Deng Xiaoping's negation of "class struggle" (*jieji douzheng*) from which many people, including my family, suffered in the Mao Zedong era. However, my discussions with local people and observation of their activities somehow made me repossess my childhood memories of some domestic scenes of struggle during the Cultural Revolution. When I was small, my grandmother who lived with us was a "superstitious" person. However, she could not worship deities without shutting the front door — otherwise the Red Guards, neighborhood committee officers, and even my parents would smash the dishes that she took a long time to prepare for all kinds of divinity. During those years, "destruction" (*dapo*) was a keyword brushed all over the walls of the city. Many temples were torn down, and activities with even only a little "feudal color" (*fengjian secai*) were forbidden.

Compared with those "mad years" (*fengkuang niandai*), as many people say in Quanzhou, now the people know how to enjoy greater "freedom" (*ziyou*) or in fact know how to avoid doing what the Party-state tells them to do. Nowadays, most households in Quanzhou have re-created their domestic shrines for ancestor and deity worship. In the public places of the city's neighborhood areas, temples of different sizes, names, and deities have been rebuilt. Tales that even the local government has engaged in "superstitious activities" have become widespread. One example of this is that since the early 1980s, the Bureau of Culture has been assigned by its superiors to protect relics of Chinese tradition that were designated as "places of superstitious activities" (*mixin huodong changsuo*) just a few years ago. To do that, some old temples have been included in the Bureau's cultural conservation projects and have been rebuilt. Local operatic and ritual performances are organized to sanctify both new and old national holidays of China.

The revival of tradition in both the domestic and public domains intrigued me,[2] and a "practical paradox" (*shiji maodun*) also came to my attention. "Tradition" (*chuantong*), "heritage" (*wenhua yichan*), "culture" (*wenhua*), and whatever is associated with the greatness of "being Chinese" is now highly valued by government officials. Nonetheless, the word "superstition," which Western anthropology has treated as the core aspect of the concept "culture," was still widely used in the 1990s in newspapers, on TV, and in other forms of state-owned media to describe the backwardness of the "masses" (*qunzhong*). Constant effort is still made by government agencies to prohibit popular ritual activities. Although the government has generally permitted popular worship of ancestors, the system of territorial temples, the deity cults, and festivals are still defined as "manifestations of superstition" (*mixin de biaoxian*). Annually, around popular festival times, official campaigns against them are organized. These ideological and political actions are often not effective, but they have continued to convey the message that the cultural front (*wenhua zhendi*) should still be "fought for" (*zhengduo*) in the phase of reform. They thus validate the observation that Chinese state socialism and capitalism are "modernizing forces which have brought about the radical 'eradication' or 'uprooting' of tradition" (Yang 1996: 110).

Temples, cultural halls (*wenhua gong*), and museums are "memory places," which people construct to remind themselves of their past. How and why has the Bureau of Culture on the one hand promoted tradition and on the other excluded from its projects of "cultural construction" (*wenhua jianshe*) those equally traditional and cultural practices of the ordinary people? Equally important, why, under government prohibition, do the ordinary residents of Quanzhou spend so much time and resources on reshaping the images of their deities, rebuilding temples, and celebrating festivals?

In answering my questions, historians and officials in Quanzhou often used Deng Xiaoping's conception of the "preliminary stage of socialism" (*shehui zhuyi de chuji jieduan*) to disguise a self-contradiction. It seems to them that in the "preliminary stage of socialism," one has to allow "practical paradoxes" to exist. To the official-scholars, social progress will ultimately lead the country out of chaos, while at the current stage, the pursuit of "logic" (*luoji*) is unimportant. In others words, these scholars and officials see my questions as a manifestation of the "naïveté" (*tianzhen*), which, they say, stems from my being in the West too long.

But I have talked to many other local people who insisted on an explanation. As one of them put it, since the Liberation in 1949, the people (*baixing*) have always been said by the Party to be the masters of the country (*guojia de zhuren*). However, even today, the government still acts in an "old society manner" (*jiu shehui zuofeng*) when "allowing the officials to set [the people's houses] on fire while prohibiting the people to light their lanterns" (*zhixu guanjia fanghuo, buxu baixing diandeng*). Why can this be so?

To work out a "scholarly solution" to the "practical paradoxes," I now turn to more details of the interactive drama of official and popular traditions, which, in my view, has been essential to what has been called "the changing meaning of being Chinese today" (Tu 1991).

Historical Traces of the City

Later it will become clearer that both the official and non-official kinds of temple and festival claim to be the continuities of the "ancient dynasties" (*gudai*). The historical claims of the ancient and the authentic are representations of what is going on in social practice. However, we should not ignore the fact that the history-as-process is the realm in which artificial histories are made and the core source from which these histories absorb their vitality. To begin my explanation, I thus feel that it is important to first provide a brief overview of the regional historical process.

To take G. William Skinner's elegant outline (1985), by the 20th century, Quanzhou had experienced several phases of socioeconomic change. First, from the 3rd century onward, gradual development and commercialization enhanced the urbanization of the region. By the 10th century, the economy of the southeast coast was highly commercialized, and a supra-local network of overseas trade centered in Quanzhou, reaching as far as the Middle East, India, Africa, and Europe, was created (see also Clark 1991). Throughout most of the period between the 10th and 14th centuries, due to government's encouragement and further expansion of merchants' power, the economy of Quanzhou developed and reached its peak. In Skinner's words, it reached such a degree that regional economy was "over-heated by foreign trade" (Skinner 1985: 276). From the establishment of the Ming Dynasty onward, coastal traders were forbidden to trade with the outside world; as a consequence, the Quanzhou-centered network declined. From the perspective of the macro-region, it was replaced in the 16th century by the newly established Port of Yuegang in the Zhangzhou area, which in turn was substituted by a Xiamen-centered network "inspired" by the coming of foreign imperialism in the mid-19th century.

Elsewhere I have described in detail how religion, cosmology, and ritual formed an essential part of the regional history of Quanzhou that Skinner ignores (Wang 1999). If what I have said is right, for the city of Quanzhou the most critical transitional phase is the establishment of the Ming Dynasty in 1368. The walled city of Quanzhou constructed in the Tang Dynasty mainly enclosed an administrative core and residential neighborhoods. On the basis of the old city, later an outer wall (*luoqiang*) was built to extend the city from its administrative core to include the commercial area and its attached religious sites in the south. The government headquarters of the prefecture (*zhou*) and the county were planned on the north-central axial line; on the two portions beside the line, state cult temples, including a "literati temple" (*wenmiao*) and a "martial temple" (*wumiao*), were located and were accompanied by official Buddhist and Taoist temples (see details in So 1991).

Urban planning in ancient Quanzhou represented a local projection of the central order, and this projection remained unchanged even after the Mongol Yuan Dynasty's takeover. However, before the Ming Dynasty, the city of Quanzhou may well be described as a special kind of "multiculturalism." Between the Tang and Yuan Dynasties, Quanzhou's regional system of "world trade" facilitated profound cultural contact between local Chinese cultural forms and religious traditions brought by foreign merchants, settlers, and religious specialists (including missionaries).

Buddhism was the earliest foreign religion accepted by local people. In the Tang Dynasty, Hinduism came to Quanzhou with Indian merchants. Between the 12th and the early 14th centuries, there were also European religious influences in Quanzhou. In the Song and Yuan Dynasties, trade with the Arab world via the Maritime Silk Road was important to local economy and the government's tax income (in the name of tribute). In the Northern Song, Southern Song, and Yuan Dynasties, many West Asian and possibly Southeast Asian Muslim merchants were allowed to build as many as six mosques in Quanzhou (Zhuang and Chen 1980). Even Manichaeism had a place in the suburb of the city (a Manichaest temple dated to the 15th century still exists).

Currently, there is a great number of local historians who are keen to re-envisage the multiculturalism of ancient Quanzhou. To me, this is important, but attention should also be paid to the end of commercial prosperity and cultural diversity and to the emergence of a new kind of cultural politics in the Ming Dynasty. The prominent Chinese thinker, Qian Mu (1939: 663–703), observed that the establishment of the Ming Dynasty signaled a drastic change in the élite view of cultural values. Qian Mu describes this change by the transformation of Confucian philosophical politics from "kingly Confucianism" (*wangdao zhi ru*) to "civilizing Confucianism" (*jiaohua zhi ru*). The substitute of "civilizing Confucianism" for "kingly Confucianism" implicated a new dynastic concern with education and culture, or with creating dynastic order, through what we may call the body politics of Confucian "text/performance" (Zito 1997). Its overall historical consequence is the emergence of "Chinese nativism" as briefly discussed by the anthropologist Eric R. Wolf in his masterpiece *Europe and the People without History* (1982). In my view, this historical change in turn led to several cultural and political inventions in the late imperial dynasties of the Ming and Qing (1368–1911).

After having been ruled by the Mongols, the Han Chinese Ming Dynasty had come to view foreigners as devils and treated Han Chinese trade with them as morally incorrect. Along the coast of southern Fujian, more than 20 garrison towns were built to protect the "Divine Prefectures" (*shenzhou*; an intellectual and official name for what is known in English as China) from piracy, invasion, and illegal trade from the sea. In the sphere of public sacred land in Quanzhou, for example, the portions of Chinese government buildings, temples (*miao*), altars (*tan*), city gates (*men*), and walls (*qiang*) were emphasized. Seven Guandi Miao, temples of the Military God, were constructed in the early Ming to represent the authority and protectiveness of the Chinese state (Wang 1994). Within the city, a network of place administration called "*pujing*" (administrative wards and precincts) was created to function like the *li* (township) and *she* (community) systems in the countryside (Wang 1995). In these *pujing* neighborhoods, temples and memorial halls (*ci*) of war heroes who died in action against "short pirates" (*wokou*; Japanese) and model Confucianist disciples were constructed.

The "maritime prohibition policy" (*haijin zhengce*) that the Ming Dynasty adopted was evidently contested. One indication is the expansion of the smuggling business near the garrison towns on the coast of Fujian, which eventually led to the government's ironic recognition of the Port of Yuegang in Zhangzhou. The second aspect of popular resistance to the maritime prohibition policy was the development of illegal immigration to Southeast Asia. Along with the growth of the merchants' resistance, by the late Ming and early Qing Dynasties, local residents had turned the ward administration system (*pujing*) into territorial deity cult areas. Images and documents originally kept in the community hall, the memorial halls of model Confucian disciples, and the official temples of war heroes were removed and replaced by statues of popular deity cults such as Wangye (Marshal Lords). By the late Qing Dynasty, the *pujing* system had already regrouped into two rival factions, the East and West cult organizations (*dongxi fo*), and had become a system of territorial feuds that created many troubles for the government.

From around 1840 to the Republican era (ending in the mainland in 1949), Quanzhou seemed to have gained a new opportunity to re-create its multiculturalism. Skinner (1985: 279) suggests that the years around 1840s signaled "the end of the dark age of the Southeast." Indeed, from the perspective of the southeastern macro-region, it was a time when Fuzhou and Xiamen in the same macro-region were opened as treaty ports and when such ports began to "inspire the return of overseas trade and the reconstruction of urban systems" (Skinner 1985: 279). However, Skinner is perhaps too concerned with the southeast coast as a macro-region to treat the city of Quanzhou as a center of his regional economic geographic history. If we localize our perspective a little, it should be clear that for Fuzhou and Xiamen, where treaty ports were located, the fortune of economy and urbanism was a great deal better than in the old abandoned harbor of Quanzhou.

More importantly, by the 19th century, local Chinese contacts with foreign cultures had somehow lost their open characteristics. Admittedly, some Chinese intellectuals and officials had by the late 19th century adopted modern social theories of capitalism and socialism as the cure for China's ills. This may serve as an indication of the resurgence of cultural openness in the new age. However, such a culturally open attitude was for a whole century coupled by extremist intellectual-political nationalism and popular moral-cultural panic toward "foreign devils" (*waiguo guizi*). Consequently, on the one hand, as Myron Cohen (1993: 151) brilliantly puts it, in order to create a new society and to justify its creation, "it also required that the 'old' society be defined in such a way as to provide the basis for its thorough rejection." On the other hand, a sense of Chinese cultural essence was re-envisaged as the opposite of foreign imperialism.

Overseas Chinese sojourners (*huaqiao*), who left their homelands in the Ming and Qing Dynasties as a consequence of what Skinner (1985) terms "dramatic centrifugal effects" of the contradiction between economic decline and population growth, became the link between the old and the new, the foreign and the Chinese. In Quanzhou, *huaqiao* were the first generation of Republican revolutionaries and the first to invest in the destruction of the imperial city walls and in the remaking of the city as something entirely "modern and commercial." Meanwhile, *huaqiao* also ironically served to protect and rebuild the public temples of their native places.

Another stream of new social forces was the Republican army from Guangdong and students in the new schools set up either by overseas Chinese or foreign missionaries. According to Su Tao (1982), in 1923, 1926, and 1932, these new social forces respectively organized three major campaigns against superstition in the city. The first campaign was organized by the Eastern Army from Guangdong to revolutionize the city. The second was organized by students in Liming College to destroy religion (*fan zongjiao*). The third was organized by anti-Japanese military organizations to stop a religious parade organized by several popular religious temples aimed at eliminating life-threatening epidemics (Su 1982; Wang 1999: 389–93).

The "Culture" of the Bureau of Culture

When Chinese Communists were still underground in the city of Quanzhou (in the 1930s and 1940s), they were engaged in military and political struggles against the KMT (Kuomintang), the Nationalist Party. Among them were schoolteachers and modern theater performers who were mostly involved in transmitting new ideas and advocating "class-consciousness" (*jieji yishi*). During the anti-Japanese war (1937–45), the force of the CCP's (Chinese Communist Party) underground members in Quanzhou expanded through the patriotic modern theater movement (*huaju yundong*). This was supposed to replace local traditional operas with a new performing art in service of propaganda against the Japanese and the KMT. Later, in 1949, they joined the People's Liberation Army to take control of the city soon after the Liberation.[3] A small group of men and women who led the anti-Japanese modern theater movement were selected to work with a "sent-south cadre" (*nanxia ganbu*) to form "a team of cultural workers" (*wenhua gongzuo xiaozu*), which in 1952 was formally announced to be the Bureau of Culture of Quanzhou (Quanzhou Wenhua Ju 1990).

Because of the interruption of "total destruction" in the 10 years of the Cultural Revolution (1966–76), the Bureau of Culture worked toward transforming old traditions into a new culture. Other governmental organizations such as the Public Security Bureau (Gong'an Ju) and its affiliates worked in a more violent manner to eliminate what the Party had decided to destroy. In comparison, the Bureau of Culture has played a relatively "soft" role by insisting on the enhancement of culture. It has led to the invention of some new spaces for mass cultural activities. These include modern theaters, theatrical troupes, cinemas, dance halls, radio stations, and now TV stations and cable networks (together with the new Bureau of Broadcasting and Television (Guangdian Ju), which was not set up until 1988). It has also worked to protect local traditional "cultural properties" (*wenwu*). The latter aspect of its work in turn involves the reorganization of traditional operatic troupes, the managing of performances and art festivals, and the protection of officially recognized "cultural properties" such as archaeological findings and sites, museums, and great ancient temples.

In any Chinese work unit (*danwei*), internal factionalism has not only created personal or small group divisions among officials but also has influenced the formation of the officials' reading of national policy. For example, during my fieldwork, Director Chen, with a native background, and his newly arrived rival, an ex-army officer who was sent to work with him as a joint director in 1991, quarreled over what kind of "culture" the Bureau should develop. Director Chen was more inclined to promote local traditional culture, whereas the outsider-cadre was much more interested in gaining profit from managing the new cultural forms such as dance halls, cinemas, and sports centers.

There has been some tension and conflict of opinion between the officials of the Bureau of Culture and the subcommittees. For instance, the head of the Cultural Property Management Committee (Wenguanhui) under the Bureau was not obedient to his superiors, the directors of the Bureau of Culture. He demanded greater support for more and more historical cultural properties, of which the directors of the Bureau of Culture would be willing to cover only a small part. A separate analysis of diverse readings of cultural policy within officialdom would reveal the "practical paradoxes" within the government. However, here, while noting its importance, I would concentrate on some more institutionalized spaces and cultural rhythms that have served to signify "tradition" for the state apparatuses of politics and ideology since the 1980s.

A slogan that has been the guideline for cultural work in Quanzhou since the 1980s states: "Let the world come to Quanzhou, let Quanzhou go to the world" (*rang shijie zouxiang Quanzhou, rang Quanzhou zouxiang shijie*). This call for cultural openness is derived from the national open-door policy. However, it has somehow led to a closer link to the city's commercial prosperity and cultural diversity in ancient times. What has excited the officials and many local residents has been the Song junk excavated in the later years of the Cultural Revolution (Zhuang 1991). In 1974, when the junk was being unearthed, a thread of light penetrated the dark age of commerce, the Cultural Revolution, to remind local historians and common residents of Quanzhou's historic prosperity that had been forgotten during class struggle. Recently, a prominent local historian suggested to the municipal government that a large boat-like building should be constructed on the Jinjiang River, the gateway to Quanzhou. He said that within this building, all authentic cultural properties of the city could be displayed and they should serve to inform tourists from other parts of China and foreign countries of the openness of ancient Quanzhou.[4]

The Bureau of Culture, together with its subcommittees, currently manages two categories of building. The first category consists of museums, such as the Quanzhou Maritime Museum, the Museum of Overseas Chinese History in the eastern part of the city, and the Museum of Fujian and Taiwan Relations at the Temple of Tianhou (Heavenly Queen Temple). The second category consists of the nationally and provincially listed important religious temples, such as the Buddhist temples of Kaiyuansi and Chengtiansi; the remaining mosque (Qingzhensi); the Manichaest temple of Cao'an; the Taoist temples of Tonghuai Street, Guandi Miao, and the newly rebuilt and refurbished temple of Yuanmiao Guan; and the state cults temple of Confucius and of the Heavenly Queen (which also serves as a museum).[5] All of these museums and historic buildings have been listed in the national, provincial, and municipal plans of cultural properties. They are officially recognized places where the historical and cultural characteristics of the city are exhibited.

To be more specific, the first category of buildings contains mainly items of material culture and photographic representations of people, costumes, and ritual. These serve to forge a history of Quanzhou's historical relationships with different zones of the "overseas," such as the non-Chinese world, the overseas Chinese communities, and Taiwan. Such museum displays reflect long-term archaeological and archival studies and to a great extent also reflect available historical facts. By visiting these museums, one indeed learns a lot about Quanzhou's important position in world trade in the Song and Yuan Dynasties, its waves of emigration in the Ming and Qing Dynasties, and its people's settlement in Taiwan from the early Qing.

For the cultural workers and historians who work in the museums, the exhibition of their discovered material cultural remains of the past may be their prime concern. However, to the Bureau of Culture, the exhibitions are meaningless without reference to contemporary practice. Quanzhou is the homeland of Taiwanese and overseas Chinese — this is emphasized in the guidelines for museum display. As Director Chen explained, these temples "symbolize the advance (*xianjin*) of Quanzhou people in ancient

1. The Museum of Fujian and Taiwan Relations at the Temple of Tianhou in Quanzhou (photograph by Tan C. B., 1998).

times," and equally important, they "symbolize the predestined ties (*yuan*) between Quanzhou and the three Chinese siblings (*sanbao*)." By the "three Chinese siblings," he means the "overseas" Chinese siblings of Hong Kong, Macao, and Taiwan.

The "institutionalized religious temples," to use C. K. Yang's (1961) terminology, included in the cultural property lists of the Bureau of Culture are museums of such "progressiveness" and "predestined ties." Since the 1980s, it has been widely believed among the "cultural cadres" and local historians that the whole world has recognized Quanzhou as "the museum of world religions" (*shijie zongjiao bowuguan*). It is true that in the past two decades, many foreign scholars have visited Quanzhou and are intrigued by its wealth of religious traditions. However, "the museum of world religions" is a label that the official scholars of the city have promoted. To shape Quanzhou into such a "museum," the Bureau of Culture and its museum workers and historians have mobilized many resources from the Ministry of Culture, the provincial government, and the municipal finance department.

Meanwhile, the "predestined ties" between Quanzhou and Taiwanese as well as overseas Chinese have proven to be useful. For example, the reconstruction of the Heavenly Queen Temple was made possible by donations from its two main branch temples in Taiwan, and Chengtiansi was rebuilt thanks to the joint donations of a number of Southeast Asian Chinese Buddhist masters originally from Quanzhou.

"The cultural work directed by the Bureau of Culture has not stopped at the level of maintaining some exhibitions of materials or dead data," said Director Chen; "it should shape Quanzhou into a lively city and should fill its streets with cultural activities." For this purpose, every year, the Bureau of Culture organizes several art festivals. In 1991, the Grand Concert of Southern Music (Nanyin Dahuichang) around the traditional Lantern Festival (on the 15th day of the 1st lunar month), the Summer of Weiyuanlou Building (Operatic Performances Festival) around the Universal Salvation Festival (on the 15th day of the 7th lunar month), and the International Puppet Festival around the Mid-Autumn Festival (on the 15th day of the 8th lunar month) were organized (Wang 1993: 164–96). The sites of these performing art festivals were chosen to be cinemas, courtyards of museum-temples, and imperial government gate-buildings. However, the performances were distributed throughout the main streets and religious buildings. Each festival also involved a kind of "cultural and art parades" (*wenyi caijie*) which resembled either the marches of imperial spring celebration or popular territorial procession rituals (*yingshen saihui*) in ancient times.

If the rhythmic tradition of performing art festivals was entirely invented by the Bureau of Culture, then why should such a new tradition relate itself to popular religious festivals? The "flavor" of tradition that popular religious festivals provides is of course one ingredient considered by the Bureau of Culture. "More subtly than this," Director Chen told me, "our choosing such dates is based upon the consideration that there is a return of superstitious activities in these years." He continued, "many Quanzhou people love festivity (*re'nao*); so by way of creating festive events, we can reduce the opportunity for their superstitious practices — this is more effective than forcing them to stop their old habits." This explanation conveys several messages that are significant to our understanding of the official discourse of culture. The willingness of a post-Mao government agency to accommodate itself to local popular cultural practices is of course one message. However, using popular skills of mobilization to serve the government purpose of cultural renewal is one more important message.

A middle-aged man with a rather strong spirit of social critique once told me, "The government is wasting our money." Why? "The government's festivals only entertain foreigners and overseas Chinese and have nothing to do with our lives. We ordinary people are still quite poor.

2. A Nanyin performance in Quanzhou (photograph by Tan C. B., 2002).

However, the officials (*dangguan de*) are not concerned with this. They are more concerned with the face (*mianzi*) of the state." I could agree with this critique, but it seems to be untrue that the officials in the Bureau of Culture are spending money in vain. In the past two decades, one important guideline for the work of the Bureau of Culture has been to "let culture set up a stage on which economy can perform the opera" (*wenhua datai jingji changxi*). It is true that the official performing art festivals are mainly designed for foreign tourists and returned overseas and Taiwanese Chinese, but the organizers do not intend to waste money. The development of tourism and the enhancement of overseas investment are other two explicitly expressed purposes of the cultural activities (besides reducing the frequency of superstitious practices).

In Quanzhou, when we observe the keen interest on the part of the Bureau of Culture in creating a local "museum" or a "theater" for the reunion of cultures in plural, we are observing a neat convergence of China's open-door policy and Quanzhou's local élite view of their own history. The symbolic resources that the Bureau of Culture and its officials and committees mobilize to mark the greatness of Quanzhou varied considerably in form and historical origin. Whether a newly established museum or an old temple, whether the new theaters or the old Song Dynasty operatic arts (the Liyuan Opera, for instance), cultural forms serve in their joint force to make a history. This is a history of overseas trade, emigration, and expansion through "ungrounded empires" (Ong and Nonini 1997), which were for centuries ignored but which are by now part of a national politics of cultural revitalization. This particular politics of culture can of course be reviewed as an effort to imagine out of the ruins of history a "community" (Anderson 1983). However, it is a particular kind of "imagined community." It is envisioned on the southeastern coastal margin of Chinese culture with "extraterritorial narratives" of race and culture, or the loyalties of deracinated "transnational communities" (Duara 1997) that contain certain raw materials that may also be interpreted into a rival view.

Small Places, Big Problems: Popular Territorial Temples and Their Festivals

One day in October 1991, I chatted with Director Chen and an American academic, Kenneth Dean, who was also conducting research in the southern Fujian region. We watched a performing art event together, and Director Chen asked for our opinions. Kenneth Dean had spent years in the area and keenly observed the reviving religious traditions. He said that it seemed to him that the performance was "not quite the same as its original traditional form." It was over-reformed, he meant, and was more modern than those "real traditional forms" which he saw in the popular temples. (He had told me that he treated these temples as "real cultural centers.") Director Chen showed a gesture of respect to the foreign sinologist, but he disagreed with him. He said that those small temples that the foreign scholar had regarded as "real traditional forms" did not have sufficient "historical depth" (*lishi shendu*), and as such they did not deserve serious attention. "Most of these temples are only 100 years old, having been built in the late Qing," he said, "but the operas and large temples that we protect are around 1000 years old, mostly." He asked, "Why, then, should we drop the more valuable for the trivial?"

This conversation reveals an important difference between an outsider who has studied and become sympathetic to the long repressed popular religious traditions and an official who has served in his office for years to *only selectively* enhance tradition. I should say that Director Chen's view is only a soft line of official negation of unofficial cultures. In Quanzhou, most officials, local historians, and museum specialists are ready to draw a demarcation line between old cultural forms with "historical depth" and those without it. In most cases, the latter, that is the traditional cultural forms without "historical depth," are simply not treated as "culture" but as "superstitious manifestations." "Superstitious manifestations" are to a great extent defined as "misguided beliefs," "wastefulness," "chaos," and "backwardness" which set up certain counter-versions of what the state seeks to establish (Anagnost 1987; Feuchtwang 1989).

Just a decade before I started to conduct fieldwork, any such manifestations were treated as reactionary to the new society and were eliminated the moment they appeared. Since the 1980s, the government has adopted a relatively softened policy, allowing some of the so-called normal and useful practices to exist or even to be absorbed in its cultural schemes. However, a category of ritual practices and places of commemoration are still prohibited (though often not at all effectively). As I mentioned earlier, this category of popular religious practices is organized within the framework of the *pujing* system, and *pujing* is associated with the popular cults locally classified roughly as Wangye (Marshal Lords) as well as with the Universal Salvation Festival that takes place every year from the 6th to the 8th months in the lunar calendar.

According to the Qianlong Reign edition of *Quanzhou Prefecture*

Gazetteer, *pujing* consists of 36 *pu* (wards) and each *pu* is further divided into two or more *jing* (precincts) (the total number of *jing* recorded is 94) (Wang 1999: 179–243). I visited most of the *pujing* temples and found them to be focal points of popular public ceremonies. Presently, precise statistics have not been kept of the numbers of *pu* (wards) and *jing* (precincts). *Pujing* rituals are practiced today in accordance to the spatial divisions memorialized by the elderly and enhanced by keenly interested people who checked the *Gazetteer*. The oldest *pujing* temples could only be dated to the early Ming, despite the fact that some of these had derived from reconstruction or substantial amendments in the early Qing. The deity cults of *pujing* temples have been known as the Lords of Pu or Jing (Puzhu or Jingzhu) since mid-Qing. These deity cults consist of the following categories:

(1) Regional cults such as Xianggong Ye (Opera God), Baosheng Dadi (the Great Emperor Who Protects Life), and so on;

(2) Popular Taoist cults such as San Qing (Three Purities), San Guan (Three Officials), Immortal Lü Dongbin, and various Xingjun (Star Messengers);

(3) Patriotic heroes who were endorsed as official cults in the Ming and Qing Dynasties;

(4) Historical figures such as Guangong, Wu Zixu, and Generals of the Yang Family; and

(5) Marshal Lords with various surnames.

Some of the deity cults whose origins could well be dated to as far as the Tang and Song Dynasties, and many of the temple managers whom I interviewed, had a common tendency to insist on the ancientness and authenticity of their cults and temples without concrete evidence. However, available data indicate that the temples and their cults were in fact invented through the years between the late Ming and early Qing, and they had experienced changes in the Qing Dynasty and the Republican era (Wang 1995).

Pujing as a systematic order was invented in the early Ming as a semi-governmental organization. For the government, its intended function in the Ming and Qing was household registration, neighborhood watch, and maintenance of "civilization" (*jiaohua*). *Pujing* was thus a regional version of *li* and *she* systems, practiced in other parts of China, mainly in the rural areas. What we now know as *lishe zhidu* (the system of *li* and *she*) was a Song invention of rural social control (McKnight 1971). In the early Ming, it was adopted as part of the imperial state's scheme of *jiaohua*. It is evident that in the early Ming, *pujing* halls had already been built to keep household registration records, hold community meetings, punish misconduct, worship the official cult of the locality, and resolve local disputes. Gazetteer materials also indicate that some of the *pujing* cults were listed in the official local state cults. The cults of the war heroes and civilian models were the core content of this official *pujing* worship system.

From the late Ming Dynasty onward, such a semi-governmental system of place administration and *jiaohua* had begun to be contested. An interesting phenomenon in this local process of resistance is the fact that instead of destroying the official *pujing* system, the local people somehow transformed it into an order of territorial deity cults. This cult order, on the one hand, claimed itself an origin in the official *jiaohua* project and, on the other hand, differed greatly from this specific official scheme in its operations and meaning. The transformed *pujing* system as we now observe in Quanzhou has been a temporal and spatial order of festivals instead of being a strategy for surveillance. The compilers of the Qianlong Reign edition of *Quanzhou Prefecture Gazetteer* were still viewing *pujing* as a local version of *li* and *she*. However, their edited materials show us that they were clearly aware of some unofficial currents surrounding the *pujing* public halls. Popular festivals that often created "chaos" (*luan*) among *pujing*-divided neighborhoods formed one of the main concerns of the imperial scholar-officials. "Madness" (*kuang*) was thus used in their description of them.

Pujing festivals from the Qing to the Republican era occurred at three different kinds of annual event. First, each temple of *pu* or *jing* had one or more "lords" who had birth and death (rebirth) anniversaries. These anniversaries served as neighborhood public events of festivity. At these events, offerings to gods were made in front of *pu* or *jing* temples; the gods' images were carried out of the temple to "survey" the neighborhood territories, and operas were sung day and night at the temple stage.

Second, during the annual celebrations at the major Taoist or regional cult temples, *pu* or *jing* neighborhoods would go on collective pilgrimages to these great temples. They did this in order for their local cults to return to their root temples or to be recharged with new efficacy in larger temples. The key ritual of pilgrimage was procession, whereby selected local young men carried the images of local gods on the streets and marched together with all household representatives toward the great regional religious temples.

Third, between the 6th and 8th months, or more precisely the three full months around the 15th day of the 7th month, *pudu*, or the Universal Salvation Festival, took place. The three months were treated as three phases of rotation, and each phase was divided into 30 units (days). The three phases were known as "setting up the banner" (*shuqi*), "universal salvation" (*pudu*), and "re-salvation" (*chongpu*). During each of the three phases, *pujing* was redivided into 30 temporal units, which formed a monthly cycle of rotation for *pujing* units to take turns to offer meals to ghosts outside *pu* or *jing* temples and in front of household front gates.

Stephan Feuchtwang, who has worked in the same cultural area, has provided a useful conceptual framework with which Chinese gods and ghosts could be analyzed as two mutually constructive cosmologies of community. Gods define the public face of community from the inside, whereas offerings to ghosts serve to shape the same imagery of community from the outside (Feuchtwang 1974). Popular religious practices surrounding the *pujing* system as I briefly outlined above could be analyzed with the same framework as deity-ritual definitions of social space and communal identity. However, the imperial *Gazetteer* compilers add to our analysis a right observation; that is, *pujing* festivals were "chaotic" and their participants were "mad." In other words, it seems to be true that after having been turned into a popular religious system, *pujing* represented something that comprised more than cosmological orders of place. To me, it has been a system of place-centered deity cults that also transcended neighborhood identity and contested the imperial top-down mode of civilization.

In a brilliant historical discussion on Marshal Wen and other deity cults in late imperial China, Paul Katz argues for the presence of "civil society" in popular religious temples. As he suggests:

> In considering the public nature of rituals performed at temples or during festivals, it might be helpful to treat these events as performances that brought differing representations and conflicting ideologies into public space where they could be examined critically. Such performances had the potential to shape speech, influence behavior, and generally contribute to the construction and assumption of social power (Katz 1995: 185).

Following Prasenjit Duara's "genealogy of feudalism" (*fengjian*), one may also look into the public nature of territorial festivals to find their "autonomous societal initiative" which was absorbed in early modern state-building "New Policy" reform (Xinzheng) (1902–08), and in a failed intellectual "civil society" projection (Duara 1995: 147–75). Duara also indicates that "the accommodationist language of the *fengjian*" which was projected at the turn of the 20th century was "soon eclipsed by that of a highly interventionist state" (Duara 1995: 170).

In the late Qing, a handful of local officials did try to find some useful aspects in *pujing* divisions in Quanzhou, and these officials proposed to the emperor that *pujing* should be used as an instrument of "rule by division" (*fen er zhi zhi*) (Fu 1992: 149–55). Nonetheless, what Duara has seen as the "feudalist" and "accommodationist school" of modern state-builders did not really have a major influence upon the political transformation of the city. Instead, there were constant government and intellectual efforts in denouncing and abolishing the "segmentary characteristic" of popular religious cults and their rituals throughout the 20th century.

In the late imperial times, territorial cults and festivals were treated as relatively minor problems in local society by the officialdom. Comparatively, from the "dawn" of the 20th century until the 1990s, similar problems have been viewed as serious. Not long after the city was "liberated" in 1949, systematic inquiries were conducted under the leadership of the Party commission and the newly established municipal government. In the reports of investigation, the "chaotic" and "mad" aspects of *pujing* are emphasized to an extreme extent; the social roots of *pujing* problems were highlighted for purposes of their elimination (e.g., Wu 1985 [reprint]; Ke 1985 [reprint]). A report carried in the *Renmin Ribao* (People's Daily) on 13 December 1989 summarizes for us the 20th-century Chinese state's views for abolishing "superstition":

> The government in the city of Quanzhou, Fujian province, has tightly controlled the out-of-date harmful customs of *pudu* festivals and gained the achievement of saving RMB300 million in the past three years.

> *Pudu* is an old and feudal kind of custom popular in southern Fujian ... Every year, in the high summer, local households used to engage themselves in preparing rich feasts to offer to ghosts ... The custom was once eliminated in the earlier phase of New China. However, recently, it was revived and the revival has become more and more dramatic. Festivals induced expenditures to cover feasts and firecrackers. The annual total expenditure on *pudu* reaches as much as RMB100 million. Accompanying the festivals, there are phenomena of alcoholism, violence, and gambling, which have harmful effects on societal stability ...

> Since 1986, to implement the central committee's policy of socialist spiritual civilization, the Quanzhou municipal government has carried out measures to prevent *pudu* activities from taking place. It has organized propaganda and

inspection teams that have been actively involved in advocating policy and educating the masses in all streets and villages before the beginning of each festival.

[My translation]

Obviously, here "wastefulness" of *pudu* as depicted in the report in a persuasive tone has to do with "societal stability" (*shehui wending*), which is the main issue that the state is really concerned with. The report also describes several forms of the harm of *pudu* to public order — alcoholism, violence, and gambling. I can agree with the argument that *pudu* and other *pujing*-centered festivals are like "carnivals" (*kuanghuan*) that wound the state-projected social order.[6] However, the reason why such "carnivals" have been constantly "nationalized" by the Party-state's "throat and tongue" (*houshe*) as serious problems can be better explained by the failure of the anti-superstitious campaigns conducted by the teams of propaganda, persuasion, and inspection.

The *Renmin Ribao* report is right in saying that "the custom was once eliminated in the earlier phase of New China," and recently it was "revived and the revival has become more and more dramatic." In the past two decades, I have personally witnessed the gradual process of "superstitious" revival in Quanzhou. From the aftermath of the Cultural Revolution to the mid-1980s, I noticed the quiet return of many popular religious practices. In the early 1980s, *pudu* festivals had not yet gone public. They were celebrated at home with rotational feasts among relatives and friends, which conformed to the rhythms of territorial rotations in the late Qing and the Republican era. Although hardly any *pujing* temples were reconstructed, I sometimes saw individuals burning incense at the ruins of temple sites.[7]

By the time of my return in 1990, most *pujing* temples had been rebuilt. Public festivals at these temples had also been fully revived. Operatic and Taoist ritual performances which I did not see occurring at temples in the early 1980s had, by the late 1980s, turned out to be a major part of the cultural landscape of the city. The amount of money donated to temple festivals had increased to such a scale that even the formal theatrical troupes controlled, but poorly financed, by the Bureau of Culture had become interested in making money from "superstitious activities."

From 1994 to 1999, I visited Quanzhou several times. Each time, I saw an increase of festivities in the city. Now, firecrackers have been banned and the Party boss of the city, who has been aptly called a "Doctor of Architectural Destruction" (Pohuai Jianzhu Boshi) by discontented "masses" (*qunzhong*), has implemented an urban reform project. The old houses along the main streets have been torn down and new buildings with a pretentious traditional look have been constructed. Many old *pujing* temples are destroyed in the course of the government's planned urban reform process. However, we now see most *pujing* have new temples that are larger and better looking. They are the fruit of successful negotiations between *pujing* neighborhood residents and real estate developers who were contracted to build the new street blocks. A friend, the president of a construction group, told me, "to do this kind of business [street block rebuilding] is naturally profitable, but it is also rather difficult." Not only does he have to give the government officials bribes, but he also has to compromise to *pujing* groups who normally would demand the return of their local temples, which to him, means spending some extra money.

In part of his wonderful work on cultural heritage, David Lowenthal (1998) critiques "heritage apes scholarship" for seeking to persuade people to believe in the legacy that they have created and "proved." He argues that this special kind of scholarship has done this "all in vain" for a number of reasons. One of these reasons, he points out, is the fact that "adherents of rival heritages simultaneously construct versions that are equally well-grounded (and equally spurious)" (Lowenthal 1998: 249–55). What Lowenthal argues is also true of Quanzhou.

In the course of reconstructing their *pujing* heritages, "superstitious activists" in the city have resorted to the method of "imitation." The "heritage apes scholarship" in the Bureau of Culture has applied "factoids and footnotes" — to use Lowenthal's words again — to prove the authenticity of its re-enhanced tradition. Here, historic relations with the outside world and the nation are emphasized. Once such a tactic of discourse has been invented, it is available to the "broad masses" (*guangda qunzhong*). "Superstitious masses" that belong to the rebuilt *pujing* temples often claim that their temples are as old as the grand temples that the government protects.[8] So, "Why couldn't we rebuild them?" The question was most frequently posed to those who doubt the authenticity of what the Bureau of Culture and other government agencies have called the "places of superstitious activities" (*mixin huodong changsuo*).

Apart from authentication, connection between *pujing* temples and overseas Chinese community has been one other major excuse that "adherents of rival heritages" have often used to persuade officials to recognize the historic values of their heritages. For example, the Huaqiao Ciji Gong (Huaqiao Temple of the God Who Protects Life) has now gained official recognition as a historically valuable territorial temple, thanks to its connection with a charitable overseas Chinese family. Like many other *pujing* temples, Huaqiao Ciji Gong was established on the basis of a Ming Dynasty official community hall. In the late Qing, an emigrant who belonged to the *pu* returned home and established a charitable medical service within the temple. In the late 1980s, her descendants who still live in Singapore expressed the strong hope to revive their family tradition of medical charity. They gained support from the United Front Department of the Party Commission that authorized the refurbishment of the temple and its medical service. The temple now serves as a joint-venture charity organization and a *pu* territorial cult temple. This model was, however, imitated by another Baosheng Dadi temple in the northern part of the city, which could not actually find a strong overseas Chinese connection but insisted that it had one.[9]

Conclusion: "Great Tradition" and Its Enemy

In Quanzhou, what may be called "identity politics" is deeply embedded in a complex process of modern civilization that paradoxically entertains, to use Jenner's (1994) words, the "tyranny of history." The new notion of culture that the Bureau of Culture seeks to designate and promote stems from the project that is aimed at "letting Quanzhou go to the world." However, by also trying to "let the world come to Quanzhou," the government agency creates a mode of cultural production that resembles that of the late imperial civilization (*jiaohua*) in the Ming and Qing Dynasties. The observation that "many other forces for backwardness in the culture have been strengthened" (Jenner 1994: 263) could be explained within this same frame of the irony of modern civilization.

In the social anthropological studies of Chinese culture that I myself undertake, efforts have been made to accommodate fieldwork and archival findings in local cultural settings to the "great tradition" of Chinese civilization. In the late 1930s and 1940s, when the first generation of native Chinese anthropologists went to the West to write up their "community studies," Robert Redfield's distinction between "great" and "little traditions" was not yet fully developed. Nonetheless, as Edmund Leach (1982: 27) notes in his *Social Anthropology*, four core members of this group were already thinking of representing China by doing fieldwork in small places and about "little traditions."

Deriving his observation from a Kaixiangong village, Fei Xiaotong

(1939) was treating the place as a typical example of how "peasant life in China" changed. Writing in the style of the experimental ethnographic novel, Lin Yueh-hwa (1947) sought to deploy Chinese lives in a culturally peculiar world of geomancy and lineage. Treating a Chinese place like an African tribe, Martin Yang (1945) demonstrated a total surrender of China to the ethnology of archaic social mode. Turning a Bai ethnic minority township into a typical place of Chinese ancestral worship, Francis L. K. Hsü (1949) placed his image of China under "the ancestral shadow." Exempting Fei Xiaotong a little from his criticism in consideration of his loyalty to the functionalist school of anthropology, Leach (1982: 122–48) denounces such efforts, of their failures to decipher a place as a holistic cosmology, and/or a "functionally related whole (and 'in its own right')."

However, 20 years before Leach, Maurice Freedman (1963) had written of a "Chinese phase in social anthropology." Trying to escape from the trap of the "bifurcated histories" (Duara 1995) of both sinological great traditions of "oriental despotism" and the African model of segmentation (Wang 1997: 65–111), Freedman was able to become self-reflexive of his life work about "Chinese religion." Past ethnographies of China, as Freedman saw it, were full of pitfalls and weaknesses when concerning themselves only with small places and not being enlightened by classic traditions of the *Book of Odes* and the *Book of Rites*. By way of a mutation of J. J. M. de Groot's top-down model of the *Book of Rites* and Marcel Granet's bottom-up model of the *Book of Odes*, Freedman (1974) was looking at something that he thought would allow an anthropology of civilization to emerge in the theoretical frontiers of anthropology.

Political scientists included in their ethnographic descriptions their concerns about political change (e.g., Chan, Madsen, and Unger 1992; Madsen 1984). Social anthropologists working in the field in the 1970s and 1980s engaged themselves somewhat differently in an ambitious effort to discover what Freedman saw as the "Chinese essence" from the bottom up again. The diversity of peasant cultures in different localities was described in accordance with Freedman's A–Z model of variation of the lineage (Pasternak 1972) or in accordance with hermeneutics through and about social stratification (Weller 1987). Nonetheless, the ambition to discover a peculiarly Chinese cultural logic of gods, ancestors, and ghosts dominated many of the works of anthropologists (e.g., Wolf 1974; Ahern 1981; Sangren 1984, 1987).

As one of the fruits of this ambitious effort, the project of Robert Redfield (1941), which had rarely been mentioned before the 1970s in

Chinese anthropology, had become by the 1980s a prime object of critique. Writing in the new phase of Chinese anthropology, Catherine Bell and P. Steven Sangren have applied the outcomes of Chinese anthropology to work out a reflection on the notorious dichotomy of great/little traditions. They have done so paradoxically with reference to the conjunction of the Chinese élite (Bell 1989) and to place-linking pilgrimages (Sangren 1984). Meanwhile, as we should also note, the Gramscian idea of hegemony had caught a great deal of attention among the core researchers of "Chinese folk religion [or religions, as it is sometimes called]" (Gates and Weller 1987).

A notion of a unified religion in China implicates, though in various ways, a notion of unified ethnicity (Feuchtwang 1991), which ironically only exists as an "imperial metaphor" (Feuchtwang 1992). This much said, the enemy of a "great tradition" is simply within this great tradition itself. Heterodox derivatives of a supposed singular "historical metaphor" are always possible, and such heterodox versions could convey an alternative order by turning the kingly to the demonic and vice versa (Feuchtwang 1992).

It is in the quest for an alternative culture that recently Myron Cohen (1991) has called for "the peripheralization of traditional [Chinese] identity," whereby we are somehow pushed toward a recognition of the heterodoxy as the center of the Chinese nation and culture. Nonetheless, to me, this could hardly mean that anthropologists who work in small communities should entirely follow Leach's suggestion that their places should be constructed into cosmological or political system models to become sufficiently anthropological or representative. Dynastic projects of absorbing heritages either from local popular culture (Watson 1985) or from a ready-made model of the middle-realm of philosophical élitism (Zito 1997) have formed an important part of the "imperial metaphor" which is equally productive in the making of heterodoxies.

However, social anthropologists do not live in the world of the "late imperial China," despite the fact that studies of such a world may shed light on our conceptions of what is called "the new" by the new state. Extending our scope to include a "world system," the transmission of modernity and its consequential "globalization" has been a broadcast epoch. Studies, the number of which is too large to be indicated here, have shown that such a world system of modernity is not quite complete. As a consequence of modernity, a historicity that entirely breaks with history has come about in human "universal knowledge" and practice (Giddens 1990). Ironically, talks of devils, that could only be rediscovered in "traditional societies" as anthropologists used to think, have returned to Anglo-American societies, the centers of modernity's cultural diffusion (La Fontaine 1998). Communication technology has facilitated the expansion of folk culture across the horizons of temporality and space (Bausinger 1990). While linear historians of all kinds are struggling to trace the historical trajectory of cultural breakthroughs, they are ironically also inventing everything from Disneyland to the Holocaust Museum, which highlights the value of our "heritages" (Lowenthal 1998).

Scholars of Chinese culture have for long blamed post–May Fourth Movement Chinese intellectuals and the political mainstream for their peculiar minds of forgetting. "The Chinese had a traditional system" that "was a total configuration that linked the people to the nation ... linked the people to the élite." Myron Cohen thus continues in his informal remarks to the conference on the "Meaning of Being Chinese Today," "this was destroyed by the same individuals who created modern Chinese nationalism, which has had the ironic effect of not providing a replacement" (cited in Tu 1991: 63). It seems important for Chinese intellectuals to be self-reflexive, because it sounds true that they are responsible for introducing a radical enlightenment after having been converted to the religion of modernity.

Ironic as it is, anthropological investigations carried out in the 1990s have demonstrated the usefulness of the conception of persisting culture. Observations of the flow of gifts and the art of *guanxi* (human relations) lead us to believe in the vitality of traditional sociality or what we call "culture of the people" in the new age of socialist state capitalism (Yang 1994; Yan 1996). Meanwhile, Jing Jun, an anthropologist who has focused on the effect of the state-built and state-owned hydroelectric dams in the northwestern China, has not seen the triumph of the project. He thus shifted his attention to the villagers' memorial movement of "locality repossession," which during his fieldwork turned out to be more elaborate than the hydroelectric projection of the future (Jing 1999).

Looking *"up"* to the mainstream, both the official discourse of culture and the scholarly Chinese cultural studies would highly value the spirituality of foreign sinologists (including the anthropologist Maurice Freedman) who have taught how to discover a Chinese cultural essence. Studies of Chinese culture within China have only been allowed after the collapse of the "Gang of Four"; but they have by now developed significant arguments that would have shocked Mao Zedong if he were to hear them. Confucius as sage-kingship and neo-Confucianism form the core pursuits of a young generation of liberal intellectuals who seek to find capitalist spirit and democratic culture in native Chinese "high" religious philosophy (but not popular religion).[10]

To a great extent, what I have learned from studying Quanzhou has its links to the grand scenarios of culture. The two or more versions of heritage that I presented in the bulk of this article are not intended to revitalize the distinction between "great and little traditions." It admits the distinction only when it helps us illuminate a contesting confusion of histories. By looking at the scales of architecture and at the spectacles of performances, we find official symbols to be greater than what may be termed "folk culture" ("superstitious festivals" in this case). The history that the Bureau of Culture is trying to make also resembles the "great tradition" that Redfield was advocating. Being aimed at driving local society toward a linear history of regional and, ultimately, national as well as transnational progress (now viewed as economic development in China), such a "great tradition" does look a lot more cosmopolitan than the local celebrations. However, it is "sadly," as some officials say, not the only tradition, and the cultures (or perhaps the "lesser cultures" or "non-cultures") of superstition "dirty the face of socialism" by setting up obstacles to its realization of the intended break-with-history history.

Robert Redfield (1941: 360) was looking forward to seeing "the extension of modern Euro-American ways into old societies." In contrast, ambivalence has been widely felt among the cultural cadres in Quanzhou. While being glorified by the tradition that they invented, officials in the Bureau of Culture also have a feeling of "sadness" (*bei'ai*). As one of them said, "after more than 40 years of cultural reconstruction, we still see backward masses who tie themselves to superstition and by so doing become indifferent to the real culture of the Bureau of Culture." As I have tried to point out here, such a sense of "sadness" has sprung less from "social reality" itself than from the official ignorance of the fact that both "great and little traditions" are based upon a "time-before."

Anthropological researchers of culture are indeed enabled by our discipline to look at the peripheries of societies and nations as their cores. Living and working with local persons and materials, I have, to use a Chinese concept, "sensed" (*tihui*) the centrality of the natives' points of view of ordinary people and the micro-cosmology of work units of the state apparatus. However, the sense of centrality on the margin does not induce a requirement to find a unitary essence in the cultures that we study; nor does it require us to adopt the tactic of treating popular little tradition as the great one (and attempting to centralize it). What I have found to be a demand is not to pose the natives' points of view against foreign imperialism but is the necessity to "articulate that archaic ambivalence that informs modernity" (Bhabha 1990: 294) within my home country.

Almost a century ago, the first generation of modern Chinese nationalists engaged themselves in searching for a modern state for the old "central kingdom" (*zhongguo*). Then, these ancestors of revolution were faced with a dilemma. Most of them chose to become Republicans instead of adopting a constitutional monarchist line of reform like Yuan Shikai did. To build a republic, emperors were forced to leave the Forbidden City. Unlike the old peasant rebels, the new Chinese politicians refused (most of the time pretentiously) to become new emperors, perhaps because they held the revolutionary faith that "the people" (*renmin*) should be the collective master of the country. Yet, it was the large group that was called *renmin* that induced a great suspicion among the nationalists. "The people" were like "a dish of loose sand" (*yipan sansha*). There was a long tradition of familialism among them. Belonging to the family, the extended family, the lineage, and native place was the sense of identity prevalent among ordinary people. Such kind of identity represented not simply a difficulty for national mobilization; it was in addition an ideological obstacle or an imagined enemy to the new project of state-builders and to the formation of "state-national race" (*guozu*), to use Sun Yat-sen's term.[11]

For the entire 20th century, mass mobilization campaigns known as *yundong* have dominated the national politics of China. Each campaign has its distinctive call and mode of motion. However, the campaigns have a common target, which is the people or the masses. The people are like the uncooked barbarians of the imperial phase. Moved by the callings of campaigns, they may become, like cooked barbarians, the dynamics of civilization. Remaining as uncookable "hard rocks" (*shitou*) or "uncraftable rotten trees" (*xiumu*) to the progressive cultural apparatus of the state, they may just push the present into the past and reproduce the "tyranny of history" in China. So, what we have observed on the economically advanced coastal region is in fact two or more manifestations of the "tyranny of history." The *yundong* culture of 20th-century China resembles that of the late imperial Chinese civilizing (*jiaohua*) project, despite the fact that it has always been described as a historical breakthrough.[12] The enemy — whether imagined or real — of the "great tradition" invented by the Bureau of Culture of Quanzhou is the uncookable "hard rocks" of local bonds, which form an order of chaos and endanger the delocalizing nation-state.

What has just been said does not lead to the argument that the particular historical heritages of Quanzhou can easily be distinguished into localist and supra-localist traditions. In fact, throughout the imperial dynasties until the late 20th century, local bonds in this area have not simply meant territorially confined relationships. Demographic and cultural mobility within and beyond the confines of China have been demonstrated to be one of their core aspects. To a great extent, the open-door policy in the last two decades has relied heavily on the overseas Chinese communities, whose "predestined ties" in history have been initially reconnected to China through the prohibited lineage and territorial bonds and their folklore. The despotic character of the "great tradition" is thus manifested in the way in which it refuses to render recognition to what it has treated as its own "cultural capital."

Notes

1. Much of the materials amassed during the period are included in my thesis (Wang 1993) and two articles (Wang 1994, 1995). With regard to the history and cultural change of Quanzhou, I have published a book (Wang 1999). My fieldwork was made possible by the British Council, London University Central Research Fund, and a Postgraduate Research Award from SOAS. I am grateful to these institutions as well as to those who helped with my studies in London and with my fieldwork in Quanzhou. I am grateful to Mr. Chen, the former Director of the Bureau of Culture of Quanzhou, who offered his help. Nevertheless, my view of culture is quite different from his.
2. Field researchers in other parts of southeast China have observed similar phenomenon. For example, see Dean (1993) and Yang (1996).
3. I interviewed the leader of the movement Mr. Lu, who was still alive in 1991.
4. This is from a personal communication.
5. Richard Pearson, Li Min, and Li Guo (1999) have furnished a comprehensive survey of these temple relics.
6. In fact, Duara (1995: 236) has argued that Chinese carnivals such as that of *gelaohui* are the "signs of the dispersed real" which fail the national narrative of linear history.
7. It was widely known that these sites were deserted. Private households, including those of the officials, were too scared of the spirits of gods and demons to occupy the places. Thus, only a handful of small factories dared to take these places for their use. Tales were also widespread about the revenge that gods might impose upon those who transgressed or "wounded" (*shang*) the walls and floors of the temples. For example, a local leader in a *pu* in south

Quanzhou was said to have died of cancer after having torn down a wall of a small temple.

8. In the interesting article "Villagers and Popular Resistance in Contemporary China," Li Lianjiang and Kevin J. O'Brien (1996) examine three possible groupings of popular attitudes toward policy in the countryside. These include "complaint villagers" (*shunmin*), "recalcitrants" (*dingzihu*), and "policy-based resisters" (*diaomin*) who have reacted quite differently in their encounters with policy implementation teams. In the local resistance to government's urban reform project, these three groupings of ordinary residents can also be found. However, I have found that the difference between popular compliance and opposition has not influenced the general outcome, the revival of "superstition."

9. In addition to the problem of popular "imitation," today, officials working in the sphere of culture in Quanzhou are faced with several other difficult problems. It seems to be a tendency for the *pujing* system to merge with the semi-government organization of residents' committees (*juweihui*). Originally, *pujing* spatial divisions corresponded with those of *juweihui*, which were in effect invented in the early 1950s as replacements of the Republican place organization system, modeled on the Ming and Qing *pujing* system. Since the establishment of *juweihui* in the 1950s (once renamed rural communes and brigade in Mao's time), *pujing* has been defined and treated in official discourse and political practice as something reactionary to the new local administration system. However, nowadays, those who work in the *juweihui* are normally those who notify local households about the happenings of *pujing* temples and dates of *pudu* territorial rotation. Furthermore, temple areas with better economic conditions tend to attract local historians and archaeologists to write historical records for their temples and deities. In fact, the Quanzhou Taoist Culture Research Society has accepted several such requests, and its informal journal *Taoist Culture in Quanzhou* has published a number of articles based on privately funded projects. Moreover, the official opera troupes under the control and finance of the Bureau of Culture are now benefiting financially by performing for "places of superstitious activities."

10. I have critically outlined schools of Chinese cultural studies that have developed since the late 1990s (Wang 2000).

11. The concept "the people" has been treated in Chinese studies mainly as "peasantry," and in recent discussions, we see interesting differences between two ways of treating the people's conception of emperorship. Faure (1999) seems to argue that a concept of the emperor exists in the peasant Chinese conception of society. Anagnost (1987) in her earlier discussion describes instead a dramatic performance of the emperor as opposition to the contemporary state politics of culture.

12. Of course we should try to suggest that *jiaohua* was a kind of nativist

movement aimed at creating a modern Chinese national citizenship; but it was obviously intended as a project of "universal knowledge" (Gellner 1983) that inspired modern Chinese self-consciousness of a "universal Chinese culture."

References

Ahern, Emily Martin. 1981. *Chinese Ritual and Politics*. Cambridge: Cambridge University Press.

Anagnost, Ann. 1987. Politics and Magic in Contemporary China. *Modern China* 13(1): 40–61.

Anderson, Benedict. 1983. *Imagined Communities: Reflection on the Origin and Spread of Nationalism*. London: Verso.

Bausinger, Hermann. 1990. *Folk Culture in a World of Technology*. Elke Dettmer, trans. Bloomington, IN: Indiana University Press.

Bell, Catherine. 1989. Religion and Chinese Culture: Toward an Assessment of Popular Religion. *History of Religions* 29(1): 37–57.

Bhabha, Homi K. 1990. DissemiNation: Time, Narrative, and the Margins of the Modern Nation. In Homi K. Bhabha, ed., *Nation and Narration*, pp. 291–322. London: Routledge.

Chan, Anita, Richard Madsen, and Jonathan Unger. 1992. *Chen Village under Mao and Deng*. Berkeley: University of California Press.

Clark, Hugh. 1991. *Community, Trade, and Networks: Southern Fujian Province from the Third to the Thirteenth Century*. New York: Cambridge University Press.

Cohen, Myron. 1991. Being Chinese: The Peripheralization of Traditional Identity. In Tu Wei-ming, ed., *The Living Tree: The Changing Meaning of Being Chinese Today*, pp. 88–108. Stanford: Stanford University Press.

———. 1993. Cultural and Political Inventions in Modern China: The Case of the Chinese "Peasant." *Daedalus* 122(2): 151–70.

Dean, Kenneth. 1993. *Taoist Ritual and Popular Cults of Southeast China*. Princeton, NJ: Princeton University Press.

Duara, Prasenjit. 1995. *Rescuing History from the Nation: Questioning Narratives of Modern China*. Chicago: University of Chicago Press.

———. 1997. Nationalists among Transnationals: Overseas Chinese and the Idea of China, 1900–1911. In Ong Aihwa and Donald M. Nonini, eds., *Ungrounded Empires: The Cultural Politics of Modern Chinese Transnationalism*, pp. 39–60. New York: Routledge.

Faure, David. 1999. The Emperor in the Village: Representing the State in South China. In Joseph P. McDermott, ed., *State and Court Ritual in China*, pp. 267–98. Cambridge: Cambridge University Press.

Fei, Xiaotong. 1939. *Peasant Life in China: A Field Study of Country Life in the Yangtze Valley*. London: Routledge and Kegan Paul.

Feuchtwang, Stephan. 1974. Domestic and Communal Worship in Taiwan. In Arthur P. Wolf, ed., *Religion and Ritual in Chinese Society*, pp. 105–29. Stanford: Stanford University Press.

———. 1989. The Study of Chinese Popular Religion in the PRC. *Revue Européenne des Sciences Sociales*, no. 84.

———. 1991. A Chinese Religion Exists. In Hugh Baker and Stephan Feuchtwang, eds., *An Old State in New Settings: Studies in the Social Anthropology of China in Memory of Maurice Freedman*, pp. 139–61. Oxford: JASO.

———. 1992. *The Imperial Metaphor: Popular Religion in China*. London: Routledge.

Freedman, Maurice. 1963. A Chinese Phase in Social Anthropology. *The British Journal of Sociology* 14(1): 1–19.

———. 1974. On the Sociological Study of Chinese Religion. In Arthur P. Wolf, ed., *Religion and Ritual in Chinese Society*, pp. 19–41. Stanford: Stanford University Press.

Fu, Jin Xing. 1992. *Quanshan Caipu* (Picking up Jades in the Mountains of Quanzhou). Quanzhou: Office of Local Gazetteers.

Gates, Hill and Robert P. Weller. 1987. Hegemony and Chinese Folk Ideologies: An Introduction. *Modern China* 13(1): 3–16.

Gellner, Ernest. 1983. *Nations and Nationalism*. Oxford: Blackwell.

Giddens, Anthony. 1990. *The Consequences of Modernity*. Cambridge: Polity.

Hsü, Francis L. K. 1949. *Under the Ancestors' Shadow: Chinese Culture and Personality*. London: Routledge and Kegan Paul.

Jenner, William J. F. 1994. *The Tyranny of History: The Roots of China's Crisis*. Harmondsworth: Penguin Books.

Jing, Jun. 1999. Villages Dammed, Villages Repossessed: A Memorial Movement in Northwest China. *American Ethnologist* 26(2): 324–43.

Katz, Paul. 1995. *Demon Hordes and Burning Boats: The Cult of Marshal Wen in Late Imperial Chekiang*. New York: The State University of New York Press.

Ke, Jianrui. 1985 [reprint]. Quanzhou Pudu Fengsu Kao (An Investigation of Pudu Customs in Quanzhou). In *Quanzhou Jiu Fengsu Ziliao Huibian* (A Collection of Materials of Old Customs in Quanzhou), pp. 143–50. Quanzhou: Minzheng Ju and Fangzhiban.

La Fontaine, Jean S. 1998. *Speak of the Devil: Tales of Satanic Abuse in Contemporary England*. Cambridge: Cambridge University Press.

Leach, Edmund. 1982. *Social Anthropology*. London: Fontana.

Li, Lianjiang and Kevin J. O'Brien. 1996. Villagers and Popular Resistance in Contemporary China. *Modern China* 22(1): 28–61.

Lin, Yueh-hwa. 1947. *The Golden Wing: A Sociological Study of Chinese Familism*. London: Kegan Paul.

Lowenthal, David. 1998. *The Heritage Crusade and the Spoils of History*. Cambridge: Cambridge University Press.

Madsen, Richard. 1984. *Morality and Power in a Chinese Village*. Berkeley: University of California Press.

McKnight, Brian K. 1971. *Village and Bureaucracy in Southern Song China*. Chicago: University of Chicago Press.

Ong, Aihwa and Donald M. Nonini, eds. 1997. *Ungrounded Empires: The Cultural Politics of Modern Chinese Transnationalism*. New York: Routledge.

Pasternak, Burton. 1972. *Kinship and Community in Two Chinese Villages*. Stanford: Stanford University Press.

Pearson, Richard, Li Min, and Li Guo. 1999. Quanzhou: Archaeology and Political Economy of an Ancient World Port City. Unpublished manuscript.

Qian, Mu. 1939. *Guoshi Dagang* (Outline of National History). Shanghai and Beiping: Shangwu Yinshuguan.

Quanzhou Wenhua Ju. 1990. Quanzhou Wenhua Ju Gongzuo Huibao (A Work Report of the Bureau of Culture in Quanzhou). Unpublished document.

Redfield, Robert. 1941. *The Folk Culture of Yucatan*. Chicago: University of Chicago Press.

Sangren, P. Steven. 1984. Great and Little Traditions Reconsidered: The Question of Cultural Integration in China. *Journal of Chinese Studies* 1(5): 1–24.

———. 1987. *History and Magical Power in a Chinese Community*. Stanford: Stanford University Press.

Skinner, G. William. 1985. Presidential Address: The Structure of Chinese History. *The Journal of Asian Studies* 44(2): 271–92.

So, Kee-Long. 1991. *Tang Song Shidai Minnan Quanzhou Shidi Lungao* (Papers on the Historical Geography of Quanzhou, Southern Fujian during the Tang and Song Periods). Taipei: Shangwu Yinshuguan.

Su, Tao. 1982. Dageming Hou Quanzhou de Sanci Pomie Yundong (Three Campaigns Aimed at Abolishing Superstition in Quanzhou after the Great Revolution). *Quanzhou Wenshi Ziliao* (Historical and Cultural Materials of Quanzhou), issue 13.

Tu, Wei-ming, ed. 1991. *The Living Tree: The Changing Meaning of Being Chinese Today*. Stanford: Stanford University Press.

Wang, Mingming. 1993. Flowers of the State, Grasses of the People: Yearly Rites and Aesthetics of Power in Quanzhou, Southeast China. Ph.D. Thesis. London University.

———. 1994. Quanzhou: The Chinese City as Cosmogram. *Cosmos* 16(1): 3–25.

———. 1995. Place, Administration, and Territorial Cults in Late Imperial China: A Case Study from South Fujian. *Late Imperial China* 16: 33–78.

———. 1997. *Shehui Renleixue yu Zhongguo Yanjiu* (Social Anthropology and Sinology). Beijing: Sanlian Shudian.

———. 1999. *Shiqu de Fanrong: Yizuo Laocheng de Lishi Renleixue Kaocha* (The

Declined Prosperity: A Historical Anthropology of an Old City). Hangzhou: Zhejiang Renmin Chubanshe.

——. 2000. Guoqu Shinian Wenhua Yanjiu de Neizai Kunjing (The Internal Crises of Cultural Studies in the Past Ten Years). *Nanfang Wentan* (Southern Forum) 2000(1): 2–11.

Watson, James. 1985. Standardizing the Gods: The Promotion of T'ien Hau (Empress of Heaven) along the South China Coast, 960–1960. In David Johnson, Andrew J. Nathan, and Evelyn S. Rawski, eds., *Popular Culture in Late Imperial China*, pp. 292–324. Berkeley: University of California Press.

Weller, Robert P. 1987. *Unities and Diversities in Chinese Religion*. London and New York: Macmillan.

Wolf, Arthur P., ed. 1974. *Religion and Ritual in Chinese Society*. Stanford: Stanford University Press.

Wolf, Eric R. 1982. *Europe and the People without History*. Berkeley: University of California Press.

Wu, Zaoting. 1985 [reprint]. Quanzhou Dongxi Fo (The Eastern and Western Cult Factions in Quanzhou.) In *Quanzhou Jiu Fengsu Ziliao Huibian* (A Collection of Materials of Old Customs in Quanzhou), pp. 165–71. Quanzhou: Minzheng Ju and Fangzhiban.

Yan, Yunxiang. 1996. *The Flow of Gifts: Reciprocity and Social Networks in a Chinese Village*. Stanford: Stanford University Press.

Yang, C. K. 1961. *Religion in Chinese Society: A Study of Contemporary Social Functions of Religion and Some of Their Historical Factors*. Berkeley: University of California Press.

Yang, Martin M. C. 1945. *A Chinese Village: Taitou, Shantung Province*. New York: Columbia University Press.

Yang, Mayfair M. H. 1994. *Gifts, Favors, and Banquets: The Art of Social Relationship in China*. Ithaca, NY: Cornell University Press.

——. 1996. Tradition, Travelling Anthropology, and the Discourse of Modernity in China. In Henrietta L. Moore, ed., *The Future of Anthropological Knowledge*, pp. 93–114. London: Routledge.

Zhuang, Weiji. 1991. Quanzhou Songchuan Wei Pujia Sichuan Kao (The Belonging of the Song Boat in Quanzhou to the Family of the Pus: An Investigation). In *China and the Maritime Silk Roads, Vol. 1*, pp. 344–53. Fuzhou: People's Publishing House.

Zhuang, Weiji and Chen Dasheng. 1980. Quanzhou Yisilanjiao Sizhi de Xin Yanjiu (A New Study of Islamic Mosques in Quanzhou). *Quanzhou Wenshi* (Culture and History in Quanzhou) 4: 1–110.

Zito, Angela. 1997. *Of Body and Brush: Grand Sacrifice as Text/Performance in Eighteenth-Century China*. Chicago: University of Chicago Press.

Glossary

Baosheng Dadi	保生大帝
Cao'an	草庵
Chengtiansi	承天寺
chongpu	重普
dongxi fo	東西佛
Guangdian Ju	廣電局
Guangong	關公
Huaqiao Ciji Gong	花橋慈濟宮
Kaiyuansi	開元寺
Liyuan	梨園
Lü Dongbin	呂洞賓
Nanyin Dahuichang	南音大會唱
pudu	普度
pujing miao	鋪境廟
San Guan	三官
San Qing	三清
Tonghuai Street	通淮街
wenyi caijie	文藝踩街
Wu Zixu	伍子胥
Xingjun	星君
Yuanmiao Guan	元妙觀

2

Traditionalism and Identity Politics among the Ding Hui Community in Southern Fujian

■ Fan Ke

Introduction

This paper examines traditionalism, political legitimization, and identity politics among a Hui community in southern Fujian.[1] I use the term traditionalism in Max Weber's sense. According to Weber (1973 [1946]: 296), traditionalism "should refer to the psychic attitude-set for the habitual workday and to the belief in the everyday routine as an inviolable norm of conduct." In other words, traditionalism could be considered an aspiration to preserve, stabilize, and strengthen tradition (Fan 2001: 8), and it involves social continuity and cohesion (see Shils 1981).

There are several concepts or notions in the field of China study that refer to this humanistic aspiration, such as "cultural grammar" (Metzger 1977: 15) and "familism" (Yang 1965 [1945]). More specifically, Fei Xiaotong (Fei and Li 1998) addresses it by the notion of cultural driving force. It is this force that drives people to realize their ambition in life. As Fei (1939) points out, people in a Chinese context are concerned about how to "honor ancestors" (*guangzong yaozu*) and how to "benefit later generations" (*huiji zisun*). Familism is thus something genealogical, involving an idea of continuation of family lineage (Harrell 1985) in a manner ethically expected to be recognized by outsiders. This Chinese familism is, to a great extent, characterized by a set of relationships related to the practice of ancestor worship.

Sinological anthropologists are familiar with this topic, having been influenced by British political anthropology. However, lineage organization as social construction determined by this cultural grammar still needs exploration at the ideological level. China anthropologists in the West rarely paid attentions to this, an exception being Myron Cohen (1990), who explores symbolism and ritual arrangement of lineage organization in a north China village. Neglecting to explore the humanistic aspirations of cosmopolitan Chinese culture, many relevant works have contributed to, as James Watson (1986) noted, a Freedmanian paradigm to sinological anthropology. These anthropologists failed to identify the cultural meaning of the basic principle of the kinship system in Chinese society.

During the past two decades, however, some anthropologists have questioned the authenticity of the importance of kinship system in non-Western societies. Research topics no longer exclusively concentrate on traditional subjects such as social organization, social structure, family, marriage, and rituals. They are now more likely to be subjective, and include such areas as identity, gender, discourse, and so forth. For some anthropologists, an assumption underlying this change is that tradition is only valid as it relates to serving the present. I agree with the view of "inventing traditions" (Hobsbawm 1983), but I also think that underneath the forms of invention there is something that is essentially sustained.

Although scholars of the present generation have been paying less attention to some of the traditional concerns of anthropology, there is no reason to think that these concerns have entirely lost their significance. It is more useful to our understanding of contemporary Chinese society to revisit these concerns in conjunction with the emergence of modernity.

In the following pages, I consider familism as the core value of the lineage system that represents Chinese traditionalism. At the same time, I treat the construction of ethnic identity, which is underlined by the representation of "being ethnic" (Harrell 2001) in contemporary China, as one of the consequences of modernity (Giddens 1990). By so doing, I treat the revival of lineage activities at the center of the revitalization movement (Wallace 1956) in the past two decades, in order to exemplify the reciprocal nature of the exchange between traditionalism and modernity. In my analysis, I focus on how historical resources became a means of serving identity politics on the one hand, while pursuing ethnic representation on the other hand. In the process, people are able to strengthen familism through reviving lineage activities. Paraphrasing Bourdieu, as a manifestation of the social use of kinship, the revitalization of lineage activities taking place in the framework of ethnic construction reifies reciprocal exchange between traditionalism and modernity. Specifically, it is also a way through which relevant agencies accumulate symbolic capital (Bourdieu 1990: 112–21).

The Ding Descent Group and the Local Context

The scholarly community has recognized the importance of lineage organization to Chinese society, and much of their discussion has considered it as playing a central role in bringing other cultural and social factors into operation. This interpretation, as James Watson (1986) argues, has suggested that "corporately owned land or some other forms of material property is essential to hold people together during the formative stages of Chinese descent groups." In other words, in Watson's criticism, the lineage system for many scholars was economically determined, functioning to control both kinfolk and material properties. This assumption, however, fails to explain why the lineage activities, and of course other forms of folk tradition, have been vividly revitalized in the recent decades, after the country suffered so many waves of political movement since 1949.

The revitalization of lineage activity today shows that traditionalism has never stepped down from the historical stage. Rather, it has found a way to maintain its vitality. Traditionalism can in some ways serve modernity, as long as its validation can be confirmed by its service. The revitalization of lineage activity in contemporary China supports this suggestion. As I discuss in this article, lineage heritage for the Ding kin in Chendai township, Jinjiang city in Fujian has become a manageable social resource or a means of serving their pursuit of ethnic representation in their identity politics. Also, the Ding leadership uses this resource to underscore the construction of ethnic identity that has eventually helped the restoration of their lineage organization, which has been reinvented to articulate in a particular context of ethnic construction.

Chendai township is located in northeastern Jinjiang plain, a few miles south of Quanzhou, a city with a long period of maritime trade in Chinese history (Clark 1991; Wang 1999; Kuwabara 1935). It is said that the 19,000 residents surnamed Ding are descended from maritime foreign Muslim traders, and they now represent 27 percent of the township's population. Prior to the establishment of a dike by General Chen Hongjin of the Southern Tang Dynasty (923–36), Chendai was a beach. The place was named after Chen. The founder of the Ding community moved into Chendai at the turn of the Ming Dynasty.[2]

The establishment of the lineage system was very important to the Ding ancestors' Muslim identity change. It was essentially a fact that the ancestral cult forced the Islamic practice away from the Ding's social life. Scholarly discussion on the lineage system generally focuses on its manipulative aspect rather than on its articulation with cultural value and ideological power. Maurice Freedman (1958, 1966) suggested that the function of self-protection was an important factor for the popularity of the lineage system in a geographical and political frontier. This assumption has been challenged, since it fails to explain why an area with similar conditions did not develop a strong lineage organization (Pasternak 1969). In addition, whether or not southeast China was a frontier is problematic (Huang 1980).

In fact, large-scale lineage organization existed not only in southeast China but also in many other parts of China (Xu 1995). Historical surveys, however, document that lineage organization was highly developed in Fujian, Guangdong, Jiangxi, Zhejiang, and Jiangsu (Xu 1995). These areas contributed the most high-ranking officers and literati in Chinese history, especially since the Northern Song Dynasty (Tan 1987). In addition, when the political center and the influence of neo-Confucianism moved down to the south of the Changjiang (Yangtze River), southeast China became a cultural core in the Southern Song Dynasty (1127–1279) (Tan 1987). Some recent social-historical studies have explored the interrelation between the development of neo-Confucianism and the popularization of the lineage system (Gates 1996: 105; Davis 1986; Faure 1986). We can thus suggest that the lineage system came about in close association with the formation of the cultural center. Hence, one can consider that the lineage system reifies Chinese traditional ideology, representing the legitimate culture of literati and officialdom. However, the lineage system later became plebeian.

To understand how a lineage system was constructed, one has to consider to what extent the scenario of construction represents some humanistic aspiration informed by the traditional value system in addition to other factors in practice. Different regimes had some restrictions on the ancestral cult, depending on the levels of social hierarchy, which was in turn measured by "scholarly honors and official rankings" (*gongming*).[3] The lineage system thus metaphorically became a symbol of power. Theoretically, an ideal lineage could be achieved only through certain members passing the imperial examinations and then attaining political careers. This pursuit, among other things, would thus paradoxically form a sociocultural constraint under which construction of lineage organization became the most important way to contest symbolic capital in the locale.

Although the rulers of different dynasties issued differential stipulations to confine sizes and procedures in ancestor worship, in order to maintain hierarchical order in society, in fact, to what extent these stipulations were really obeyed is questionable. By the Ming Dynasty, according to the investigations by some Chinese social historians (Zheng 1992: 231; Chen 1991; Xu 1995), the official patriarchal system existed only in form. For one thing, the construction of ancestral halls was in vogue for a time in folk society, whether or not one had a *gongming*, because *gongming* could be pirated. Consequently, every lineage pretended to descend from some historical figures, or to have some particular kin with *gongming*.[4] This situation was an indication that the pursuit of *gongming* really became a sociocultural constraint. Therefore, in order to examine the construction of lineage in the Ding community, we should consider the role this constraint played in the whole process.

According to some historical materials, the Ding began to construct lineage quite early. It was said that their third-generation ancestor Ding Suode, who died in 1379 (Zhuang 1996: 311), suggested the building of an ancestral hall. Ding Suode's last words were orders to his sons to establish an ancestral hall (Zhuang 1996: 411). However, this message does not have to mean building an ancestral hall right after his death. In addition, the Ding ancestors were devout Muslims at that time.

Since the ancestors of the Ding were Muslim migrants, it is appropriate to argue that their establishment of a lineage system implied that their

3. The mosque in Chendai (photograph by Fan Ke).

4. Muslim graves of the Ding Hui (photograph by Fan Ke).

Muslim identity had changed. Historical materials support such an argument. It is a fact that many groups of Muslim descent in China have practiced some kinds of ritual memorializing their ancestors. Genealogical materials collected in Ma Jianzhao's edited volume (1998) prove this point. Accounts by Lin Chang-kuan (1996) and Zhang Chengzhi (1995 [1991]: 9) also suggest that the degree of Sinicization of Muslim Chinese communities varies from region to region, depending on how successful a region achieved the Confucianist accomplishments, such as the number of degree holders and literati, or the prosperity of the printing industry. In other words, as the practice of ancestor worship concerns Confucian orthodoxy, among Muslim descent groups Sinicization means downplaying Islam. However, Islam essentially excludes all forms of other religious practice, and treating ancestors like gods runs counter to Islamic monotheist doctrine. As long as Islam is a central concern, ancestor worship is not possible.

We can attribute Muslim identity change in the Ding's past to such factors as intermarriage, economic life, and participation in the imperial examinations (Fan 1990; Zhuang 1993). According to the genealogy, almost all Ding ancestors married local Han women. In the earlier generations, however, it seemed that the brides had to convert to Islam.[5] A considerable change occurred over time in their economic life, leading them closer to the local Chinese culture. This does not mean that the change of economic life itself was decisive to their Muslim identity change. Rather, as they engaged in different economic activities, the tie with other Muslim sojourners and residents in the area became less strong.

Engaging in agriculture led them to adjust their routine life; they had to start new activities other than running businesses. Economic and political interactions between the Ding and the neighboring Han people therefore became intensive. More significantly, as said in the genealogy, these neighbors were "big families" (*juxing jiating*), who have long family histories and influence in the locale. Thus, the founders of the Ding had to build networks with some of these neighbors, in order to adapt to their social surroundings (Zhuang 1996: 61).

The Ding started building their lineage organization by compiling a genealogy that followed the agnatic descent principle. An interesting piece in the genealogy describes how the Ding learned to compile their genealogy by copying the format used by one of their tutors during 1488–1505 (Zhuang 1996: 3). However, the lineage organization, as a basic unit either in the political or in the legal sense (Ch'u 1981 [1947]: 25–26), was not really established until the emergence of an élite or gentry class in the Ding community.

According to Ch'u (1962: 171), the élite or gentry class during the Qing Dynasty consisted of two groups: active, retired, or dismissed officials; and holders of the degrees or academic titles. In other words, *gongming* was the most important criterion of the definition of élite. As long as one had *gongming*, the kin group would have the privilege of building an ancestral hall according to the Ming-Qing law. Although illegally constructed, ancestral halls had been prevalent, at least in south China, since the middle Ming (Zheng 1992: 231; Chen 1991). They were manipulated to give wide publicity only after someone among the kin was awarded a certain *gongming*. The Ding genealogy does not actually indicate when the Ding built their ancestral hall, but it has an elaborate record on the event of the first "renovation" (*chongxiu*), which took place some time between 1573 and 1620 (the Wanli period of the Ming Dynasty). This renovation was undertaken in response to some kin of the Ding passing the imperial examinations at that time (Fan 1990; Zheng 1992; Zhuang 1993).

The event of renovation as noted was also a chance for the Ding élite to solidify their leadership by announcing a set of stipulations, in which the Islamic heritage was not included in the rituals of memorializing ancestors.

It was forbidden to use pork in an offering to the ancestors. Instead, sheep was the most important sacrifice used in both spring and winter ceremonies (Zhuang 1996: 193). These were the only hints that the Ding were descended from Muslims.

From the eighth generation onwards, the Ding produced degree holders in almost every generation. Accordingly, their lineage organization was fully established between the eighth and tenth generations. As a result, their Islamic practices were replaced by the ancestral cult. A genealogical record written by Ding Qing in 1699 sheds light on this. The first Ding kin to pass the imperial examination was Ding Yi. He began his career as an officer in 1505. Significantly, he was the first one to practice an appropriate ritual in order to correspond to his official status in memorializing ancestors after he brought fame (*mingsheng*) to his lineage. At this juncture, "no Muslims (*huijiaotu*) dared to disobey" (Zhuang 1996: 195). It goes without saying that the acceptance of the Confucianist education was the only way for a Ding family to promote themselves in the local political hierarchy.

In line with the consideration of the social meaning of the lineage system, one should examine the meaning of *chongxiu*, a term used in all ancestral halls. *Chongxiu* means renovation. It is supposed to be carried out regularly in accordance with the conditions of the architecture. This has not always been the case. Generally speaking, *chongxiu* would take place under two conditions. First, the buildings of the ancestral halls really needed maintenance or ornamentation. Second, grateful actions were carried out by those kin who had either passed the imperial examinations or had been officially promoted. The Ding genealogy provides us with these examples (Zhuang 1996: 311–16).

In addition, one frequently sees cases of *chongxiu* take place when some kin come home from a job for some reason. *Chongxiu* in this situation could become a chance for the lineage élite to show their authority. One can easily find that all *chongxiu* events were eventually sponsored or organized by the élite. For one thing, *chongxiu* was a project to maintain the main public property, the ancestral hall. In addition, it functioned to strengthen or revitalize the consciousness of familism. It is particularly true that the lack of maintenance of ancestral halls means that familism was in decline. The political meaning of *chongxiu* was thus significant.

Not only did the cases of *chongxiu* strengthen familism by attributing honors to the ancestors, but they also brought tremendous recognition to the lineage in the area. In fact, one can recognize the power of a lineage in local politics by measuring the size and architectural aesthetics of the ancestral halls. In other words, logically and symbolically, the degree of size and architectural aesthetics in turn could materialize the *mingsheng* of a lineage. In a sense, a lineage's *mingsheng* in the eyes of ordinary people is determined by how much the kin could do to honor the ancestors. The meaning of *chongxiu* is thus similar to Marcel Mauss's interpretation of potlatch practiced by the natives of northwestern America. According to Mauss (1950: 6), practicing potlatch actually "is a struggle between nobles to establish a hierarchy amongst themselves from which their clan will benefit at a later date."

This argument could be supported by the fact that there was no significant *chongxiu* project in Chendai from the late Qing Dynasty until the 1990s.[6] The reason for this is of course due to revolutionary movements, but the abolishment of the system of imperial examinations is also a factor.[7] This abolishment of imperial examinations, among other things, was a significant part of modern state making that began in the late 19th century (Duara 1988, 1995; Tang 1993). It undermined the legitimate foundation of producing traditional types of élite. *Chongxiu*, which provided the chance of displaying family achievement, thus declined. Except for recent events, no record of *chongxiu* or similar project can be found in the Ding community after 1889. Coincidently, from that year to 1906, the year the system of imperial examinations was officially abolished, no Ding descendant became a higher degree holder.

However, the construction of the modern state did not substantially destroy the force of lineage in the locales before 1949. Although one can trace the decline of lineages in local politics even as far as the late Qing and the early Republican era, because of modern education and the reform of administrative system at all levels, state penetration was very weak in rural areas of Fujian. Thus, to a certain degree, the system of lineage still functioned to maintain the local order.

In order to strengthen political control in the area, the regional Republican government quite often changed the divisions of administrative districts at different levels. This was in addition to carrying out some "planned social change" (Fei 1939), such as reorganizing city spatial structure, "doing away with superstitions" (*pochu mixing*), and "changing prevailing habits and customs" (*yifeng yisu*) (cf. Wang 1999: 362–93). Jinjiang county, for instance, changed at least eight times in administrative area and size after 1914 (Wang and Gao 1993: 2–3; JJSZ 1994: 14–15). All these changes were carried out with different agendas leading toward so-called regional autonomy (*difang zizhi*), back and forth between the three-level-local-system (county, township [*xiangzheng*], and neighborhood [*lulin*]) and the two-level-system (county and township), until 1949 (JJSZ 1994: 15–16).

These reforms and frequent changes in the administrative division of districts, however, did not substantially reach their goal. Rather, the local political order was to a certain degree even worse than that under Qing rule. The reason for this is that the force of lineage organizations was no longer influential enough to integrate local public order. And, as the representative of the modern state, the new regional governments lacked symbolic capital to build up authority in the locale, due to its lack of trust from the locals. Public order in the locale frequently turned into chaos. Although the traditional élite class had withered away in local politics, each lineage organization was still politically active in its territory. Consequently, warfare (*xiedou*) frequently took place between different lineages, mostly due to the limitation of local resources and the weakness of state power at the local level. Although feuding in the territory of Jinjiang was conspicuous in its scale, misery, continuity, and involvement of the local population ever since the Qing Dynasty, its heyday was in the first part of 20th century (Fu 1994: 166; JJSZ 1994: 911).

Another consequence was due to the decline of the traditional élite class in the early 20th century. Because traditional members of the élite stepped down, the lineage organizations soon became politically less cohesive, and warfare even took place frequently between different branches (*fang*) of the same lineage. In the Ding community, for example, the fighting between the so-called "strong branch" (*qiangfang*) and the "weak branch" (*ruofang*) never really stopped before 1949. This chaotic situation made the government feel weak when it came to dealing with these problems. The county government in its strongest days before 1949 had only 111 police for the whole of Jinjiang, which had about 121,420 households (JJSZ 1994: 870). Thus the government took the view that "people were fierce and tough; therefore, the quelling failed" (*minfeng manhan, tanya wuxiao*) (JJSZ 1994). Even though the area was under the power of regional warlords such as Chen Guohui and Xu Zhuoran for a while, what these originally bandit generals would do in general was to take bribes from both sides, thus ending up with nothing definite being resolved.

The description above does not mean that with the withering of the traditional élite class the core of Chinese traditional familism was losing its vitality. Rather, what I have argued is that lineage as a manipulative association was not so influential in local integration. In fact, ancestral halls were often used as a facility for other purposes. Since 1913, a couple of Ding kin initiated modern education: they established the first elementary school in the community, using their main ancestral hall as a facility. The school did not move out to its new facility until 1985, the year the ancestral hall was rearranged to become the exhibition hall for displaying Ding Hui history (Ding and Ding 1986). This case indicates that, except for its religious function, the main ancestral hall as a meeting place for the leadership of the lineage no longer existed. In the meantime, however, the branch ancestral halls were still functioning for analogous affairs but were confined to their units.

However, as one would recognize, the ancestral cult, the intensive expression of familism that has been sustained in the folk life of the people in southern Fujian, has been changing in form in accordance to varying political conditions. In reality, my informants told me that before 1949, the sacrificial offerings to the ancestors at the spring and winter seasons were sustained. They took place in the main ancestral hall even during the heyday of intra-lineage warfare (see also Ye, et al. 1990; Zhuang 1993). Even after 1913, new developments such as establishing modern schools, sending children to study overseas, and encouraging the education of women must have somehow fitted well into the requirements of familism to fulfill the humanistic aspirations of Chinese culture. Although kin welcomed the establishment of the modern elementary school, the school had to adopt the clan's literary name (*denghao*), which indicates where the family originally came from. This information was usually written on the paper lanterns hung in the ancestral halls.[8]

After the establishment of the PRC (People's Republic of China), all lineage activities were relegated to the category of feudal superstition and, therefore, forbidden by the revolutionary regime. However, as the vehicle of familism, ancestor worship has never disappeared from the common people's daily life, especially in rural areas. In the Ding community, every family performs rites and makes offerings to the ancestors on the anniversary of their death as well as practices other memorial rituals at different times according to the agricultural calendar, even though for decades these services were politically forbidden. Because of the disappearance of collective large-scale rituals of ancestral worship after 1949, the metaphor of intensifying traditionalism by means of renovation projects was of course impossible to do until the Deng era. In reality, political movements had never pushed aside the form and practice of familism from the minds of ordinary people. As I have been told, some people secretly continued to write genealogies for the lineage or for families, and some cadres were forced to resign because of their involvement in *"fengjian zongzu huodong"* (feudal lineage/family activities).[9]

During the Cultural Revolution (1966–76), fighting broke out in the Jinjiang area, as in many other parts of the country. Many devastating clashes occurred in the area in 1973, when 39 fights took place, involving 215 natural villages belonging to 163 brigades and 16 communes, and resulting in seven people dead and 249 people seriously wounded. According to the report, familism or lineage consciousness (*zongzu yishi*) was used to mobilize people to participate in the fighting (JJSZ 1994: 911–12).

Traditionalism in the Campaign for *Minzu* Identification

The Ding did not begin to construct ethnic identity through pursuing so-called ethnic flavor (*minzu fengge*) until the mid-1980s. Because they do not have different ethnic markers that can differentiate them from other local people, they resort to searching for historical resources, in addition to using the so-called Arabic elements, especially as featured in architectural representation (Fan 1999a).

Nonetheless, underneath the project of pursuing ethnic representation, traditionalism has loomed large. In the following, two issues are discussed. First, I examine the Ding leadership's campaign for their ethnic status. Second, I use the case of the Exhibition Hall of Chendai Hui History (Chendai Huizu Lishi Chenlieguan) to show that traditionalism can be used for modernity.

The Campaign for Recognition as Hui

The Ding leadership began its campaign for Hui ethnic status in late 1998, immediately after the Chinese government announced its reform policy. But, at that time, they did not really engage in searching for ethnic markers or ethnic flavor for themselves. The Ding's campaign for official *minzu* identification was linked to their desire for the benefits that are only officially given to national minorities. However, this campaign was first advanced by the urge to pursue wealth, which was repressed by the socialist system for three decades. Indeed, at that time, the leading figure of this campaign among the Ding was in charge of the License Department of Chendai Commune. He knew what could benefit the community if they were members of a minority nationality. Among other things, he told me, loyalty to the ancestors was also an encouragement. As long as the kin could get rich, it meant a great deal of honor could be attributed to the ancestors, and this would bring about considerable *mingsheng* or reputation in the locale.

I was told in the interview that, since the Ding were distributed in 13 natural villages geographically and constituted seven production brigades at that time, it would have been better if they formed a unit for self-government. The advantage was that they could have greater financial accumulation, since the annual profit tax could go directly to the county level. This meant that the people would not have to turn over part of the profit tax to the township level. The leader, Ding Guobiao, said, "As long as one retains more profits, one would have more options to do things. I did really think, in this way, we could have more money for further development and to remedy some environmental problems. Our natural surroundings were getting worse." Ding Guobiao acknowledged that the reason they asked for such autonomy after they "got their Hui identification back" was that they wanted to be in charge of "their own affairs." In other words, they wanted to be under a leadership in which the élite from their own descent group would play a more important role.

Officially, ways to identify an ethnic group as a nationality have a lot to do with the relevant people's history and other aspects of their cultural makeup. The government authority believed that the Ding were truly Hui. It also planned to tentatively set the community up as a model of *minzu* autonomy at the grassroots level, in order to accumulate some experience as well as to fulfill the political task of the Party's social policy. According to an official proposal by the Fujian People's government (FDG 178-1-144-1953), the government planned to establish 70–80 *minzu* townships in Fujian. Thus, it was not surprising that the government approved the Ding Hui identification immediately after receiving the application from the Ding community. The Ding in their appeal suggested that they considered themselves Hui, because their ancestors were foreign Muslims.

Traditionalism and the Exhibition Hall of Chendai Hui History

The establishment of an exhibition hall in the Ding community shows how traditionalism could be employed to serve modernity. In order to explore this issue, a general complexity of historical narrating in the modern era in association with the Chinese case needs first to be delineated. It will provide a historical backdrop against which to unfold the discussion.

In recent years, China studies scholars (Watson 1994; Duara 1988, 1995) have challenged the authenticity of grand narrative (Lyotard 1979) or historiography as applied to China. One thing, however, needs to be clear in this study. One should not emphasize that the voice from the margin or the grassroots level merely produces the meaning of resistance against hegemonic discourses, an approach many of the liberal left today and Marxist scholars take for granted (Fan 2000). The major problem for grand narrative is the way it generalizes things. To many post-structuralists, there are no trustable histories, because no one is able to escape the net of power relations in a changing world; all historical facts are fragmentary and discontinuous.

What concerns me here is generality. In other words, how have historical facts been selected and arranged? In the historical Exhibition Hall of Chendai Hui History, although all the specific details could be true, they have been manipulated to construct a history in a framework of grand narrative. The seemingly isolated, fragmentary, and discontinuous facts of the past and the present can be interpreted very differently, and different historical structures are provided.

The change in narrating history in post-Mao China is both spectacular and diverse. The most important change is that the nation's historicity has been projected into the country's unitary tendency in politics according to which different cultures and ethnicities have coexisted throughout the whole national history. This contrasts with an overemphasis on the historical inevitability of socialism as an evolutionary result of the country's history. From the case of the Exhibition Hall of Chendai Hui History, one could perceive the degree to which the relevant people have tried to explain their historical development in such a framework.

The exhibition hall was first established in the main ancestral hall in the spring of 1985 (Gladney 1991: 285–86). Influenced by Chinese official models of historical narrating, the Hui of Chendai have emphasized a much larger context of time and space, within which their destiny is determined by the narrative of the Hui as a whole. This argument is supported by an analysis of the structure of the display in the exhibition hall.

The sections of display include the formation and development of Chendai Hui, the historical figures, the economic achievements, and the contributions from overseas kin (*haiwai zongqing*). It goes without saying that in both rules and layout of style, the exhibition inevitably follows the way in which history has been narrated in accordance with a unilinear principle. The basic point of all the captions in the exhibition is of course a representation of the Hui historicity that is defined by the state as a subject fused into the Chinese nation, although what the exhibition displays is a specific historiography of the Ding family.

Nevertheless, the historiography of the lineage is used to support the narrative of a particular nationality. It is also an example of the social use of kinship. It is a metaphor of traditionalism and modernity. The display depicts the development of the Ding Hui as a nationality and its historicity. Interestingly, when the government just started its campaign for *minzu* categorization in 1953, many minority people did not really know what *minzu* means and identified themselves with a localized identity.[10] This situation could be regarded as what Geertz (1983) calls "local knowledge." Only after the Ding became part of an officially confirmed minority nationality did their knowledge about themselves surpass local boundaries to connect to the Hui nationwide. This is well indicated by the following introductory paragraph:

> The Ding originated from the Arabian region and moved to this place during the time of the Ming Dynasty. For over 600 years they have lived in harmony with the Han, developing Chendai together, and there emerged many excellent figures throughout history, contributing what they could for the prosperity of the Chinese nation.
>
> [My translation]

The other descriptions that introduce some outstanding kin in the past are intentionally written to relate to some well-known historical events and national historical figures, who can be found in textbooks and patriotic propaganda. Many of the achievements of some of these figures are legendary only. This does not bother the organizers of the exhibition. Rather, the legends have even become essential to the narrative. They have been combined with the discourse of familism, serving both the state political agenda and ancestral worship. Interestingly, because these descriptions are in the framework of grand narrative, the Ding historical figures are somehow promoted to national heroes:

> Ding Nan, ... a military candidate in the state-sponsored examination in Chongzhen 16th year (1643), was honored as a successful candidate after passing the highest imperial examinations. He gathered kin to help the emperor to fight the Qing, but lost the war and sacrificed his life with the highest moral integrity on Chenweng Bridge.

Ding Long was a subordinate general of Zheng Chengong. Following Zheng Chengong to recapture Taiwan, he made his contribution to the unity of the motherland and, therefore, to the advancement of historical development.

Ding Gongchen (1800–75) ... dedicated his life to the cause of the country by science (*kexue baoguo*), taking the task of rejuvenating China (*zhenxing zhonghua*) as his own career after the Opium War. His work, *Yanpao Tushuo* (Illustration of Manipulating Artillery), was held in high esteem by Wei Yuan and Lin Zexu.... He was a famous munitions scientist in the modern era.

[My translation from the captions in the exhibition hall]

Other events or figures have also been exclusively described in a similar manner, emphasizing their significance in regional or national history. The theme of the whole display, in a word, is how the Ding have made contributions to the historical development of the Chinese nation. Thus, they raised themselves to exemplify the grand narrative of the Chinese nation:

The ancestors of the Ding were Muslims from the Arabian region. Because of marriage, different laws in different periods, and many kin becoming officers in the Ming and Qing Dynasties, the Ding have been to a degree assimilated with the Han. But, they have retained certain ethnic customs that they originally had (*jiyoude minzu xisu*).[11] The history of Ding Hui is a unique history of *minzu* civilization.

[My translation]

The point of "a unique history of *minzu* civilization" (*yibu dute de minzu wenmingshi*) differentiates the ethnicity of the Ding Hui from that of the Hui in other parts of the country, who emphasize their practice of Islam rather than their ethnic origin. One might identify those Hui by looking at whether or not their practice is orthodox. In contrast, the Ding practice none of these customs. This, however, dramatically turns out to characterize the Ding's "uniqueness" (*dute*), metaphorically delivering the message to indicate their local identity, which is stated by their claim about having originated in the "Central Plain" (Zhongyuan) and their strong feelings about their ancestor worship. In the meantime, the term *minzu* in the above caption defines their uniqueness, differentiating them from the neighboring Han, with whom they share the same cultural practices. The term "civilization" (*wenming*) addresses the fact that they believe they are actually civilized; by so doing they have manifested their cultural identity.

By pursuing ethnic representation, using display to underscore ethnic identity to be an aesthetically spatio-temporal construction, the Ding as a descent group has shifted to be Ding-surnamed Hui (*Dingxing Huizu*), literally, an officially approved component part of the Hui nationality. Consequently, by so doing not only have they fused into the state narrative of multiple-nation while constructing a new identity, but they have also resumed the ideology of familism.

Revitalization of Tradition

In the past few years, the ethnographical accounts of the revitalization of folk tradition, particularly in religious practices and ancestral cults, have given invaluable insights into the scholarly understanding of Chinese society (Dean 1993; Wang 1997; Faure and Siu 1995; Huang 1998). None of these studies, however, recognizes that this movement of revitalization, which is generally treated as feudal superstition in the socialist propaganda, could take place under the state or semi-official umbrella. In the following pages, I show that the state can support this revitalization by not trying to intervene in the movement, and that the revitalization of tradition taking place in Chendai reflects the interaction between society and the state.

The Revival of Traditional Folk Life and the Government's Attitude toward It

Recent reports from the Ding community have recounted some popular religious practices that have resumed in recent decades (Chen and Ding 1997; Gladney 1991, 1998; Zhuang 1993). However, this does not mean that the government has entirely disregarded these activities, though it is true that it has been much more tolerant of them from the 1980s onwards. In addition to the traditional dynamic, the decollectivization that began in the mid-1980s is undoubtedly a factor. However, the government's power is still there. For one thing, the government does not allow people to publish genealogies through publishing houses, and generally discourages the project of rebuilding ancestral halls.[12] This shows that the government tries to find ways to downplay the influence of tradition. In southern Fujian, the government limits the scale of ancestor worship rituals and continually carries out the propaganda of "socialist spiritual civilization" (*shehui zhuyi jingshen wenming*).[13]

In other places in southern Fujian, one might recognize a local god as a source of identity and therefore form popular cults (Dean 1993). However, in the area of Jinjiang, it would be hard to find a god whose cult would even cover a scale as small as a natural village. Like all local people, the Ding collectively practice a popular cult on the birthdays of gods. The gods, however, are not the same to all Dings, although the residency of the Ding compactly formed a community for many generations. All these gods function to protect the people in their specific territories, the "corners" (*jiaotou*) in the local dialect. Thus, they are worshipped respectively by people of different locations. These small-scale popular cults have little implication for politics, and so the government in recent decades has not paid much attention to them.

However, the local government is particularly concerned about the cult of ancestor worship. The reason for this, as noted, is that it was considered the occasion of local fighting. The other factor is that the ancestor cult has been acutely attacked by all revolutionaries ever since the early 20th century, especially after 1949. Thus in practice the ancestor cult would usually be criticized as long as the government learnt of it, although sometimes the local government would turn a blind eye.

The revitalization of the ancestor cult in the Chendai Hui community is seen in the re-ornamentation of the ancestral halls and ancestral houses, the continued compilation and publication of genealogy, and the remodeling and regrouping of its ancestral graves. It is worth noting that all of these activities in the Ding community could be subsumed under the name of both *minzu* activity (*minzu huodong*) and *minzu* life (*minzu shenghuo*). Not only has the government not intervened in these activities, but it also has supported them to a great degree (Fan 1999a, 1999b).

The Revitalization of Ancestor Cult and Ritual Invention

Traditionally, the entity of patriarchal lineage organization was thought to ideally include three essential elements: the ancestral grave, the ancestral hall, and genealogy. Although a lineage organization does not have to have all three elements, having all of them is a goal that all lineage organizations want to attain. This could be the result of the social hierarchical system in which theoretically only those who had some kin who had certain *gongming* were legitimate in constructing all three. Thus, having the three key elements to a lineage organization not only means more legitimacy to engage in autonomy (Ch'u 1981 [1947]: 328–46) but also to accumulate symbolic capital in the locale.

The Ding had organized a lineage with the three elements in the middle of the Ming Dynasty and therefore became quite influential in the area, even after the abolition of the monarchy in the early 20th century. Nonetheless, as a result of the vanishing gentry class that had made up the core of power in charge of lineage affairs, and especially the pressure from the government after 1949, the influence of lineage organization as a whole declined radically. It was not revived until the post-Mao era.

Nevertheless, the sociopolitical implication of the recent revitalization of the ancestral cult in different locales should be interpreted according to the context. We should consider each case in association with the varying context defined by the different local conditions of the social economy. In addition, the meaning of this revitalization in the same area, even in the same lineage, could vary according to those who propose as well as manage the movement. In the Ding community, obviously, this movement is run separately by two agencies and could thus be divided into two structures. Both, however, cooperate and deal with their respective affairs without serious contradictions.

As one can see in all of rural southern Fujian, the first structure is underlined by the force that I call folk agency, which has nothing to do with official power. In Chendai, we find many examples of the renovation of ancestral halls that are run by local villagers. The committees of renovation consist of seniors, educated persons, wealthy individuals, and those who have some special skills in construction, decoration, etc. In general, the government does not appreciate any project run by this agency and discourages the people's commitments. However, people are always able to find some way to bypass prohibitions and continue to work on their projects. The most popular way in southern Fujian is to claim that the projects are sponsored by overseas kin (Huang 1998: 221; Kuah 1998; Fan 1999b; Pan 2000; Wang 1999), for example.

As in the past, the rebuilding or renovation of the ancestral hall symbolizes lineage revival. Today, this is more significant. Not only has it demonstrated the return of familism as Huang Shu-min (1998: 221) has rightly pointed out, but it also illustrates that the state could make concessions as it confronts the force of traditionalism (Ogden 1991; Fan 1999b).

Many factors have encouraged the revival of the ancestral cult in Chendai. But, if we compare both structures of performing ethnicity and reviving familism we would find some differences. One difference is that reviving familism does not attempt to accumulate symbolic capital from a higher level than that of the locale. Thus the meaning of it in identity

5. A newly renovated branch ancestral hall of the Ding lineage (photograph by Fan Ke).

politics is not to express ethnicity but to present the similarity with all in the locale. At this level, the revival of the ancestral cult presents the cultural identity of the Ding that they share with their neighbors, thus manifesting and emphasizing the sense of place.

Except for the main ancestral hall that has been turned into the exhibition hall, there are many ancestral halls and houses in all branches of the Ding lineage. When I was doing my recent fieldwork in Chendai, three or four ancestral halls or ancestral houses were under construction, renovation, or remodeling. I observed the construction for some time and attended the two opening ceremonies in the Spring Festival season of 1997. The people I talked to seemed to have lots of energy to engage in these projects. Many of them emphasized the importance of the projects; for example, they wanted to revive the interpersonal relationships they used to have but which appear to be increasingly lost today. For many seniors, the rebuilding of ancestral halls is one way to express their loyalty to their ancestors. These senior informants pointed out that, in the past, neither political nor financial conditions allowed them to be involved like this. Now, the policy is not so tight and finance is no longer a problem, so that it is time to fulfill the obligations they owed their ancestors for so many years.

The other reason is that many seniors are concerned about where they would go after they die. To them, ancestor worship is not only a way of dealing with spiritual life but also a response to some realistic problems. For example, they want to make sure that they would receive the offerings from later generations of their branches after they have left this world. Also, the ancestral houses are the places for dying people to live out their final days, according to local customs. I saw a dying man in a newly remodeled ancestral house and found that he was peaceful and seemed happy that he could spend his final days there.

In the past, without a certain *gongming* (scholarly honors and official rankings) one did not have the privilege of receiving offerings from kin in the main ancestral hall after one's death. This stipulation was broken even as early as the Ming Dynasty (Zheng 1992: 227–41). As long as one had made impressive contributions that led to accumulating *mingsheng* for the lineage, one would be promoted by having a tablet installed in the ancestral hall. In the Wanli period (1573–1620) of the Ming Dynasty, the ancestral cult of the Ding community stipulated that every descendant was allowed to receive the offerings from the lineage in the ancestral hall, but he or she must have *gongming* (Zhuang 1996: 159). This stipulation was changed to allow tablets to be installed for those who had donated an amount of money for the renovation of the ancestral hall. The inscriptive texts of renovation of the ancestral hall in the Kangxi and Guangxu periods, for example, indicate this message (Zhuang 1996: 312; Ye, et al. 1990). According to my informants, except for their first four generational ancestors, the main ancestral hall held the tablets of descendants with *gongming* or special contributions before the eighteenth generation only. In addition, it had a few places for those whose moral integrity was respected, reserved places paid for by someone else. For example, a place was paid for by three brothers for the tablet of their elder sister who never married in order to look after them after their parents died young (Ye, et al. 1990).

The tablets for most of those after the seventeenth generation were installed in the branch ancestral halls. The stipulation was looser in this situation. People who had no *gongming* or particular high moral conduct in their lifetime had to pay for their tablet places, if they wanted to receive offerings after leaving this world. Today, *gongming* is no longer important, and every ordinary person has the right to have a place in the branch ancestral hall, as long as he or she has money. In the opening ceremonies of two ancestral halls, I found that many people have bought places for their tablets, which are wrapped with a piece of red cloth, indicating that the persons are honored while alive.

It is not true to say that this structure of revitalization of the ancestral cult in the Ding community did not receive attention from the government. However, in most cases, the official agencies tended not to notice it. "We try not to look at them when they are doing things like this since they are a minority nationality (*shaoshu minzu*)," said a cadre in the office of Chendai township.

Cadres in the Ding community invented the second structure of revitalization. They could be considered governmental agencies, but at the same time they also represented the interests of their community. The CCHA (Committee of Chendai Hui Affairs), a semi-official agency under the leadership of the township government, has been the cornerstone underlining this structure. The other name of the CCHA is the Committee of Chendai Township Minzu Affairs, but none of its cadres is paid for his job. This committee has existed for so many years since its establishment in 1984. The members are all Ding kin.

The cadres in this body are generally trusted by the government. This puts them in a dilemma when they face a conflict of interest between their lineage group and other government agencies. Basically, as Ding Yuling (1994) put it, these cadres have a strong consciousness of lineage, so that they would naturally look for ways to make contributions to their own community, as they come across something ambiguous.

In the revitalization movement, the CCHA used their privilege of minority nationality status, inventing the ritual for ancestor worship styled in a highly hybrid form, thus entrusting the traditional ritual practice with new meaning. By doing this, the CCHA not only received credit from their kin but was also appreciated by the government for implementing ethnic representation.

This example shows that we should not consider the revitalization movement in China exclusively as resistance to a certain hegemonic power, be it the state, modernity, or globalization. Furthermore, this movement reflects the fact that not only have people actively adapted to a certain sociopolitical environment but they have also learned to manipulate this sociopolitical environment for their own purposes.

On 26 January 1997, the CCHA held a party to celebrate Spring Festival. As usual, all cadres, including those now retired, were invited to participate. But, for this year, the party was more significant; it was held in conjunction with the publication of a new genealogy of the Ding lineage, which was reedited by Zhuang Jinghui, a historian from Xiamen University. For this event, many important people were invited, too, such as university professors, the director of the Quanzhou Maritime Museum, some wealthy overseas kin, and, therefore, the major leaders of the township. At the celebration, two speakers, among others, gave very interesting speeches. This event shows the nature of interaction between the state and the society.

The Party secretary of the township began his speech with the following words: "The flourishing age calls for the compilation of a gazetteer (*shengshi xiuzhi*), as the old Chinese saying goes; the situation of today is exactly what this saying means." Why did he not say, "The flourishing age calls for the compilation of genealogy (*shengshi xiupu*)," an alternative that is also frequently heard? We do not need to examine which one is more likely to be used traditionally. What concerns us here is that the meaning of this saying could change if one character is changed for another. When the speaker used the character *zhi* (gazetteer) rather than *pu* (genealogy), he used political rhetoric. *Zhi* refers to actions like writing history that is of course acceptable to everyone, whereas *pu* gives people the impression of conjuring up the return of ancestor cults, which is not what the government wants. So the use of *zhi* indicates the Party leader's political stand: he came for the celebration of the publishing of a *zhi*, which is acceptable, although it was actually *pu*, which is in principle unacceptable to a Party leader.

The fact that the first leader of the township attended the celebration, which was in conjunction with cadres' gathering for the New Year, tells us two things. First, there could be a double standard employed by the government toward the so-called feudalistic activities. Second, from the people's standpoint, the stigma of feudalistic superstition could be rhetorically erased if these activities could be managed and articulated according to modern political legitimacy. The membership of a minority nationality thus provides the Ding people with such a form of legitimacy.

The other speech was delivered by the head of the CCHA, whose official position was Chairman of the Political Consultative Conference of Chendai Township. He spoke highly of the CCHA's three important contributions in the past years. He considered that the first contribution was that their new genealogy was published. Its high quality was reflected in the following: it was reedited by a scholar, published by a publishing house in Hong Kong, and financially sponsored by kin worldwide. Around HK$250,000 was spent on the publication. The money was donated by four kin from the United States, Hong Kong, the Philippines, and the home community.[14]

The second contribution was the regrouping of the ancestral graves and the building of a new graveyard of 5 square *mu* (1 *mu* = 0.067 hectares). The Ding are proud of this ancestral grave group (*zumu qun*), regarding it as the biggest one, even nationwide. According to the speaker, their ancestral graveyard was definitely "the biggest group of old graves (*gumu qun*) in the province."

The Ding moved all their ancestral graves to Lingshan (Holy Mountain) in 1994. Lingshan is located in the south, about a half a mile from downtown Quanzhou. It was so named because of its legendary "holy sites" (*shengmu*), which remained from the Tang Dynasty. It is said that two disciples of the Prophet Muhammad were buried there. They had been sent by Muhammad to China as missionaries and died in Quanzhou. Whether or not the story is true is not a concern here. What intrigues us is that the site in recent years has turned out to be a popular spot that attracts Muslim tourists worldwide. When the Ding leadership negotiated with the government in the late 1980s, in order to group their ancestral graves at the present site, the reason of advancing the tourism industry was given. The government soon approved their proposal for this reason. Consequently, all graves were made in the form of the so-called Arabic style. A cultural hybrid thus emerges to manifest a representation of being ethnic.[15]

These ancestral graves were originally distributed around the larger Quanzhou area. That the Ding could regroup them in Lingshan was an arrangement that shows the ingenuity of the Ding leadership. Not only have they placed their ancestors in a meaningful space, but also, because of the location, they have more opportunities to accumulate symbolic capital, making their lineage more famous in national identity politics. According to Bourdieu (1990: 120), symbolic capital "is credit, but in the broadest sense, a kind of advance, a credence." Consequently, what followed next, after moving the ancestral graves, is that the Ding invented a unique ritual for memorializing their ancestors in public.

What the CCHA has done for this, the invention of a rite, is a political-cultural performance. The traditional making of offerings (*xianji*) has been replaced by presenting bouquets (*xianhua*) and sweeping the graves (*saomu*), both of which are officially encouraged, in contrast to the traditional way that is considered *langfei* (wasting) and *mixing secai* (superstitious). Rather than practicing the rite at Qingming, the traditional day Chinese pay respects to their ancestors at their grave, the CCHA has chosen the season of Spring Festival. There are several reasons for this. First, although Qingming is the time for paying respects to the dead at their grave, people in general also visit the graves of close family members during Spring Festival.

Second, traditionally, Spring Festival is the season for people to make offerings to the ancestors in all ancestral halls and houses in a lineage. Organizing kin to pay their respects to their ancestors at the grave becomes an alternative to the traditional rite of *jizu* (offering sacrifice to the ancestors). Last, in 1997, the celebration of the end of the month of fasting (Kaizhaijie) coincided with the Spring Festival season, and members of the CCHA took advantage of this. I found there was some code switching when the CCHA called for sweeping the ancestral graveyard during the 1997 Spring Festival season. It was announced that the activity would be held in Kaizhaijie rather than in Yuanxiaojie[16]; both festivals were at about the same time of the year.

Since this event has become a chance to present ethnic representation, everyone had to dress up and wear a small white hat that represents the Hui ethnicity, on the day they went to the ancestral graves. The small white hat is thought to be a crucial component of Hui attire, but the Ding had lost this custom. Therefore, it is a representation only for cultural performance (Parking, et al. 1996), in order to accumulate recognition from others and to enable them to be "recognized as legitimate" (Bourdieu 1990: 118) to be Hui.[17]

Another of the CCHA's contributions, according to the speaker, was to turn the main ancestral hall into a "unit of provincial preservation of cultural relics" (*shengji wenwu baohu dangwei*). The CCHA also facilitated the opening of an exhibition hall, which is considered the biggest display of minority history in the province. The speaker further pointed out that the exhibition hall was "evidence of the development of Hui nationality" and "at the same time is evidence of the maritime history of China."

Although the state has been much more tolerant of the revitalization of some traditional folk practices, still, it tries to limit the scale of these practices. Now, traditional offerings to the ancestors in the Ding community have been taking place in all branch ancestral halls. It thus turns out to be private, in contrast to that under the leadership of the CCHA. Undoubtedly, the government would not appreciate the large-scale worshipping of ancestors. However, cherishing the memory of ancestors has never been discouraged in government propaganda, because it is the same way that the state conjures up the nationalist soul for the nation. Therefore, one can always find ways to do things in a direction welcomed by both the state and the ordinary people.

Conclusion: Tradition and Identity Politics

This study has explored traditionalism and legitimization. The term traditionalism, in this article, refers to some humanistic aspiration that underlines the form of tradition and social life. As Fei Xiaotong has rightly pointed out (Fei and Li 1998), Chinese traditionalism is centered on familism and is dynamic, making people realize their ambition in life. People consider their successes a way to glorify their ancestors and to profit later generations as well, in a Chinese context. Familism thus encourages people to accumulate symbolic capital. Again following Bourdieu (1990: 112–21), it is a form of power that is not perceived as power but as legitimate demands for recognition, deference, obedience, or other services to others.

The actions the Ding have taken toward identity politics thus far are of course aimed at pursuing their interests materially and spiritually. Since the community has been so successful in its economy, pursuit of material interests is no longer significant to the people. The Ding have even donated large amounts of money and materials to other minority nationality areas every year since the late 1980s. What they aspire to is some spiritual interest that can be recognized as an influential community in national identity politics. Their membership in the Hui, a minority nationality, helps them to realize this aspiration. In the past two decades, the Ding have mobilized their social capital by using kinship to underline the movement of constructing ethnic identity. It essentially is a powerful support for the state's social policy toward minority nationalities. They have corresponded so well with the state's need of writing grand narrative for national historiography. At the same time, by so doing, they have systematically revitalized traditional commitments in many aspects of their social life.

Their official *minzu* assignment functions as a charter permitting them to do things under the name of *minzu* activities. In this way, because of their economic success, the Ding have become a model for the state in its work for minority nationalities. They have accepted many visitors every year, not only from other parts of the country but also from the rest of the world. In the meantime, many of them have become celebrities in the circle of minority nationalities and have been sent abroad as a living example of the state's success in affirmative action. In viewing the Ding's success in national identity politics, it is reasonable to say that representation in being ethnic has already become great symbolic capital in a Chinese context.

According to Habermas (1996 [1962]: 7), representation "pretended to make something invisible visible through the public presence." What needs to be presented in public for those who make the invisible visible would be something that could present itself "as an embodiment of some sort of 'higher power'" (Habermas 1996 [1962]). This insight helps us to understand why ethnic representation is so popular. It also helps us to speculate on the ways in which ethnicity and "being ethnic" make sense as symbolic capital.

Notes

1. The original version of this paper was presented at the conference, "Tradition and Change: Identity, Gender and Culture in South China," The Chinese University of Hong Kong, 3–6 June 1999. I would like to express thanks to the Department of Anthropology of The Chinese University of Hong Kong for inviting me. I would also like to thank the China Program of the Jackson School of the University of Washington for providing me with the travel grant. I am grateful to Professor Kenneth Dean, whose help and encouragement has always been so invaluable to my study in the United States. I am also indebted to Professors Stevan Harrell, Ann Anagnost, Edgar Winans, and Huang Shu-min for their help at different stages during the years of my anthropological training in the United States. Last but not least, I would like to thank Professor Tan Chee-Beng and two anonymous reviewers for their constructive comments on the original version of this article.
2. We do not know when the Ding began to live in Chendai. Records from the genealogy indicate that the founder of the Ding community was a fourth-generation ancestor Ding Ren'an, who lived from 1343–1420.
3. Historically, plebeians could only practice ancestor worship in graveyards and were allowed to worship only the recent two or three generational ancestors in different periods. Up to the Ming Dynasty, the law still forbade plebeians to build an ancestral hall (Ch'u 1981 [1947]: 192–96; MS Vol. 52: Lizhi 6), although it is doubtful whether or not this stipulation really worked (Zheng 1992; Xu 1995; Chen 1991).
4. This is also the reason that many fakes were produced in genealogies in response to this sociocultural constraint. The Lin family, a neighboring lineage of the Ding in Chendai, according to my informants, never had a real *gongming* until 1995, when one of the kin was promoted to the rank of major general of the PLA (People's Liberation Army). However, they had built their ancestral hall centuries ago, indicating that they have some kin who had received *gongming* in the past.
5. According to the genealogy (Zhuang 1996: 64), after her marriage, the wife of the fourth-generation ancestor Ding Ren'an had to change her customary dress to a style preferred by Muslims: simple, white, and made from cotton cloth.
6. For why the renovation of ancestral halls resumed in the 1990s, see the section "Revitalization of Tradition" below.

7. One should note that in the historical past, although achieving a *gongming* was the most favorable chance for renovation of ancestral halls, other accomplishments, such as success in business, for example, would have enabled kin to express their gratitude by renovating ancestral halls.
8. For lineage organization, *denghao* is generally a name of the family's original place. The Ding's *denghao* is *jushu*, which means collecting books in English and which, according to the legend of the Ding, is praised and honored from an emperor in the Ming Dynasty. Use of *denghao* to decorate homes in the Ding community today indicates that the Ding have held an ambiguous attitude toward their local and ethnic identities.
9. A particular case told by some informants is about Ding Minyun, a Party secretary for the Ding's seven production brigades during the 1960s. He was criticized for organizing lineage activities after he took some kin to pay respects to the ancestors at their tombs during Qingming, the Chinese grave-sweeping festival. He was soon forced to vacate his position and was sharply criticized by the work team sent down by the prefectural government during the Movement of Socialist Education (Shejiao) in 1964.
10. Many of my informants, especially those of Baiqi Huizu township of Hui'an county, told me that the reason that they declined the *minzu* assignment planned by the government in 1953 was that they did not know what *minzu* was. They just thought that they were the same as others in the locale. The only difference, said these informants, was that their ancestors had followed Islam (*xin huijiao*).
11. Although they had built a mosque in 1990, it does not mean that the Ding people really follow Islam (Fan 1999a). The designers of the exhibition hall acknowledged that what they had written for the display functioned as a story that should have both a beginning and an end (*youtou youwei*).
12. It has been said that for publishing genealogy and rebuilding an ancestral hall, it is better to convince the government that these projects are a requirement from overseas kin. Some people suggested that this stipulation was started only in recent years, as a response by the state to the revitalization of ancestor cults (Fan 1999b; Huang 1998: 219–21).
13. It has been a task for the rural cadres in Fujian to prevent the return of lineage activities, especially during Spring Festival, traditionally the season for the practice of collective ancestor worship. As some of the cadres who were my informants said, this instruction is always announced and assigned in the workshop of the township government when Spring Festival is approaching.
14. There are different versions of genealogies in the hands of some kin or preserved by some libraries nationwide. They are all under the title of *Chendai Dingshi Zupu* (Chendai Ding Genealogy). Professor Zhuang Jinghui, an ethnohistorian at Xiamen University, based his research on these versions to compile a new one that makes use of all available historical documents from

the Ming Dynasty to the present. The genealogy was published by Xianggang Lüye Chubanshe (Hong Kong Green Leaves Educational Press) in 1996.

15. In addition to their so-called Arabic style of ancestral graves, the Ding have introduced exotic decorations featured in the architecture of "public houses" (Habermas 1996 [1962]). I have examined this elsewhere (Fan 1999a).

16. This is the 15th day of the 1st lunar month, or Lantern Festival.

17. The most dramatic episode of this is the first time they presented this invented ritual to the public in 1994. UNESCO sent an investigative team to Quanzhou for the second time, to attend the second international conference on the maritime silk route, and it was during Spring Festival. The leadership of the CCHA made a decision to pay their respects to their ancestors at the ancestral graves, only half a mile from the conference venue. The CCHA leaders mobilized several hundred people from the Ding community. Before the ceremony started, a message was delivered to the conference. The organizers of the conference therefore called for a recess, so that all conference participants could observe the ceremony. In the evening, the media in Fujian reported this news, and soon it was shown nationwide on television. Some of my informants who organized this event were still very excited when they mentioned it to me. Since then, the Ding have received foreign visitors from more than 70 countries.

References

Bourdieu, Pierre. 1990. *The Logic of Practice*. Stanford: Stanford University Press.

Chen, Xiangsui and Ding Yuling. 1997. Yujia Cun de Yujiama Xingyang Yanjiu (The Study of Mother Yu Belief in the Yu Village). *Bulletin of the Institute of Ethnology, Academia Sinica*, no. 82.

Chen, Zhiping. 1991. *Wubai Nianlai Fujian de Jiazu yu Wenhua* (Fujian's Lineages and Cultures in the Past 500 Years). Shanghai: Sanlian Shudian.

Ch'u, Tung-Tsu. 1962. *Local Government in China under the Ching*. Stanford: Stanford University Press.

———. 1981 [1947]. *Zhongguo Falü yu Zhongguo Shehui* (Law and Society in Traditional China). Beijing: Zhonghua Shuju.

Clark, Hugh R. 1991. *Community, Trade, and Networks: Southern Fujian Province from the Third to the Thirteen Century*. Cambridge: Cambridge University Press.

Cohen, Myron. 1990. Lineage Organization in North China. *The Journal of Asian Studies* 49(3): 509–34.

Davis, Richard L. 1986. Political Success and the Growth of Descent Groups: The Shih of Ming-chou during the Sung. In P. Ebrey and J. Watson, eds., *Kinship Organization in the Late Imperial China*, 1000–1940, pp. 62–94. Berkeley: University of California Press.

Dean, Kenneth. 1993. *Taoist Ritual and Popular Cults of Southeast China*. Princeton, NJ: Princeton University Press.

Ding, Mingqi and Ding Xiangshi. 1986. Jushu Huizu Xiaoxue Shihua (Stories about the Jushu Hui Primary School). In *Jinjiang Wenshi Ziliao Xuanji* (The Selection of Historical-Literary Materials of Jinjiang), no. 7: 76–85.

Ding, Yuling. 1994. Zai Tuanjie Jinbu Shiye Zhong Momo Gengyun (Working Quietly in the Course of Promoting Solidarity and Progress). *Fujian Minzu* 6: 22–23.

Duara, Prasenjit. 1988. *Culture, Power, and the State: Rural North China, 1900–1942*. Stanford: Stanford University Press.

———. 1995. *Rescuing History from the Nation: Questioning Narratives of Modern China*. Chicago: University of Chicago Press.

Fan, Ke. 1990. Guanyu Chendai Huizu de Ruogan Lishi Wenti (Some Historical Questions Regarding the Chendai Hui). In Chen Guoqiang, et al., eds., *Chendai Huizushi Yanjiu* (The Studies of the History of Chendai Hui), pp. 55–75. Beijing: Zhongguo Shehui Kexue Chubanshe.

———. 1999a. Architectural Representation as Symbolic Text. Paper presented to "Vernacular Cultures," the Center for Chinese Studies Annual Symposium, the University of California, Berkeley, 5–6 March.

———. 1999b. "Haiwai Guanxi" yu Minnan Qiaoxiang de Minjian Chuantong Fuxing (The "Overseas Networks" and Revitalization of Folk Tradition in the Overseas Chinese Native Home Villages in South Fujian). In Yang Xeling and Zhuang Guotu, eds., *Gaige Kaifang yu Fujian Huaqiao Huaren* (Liberalization and the Overseas Chinese of Fujian), pp. 155–66. Xiamen: Xiamen University Press.

———. 2000. Minzu Zhuyi yu Zuqunxing: Jianlun Ziyou Zhuyi Linian yu Zhongxi Zhishi Fenzi Chuantong (Nationalism and Ethnicity: Also on Liberalism and the Different Traditions of both Chinese and Western Intellectuals). In Zhou Daming and Xu Jieshun, eds., *Zhongguo Renleixue: Ershiyi Shiji de Qushi* (Anthropology in China: A Trend in the 21st Century). Nanning: Guangxi Minzu Chubanshe.

———. 2001. Identity Politics in South Fujian Hui Communities. Ph.D. Thesis. University of Washington.

Faure, David. 1986. *The Structure of Chinese Rural Society: Lineage and Village in the Eastern New Territories, Hong Kong*. Hong Kong: Oxford University Press.

Faure, David and Helen Siu, eds. 1995. *Down to Earth*. Stanford: Stanford University Press.

FDG. *Fujiansheng Dang'an'guan* (Fujian Provincial Archives).

Fei, Xiaotong. 1939. *Peasant Life in China: A Field Study of Country Life in the Yangtze Valley*. London: Routledge and Kegan Paul.

Fei, Xiaotong and Li Yih-yuan. 1998. Zhongguo Wenhua yu Xinshiji de Shehuixue Renleixue (Chinese Culture and the Sociology and Anthropology of the New Century). *Beijing Daxue Xuebao* (Journal of Peking University: Humanities and Social Sciences) 35(6): 80–90.

Freedman, Maurice. 1958. *Lineage Organization in Southeastern China.* London: London School of Economics.

———. 1966. *Chinese Lineage and Society: Fukien and Kwangtung.* London: London School of Economics.

Fu, Jingxing. 1994. *Quanshan Caipu* (Mining Jade in the Mountains of Quanzhou). Hong Kong: Huaxing Chubanshe.

Gates, Hill. 1996. *China's Motor: A Thousand Years of Petty Capitalism.* Ithaca, NY: Cornell University Press.

Geertz, Clifford. 1983. *Local Knowledge.* New York: Basic.

Giddens, Anthony. 1990. *Modernity and Self-Identity.* Stanford: Stanford University Press.

Gladney, Dru C. 1991. *Muslim Chinese: Ethnic Nationalism in the People's Republic.* Cambridge, MA: Council on East Asian Studies, Harvard University.

———. 1998. *Ethnic Identity in China: The Making of a Muslim Minority Nationality.* Ft. Worth, TX: Harcourt Brace College Publishers.

Habermas, Jürgen. 1996 [1962]. *The Structural Transformation of the Public Sphere.* Cambridge, MA: MIT Press.

Harrell, Stevan. 1985. Why Do the Chinese Work So Hard? Reflections on an Entrepreneurial Ethic. *Modern China* 11(2): 203–26.

———. 2001. *Ways of Being Ethnic in Southwest China.* Seattle: University of Washington Press.

Hobsbawm, Eric. 1983. Introduction: Inventing Traditions. In Eric Hobsbawm and Terence Ranger, eds., *The Invention of Tradition*, pp. 1–14. Cambridge: Cambridge University Press.

Huang, Shu-min. 1980. The Development of Regionalism in Ta-chia, Taiwan: A Non-Kinship View of Chinese Rural Society Organization. *Ethnohistory* 27(2): 243–66.

———. 1998. *The Spiral Road: Change in a Chinese Village through the Eyes of a Communist Party Leader.* Second edition. Boulder, CO: Westview Press. First edition, 1989.

JJSZ. 1994. *Jinjiang Shizhi* (Jinjiang City Gazetteer). Shanghai: Sanlian Shudian.

Kuah, Khun Eng. 1998. Doing Anthropology within a Transnational Framework: A Study of the Singapore Chinese and Emigrant Village Ties. In Sidney C. H. Cheung, ed., *On the South China Track: Perspective on Anthropological Research and Teaching.* Hong Kong: The Chinese University Press.

Kuwabara, Jitsuzo. 1935. *Tang-Song Maoyigang Yanjiu* (The Study of Port Cites in the Tang-Song Period). Chinese translation. Shanghai: Shangwu Yinshuguan.

Lin, Chang-kuan. 1996. *Zhongguo Huijiao zhi Fazhan ji qi Yundong* (The Development and Movement of Islam in China). Taipei: Zhonghua Minguo Alabo Wenhua Jingji Xiehui.

Lyotard, Jean-François. 1979. *The Post-Modern Condition: A Report on Knowledge.* Manchester: Manchester University Press.

Ma, Jianzhao. 1998. *Zhongguo Nanfang Huizu Pudie Xuanbian* (The Selection of Genealogies of the South China Hui). Nanning: Guangxi Minzu Chubanshe.

Mauss, Marcel. 1950. *The Gift*. New York and London: W. W. Norton.

Metzger, Thomas. 1977. *Escape from Predicament: Neo-Confucianism and China's Evolving Political Culture*. New York: Columbia University Press.

MS. *Mingshi* (History of the Ming Dynasty). Shanghai: Zhonghua Shuju.

Ogden, Suzanne. 1991. *China's Unresolved Issues: Politics, Development, and Culture*. Second edition. Englewood, NJ: Prentice Hall.

Pan, Hongli. 2000. Minnan Diqu Zongqinghui de Fuxing ji qi Kuaguo Wangluo (Lineage Revival in Minnan and Transnational Network). In Chen Zhiming, Zhang Xiaojun, and Zhang Zhanhong, eds., *Chuantong yu Bianqian: Huanan de Rentong yu Wenhua* (Tradition and Change: Identities and Cultures in South China). Beijing: Wenjin Chubanshe.

Parking, David, et al., eds. 1996. *The Politics of Cultural Performance*. Oxford: Berghn Books.

Pasternak, Burton. 1969. The Role of the Frontier in Chinese Lineage Development. *The Journal of Asian Studies* 23: 551–61.

Shils, Edward A. 1981. *Tradition*. London: Faber & Faber.

Tan, Qixiang. 1987. Zhongguo Wenhua de Shidai Chayi he Diqu Chayi (Time and Regional Diversity in Chinese Culture). In Department of History (Fudan University), ed., *Zhongguo Chuantong Wenhua de Zaiguji* (Reappraisal of Traditional Chinese Culture), pp. 23–42. Shanghai: Shanghai Renmin Chubanshe.

Tang, Wenquan. 1993. *Juexing yu Miwu — Zhongguo Jindai Minzu Zhuyi Sichao Yanjiu* (Awake and Loss — The Trend of Thought of Chinese Nationalist in the Modern Era). Shanghai: Shanghai Renmin Chubanshe.

Wallace, Anthony. 1956. Revitalization Movement. *American Anthropologists* 58(2): 264–81.

Wang, Mingming. 1997. *Shehui Renleixue yu Zhongguo Yanjiu* (Social Anthropology and Sinology). Beijing: Sanlian Shudian.

———. 1999. *Shiqu de Fanrong: Yizuo Laocheng de Lishi Reuleixue Kaocha* (The Declined Prosperity: A Historical Anthropology of an Old City). Hangzhou: Zhejiang Renmin Chubanshe.

Wang, Yunchuan and Gao Yuxuan. 1993. Lüetan Jinjiang Xingzheng Quyu de Yanbian (Brief Discussion on the Change of the Administrative District of Jinjiang). *Jinjiang Wenshi Ziliao Yuanji* (The Selection of Historical-Literary Materials of Jinjiang), no. 14: 1–7.

Watson, James. 1986. Anthropological Overview: The Development of Chinese Descent Group. In P. Ebrey and J. Watson, eds., *Kinship Organization in Late Imperial China, 1000–1940*, pp. 274–92. Berkeley: University of California Press.

Watson, Rubie. 1994. Memory, History, and Opposition under State Socialism: An

Introduction. In Rubie Watson, ed., *Memory, History, and Opposition under State Socialism*, pp. 1–20. Seattle: University of Washington Press.

Weber, Max. 1973 [1946]. *From Max Weber: Essays in Sociology.* H. H. Gerth and C. Wright Mills, eds. and trans. New York: Oxford University Press.

Xu, Yangjie. 1995. *Song-Ming Jiazu Zhidu Shilun* (On the History of the Song-Ming Family Institution). Beijing: Zhonghua Shuju.

Yang, Martin M. C. 1965 [1945]. *A Chinese Village: Taitou, Shantung Province.* New York: Columbia University Press.

Ye, Wencheng, et al. 1990. Chendai Zhen Andoucun Shehui Minsu Diaocha (A Social Survey on Folklore in Andou Village, Chendai Township). In Chen Guoqiang, et al., eds., *Chendai Huizushi Yanjiu* (The Studies of the Chendai Hui History), pp. 231–46. Beijing: Zhongguo Shehui Kexue Chubanshe.

Zhang, Chengzhi. 1995 [1991]. *Xinling Shi* (The Spiritual History). Haikou: Hainan Chubanshe.

Zheng, Zhenman. 1992. *Ming-Qing Fujian Jiazu Zuzhi yu Shehui Bianqian* (Social Change and Family Organization in the Ming-Qing Fujian). Changsha: Hunan Jiaoyu Chubanshe.

Zhuang, Jinghui. 1993. Chendai Dingshi Huizu Hanhua de Yanjiu (A Study of the Chendai Hui Surnamed Ding's Assimilation with the Han). In *Haijiaoshi Yanjiu* (Maritime History Studies), no. 2: 93–108.

——, ed. 1996. *Chendai Dingshi Huizu Zongpu* (The Genealogy of Ding Hui People of Chendai). Hong Kong: Lüye Chubanshe.

Glossary

Andoucun	岸兜村
Chendai	陳埭
Chen Guohui	陳國輝
denghao	燈號
Dingshi	丁氏
gongming	功名
Kaizhaijie	開齋節
jiaotou	角頭
juxing	巨姓
lulin	閭鄰
mingsheng	名聲
minfeng manhan, tanya wuxiao	民風蠻悍，彈壓無效
Quanshan caipu	泉山采璞
shengshi xiupu	盛世修譜
shengshi xiuzhi	盛世修志

xianhua	獻花
xianji	獻祭
Xu Zhuoran	許卓然
Yujiama	益家媽

3

The Old Folks' Associations and Lineage Revival in Contemporary Villages of Southern Fujian Province

■ Pan Hongli

Introduction

In the rural areas of southern Fujian province (Minnan), lineage organizations reappeared during the 1980s, following the government policy of liberalization. Since the 1990s, the lineage groups in the countryside of southern Fujian, more than in any other part of China, have experienced rapid development, going through a brand new process of "reconstruction." Such practices as compiling genealogies, building ancestral temples, holding large-scale ceremonies to "enshrine the spirit tablets of ancestors" and worshipping ancestors prevail in Jinjiang, Shishi, Nan'an, Tong'an, and other regions (Pan 1999). The lineage revival is closely related to the functions and activities of the Old Folks' Associations (Laorenhui) in these areas.

An Old Folks' Association (hereafter LRH) is a civil organization of elderly people that is recognized by the local officials. In rural south China, the LRH is in fact a sort of continuation of the local lineage gentry of the past, a reinvented form, so to speak. Indeed, the core members of the LRH are lineage elders. As the Chinese government does not recognize lineages (*zongzu*), which it sees as feudal and promoting superstition, the LRHs form a bridge between "traditional" lineages and the local government representing the state. The LRHs use their ambiguous status to help arrange lineage activities and promote their revival. The government can deal with lineages through the LRHs, and lineages use the LRHs to protect and promote their interests. Although scholars have noted the revival of lineage activities in post-1978 China, there is no systematic discussion of the role of the LRHs in this revival. The aim of this paper is to fill in this gap in the present scholarship on China.

Beginning in late 1994, I spent over a year in the southern part of rural Fujian and conducted field research on the present lineage structures. I returned there briefly each year, doing follow-up research during the period from 1997 to 2000. This long-term project traces the impact of the LRHs upon the entire process of lineage rejuvenation in the context of social, political, and cultural systems of contemporary China. It also attempts to underscore the historical, cultural, and traditional climate of southern Fujian province, with an emphasis on the distinguished features of modern lineage organizations. Relying on the material sources collected in my fieldwork, this paper discusses the LRH in the village of Rongqing of Shishi municipality, offering an analytical examination of its organizational structure, characteristics, social functions, as well as its role in promoting lineage growth and rural developments. This study shows how the LRHs have shaped the complicated interplay of the state and the society through stimulating lineage reconstruction. This will contribute to our understanding of rural China today.

The Lineage Structure in Rongqing

Rongqing had been an administrative village located in Lingxiu town, in the Shishi municipality of Fujian province. In 1994, it was divided into three smaller administrative villages named Lingshi, Lingshan, and Lingfeng.[1] The local people, nevertheless, still refer to the whole area as Rongqing. All Rongqing villagers are Han Chinese, with a single surname, Cai.[2] Their genealogy indicates explicitly that their common ancestors came to the village of Rongqing in the mid-14th century, by the end of the Yuan Dynasty. The family of Cai has lived there for 24 generations and multiplied to a population of 8,000, if we count only those concentrated in the eight "natural villages" around Mount Lingxiu on the outskirts of Shishi city.[3] These natural villages are referred to as "the eight hamlets and towns of Rongqing" (Rongqing ba xiang), comprising Qiangfang, Erfang, Xikeng, Chikeng, Shuikeng, Shanxia, Shilin, and Yulou. "Rongqing" is actually the locality of a big multi-village lineage.

The administrative village of Rongqing was established after the Liberation. Then it comprised six natural villages: Qiangfang, Erfang, Xikeng, Chikeng, Shuikeng, and Shanxia. The village of Shilin became an independent administrative village, and Yulou village was turned into a part of the administrative village of Tangyuan. The administrative village of Rongqing, as mentioned, has been broken down into three areas. The two natural villages of Qiangfang and Xikeng constitute the administrative village of Lingshi, the administrative village of Lingfeng consists of the natural villages of Erfang and Shanxia, and the administrative village of Lingshan includes the natural villages of Chikeng and Shuikeng. In short, "the eight hamlets and towns of Rongqing," as the locality of an independent agnatic kinship group, have been broken down into five administrative villages.

The Rongqing lineage, like a hierarchical organization, is differentiated into the following three distinctive strata in accordance with its kinship ties: a higher-order lineage (*dazong*), sublineages (*xiaozong*) and *fang* lineage (*fangzu*). Each stratum of this structure of agnatic kinship has its own temple to worship its ancestors. The Rongqing lineage is "a higher-order lineage" (Freedman 1971: 21); the descendants of the three sons of the second generation constitute the eldest branch, secondary branch as well as third branch respectively, known as "sublineages." They are at the secondary stratum of the lineage structure. Below the three sublineages, we see a number of grassroots units called "*fang*."

The nucleus of the lineage is the ancestral temple, which houses the spirit tablets of the Cais' first generation ancestors. Each of the three sublineages has its own ancestral hall to enshrine the spirit tablets of its own ancestors.[4] Each *fang*, in contrast, has its own ancestral house called "*zucuo*" (ancestors' mansion), where it installs the spirit tablets of those deceased *fang* members whose spirit tablets mostly cannot be promoted yet to the ancestral hall.[5] Periodically (generally every five or 10 years, but the specific period is decided by the lineage), these *fang* ancestral houses hold a ceremony, known as "the spirit tablet enshrinement" (*jinzhu*), to move accumulated tablets into the ancestral hall of their own sublineage for perpetual worship. Studies have indicated that the Rongqing lineage started organizing sacrificial rites as early as at least 200 years ago (Pan 1997). The stratified arrangement of worshipping ancestors typifies the highly developed organization of agnatic kinship in the southern Fujian.

The Rongqing lineage, like most other lineage groups in southern Fujian, binds all members together, relying on holding sacrificial rites to commemorate its ancestors. Nevertheless, since the Rongqing lineage has a highly sophisticated organizational structure, its sacrificial rites manifest a typical type of stratification. All members of the higher-order lineage hold the "Spring and Autumn Sacrificial Rites" as well as the "Grave-

Sweeping Ceremony of Qingming" every year at their ancestral temple.[6] Each sublineage holds the "Autumn Sacrificial Rite" and "Grave-Sweeping Ceremony of Qingming" every year.[7] The *fangs* worship their ancestors much more frequently, organizing as many as eight collective ceremonial activities yearly.[8] These sacrificial rites not only provide an occasion for members inside each unit of every level to socialize with each other but also, practically as well as conceptually, bind every organization within the lineage together closely. In the southern part of Fujian province, we can see such highly sophisticated ritual arrangements, as exist in Rongqing, in numerous villages dominated by powerful agnatic kinship organizations.

Before the Liberation, the Rongqing lineage had influential lineage heads and elders. At that time, the ancestral temple ran an old-style private "school" to educate family descendants. "The Rongqing School Board of Trustees" was in charge of the school affairs. The school board of trustees, in fact, functioned as lineage elders, and villagers viewed the chairman of the board as the head of their lineage. He did, indeed, play the social role of lineage head. Both the higher-order lineage and sublineages compiled their own genealogies. Each of them also possessed their own communal land known as "public estate" (*gongye*).

After the Liberation, the lineage organizations, as relics of "feudal society," were denounced. Their social and economic foundation sustaining the continuation of the lineage was therefore undermined. Meanwhile, the government set up formidable village administrative organs, which replaced the lineage to become the local authority. Furthermore, drastic political campaigns that harassed the rural areas repeatedly tended to completely destroy lineage organizations. From the 1950s to the 1980s, the Rongqing lineage declined greatly due to the severe destructive activities brought about by the political turmoil. From the 1950s, the ancestor worship rituals held by both the higher-order lineage and sublineages were banned completely, genealogies as well as spirit tablets were burned, and ancestral temples as well as ancestral halls were occupied, no longer functioning as the center of the ancestral cult.[9] Meanwhile, members of each *fang* shunned collective sacrificial rites that were once held openly. Many *fang* ancestral houses collapsed or were in a very poor condition. In other words, all public activities centering on the agnatic kinship structure were suspended, and the Rongqing lineage lingered on in an increasingly worsening condition.

After the 1980s, the Rongqing lineage was revived following the drastic political and economic changes in China. Its recovery was largely completed by the mid-1990s. The LRH played a significant role in the

Rongqing lineage revival. It was the LRH that made the first suggestion to rebuild the ancestral temple and ancestral halls; it was the members of the association who began to organize the committee in charge of the reconstruction project, and it was these elderly villagers who further facilitated all kinds of work centering on the lineage.

We can trace the Rongqing lineage revival to the reconstruction of ceremonial space initiated by each grassroots unit known as *fangzu,* a sublineage. Members of each *fangzu,* who were closely bound by blood ties, started rebuilding their *fang* ancestral houses, setting in motion the entire process of ancestral-cult reconstruction. Then members of each sublineage began to work on their own ancestral hall to "enshrine the spirit tablets of their ancestors"; and finally, the higher-order lineage decided to rebuild the ancestral temple, where it enshrined the spirit tablets of its ancestors for perpetual worship. All the activities, such as the reconstruction of ceremonial space, recovery as well as promotion of sacrificial rites, compilation of genealogies anew,[10] and amassment of lineage estate afresh,[11] followed a course that began with the basic level of *fangzu* and ended at the top stratum of the higher-order lineage.

This pattern of development demonstrated genealogical relations, which started with close relatives and ended with distant kin. The entire process of development proceeded in a manner of gradual expansion, and eventually it succeeded with the reunification of the lineage through rebuilding each branch organization. Family members reconfirmed as well as conceptualized their genealogical relations in the entire process of reconstruction, and consequently their blood ties were highlighted. In addition, when the lineage group had regained and expanded its social functions, it was increasingly involved in the daily life of local society. Nowadays in Rongqing, the lineage activities have become part and parcel of the local villagers' everyday life, and lineage organizations have adapted themselves to modern society, acting as one of the crucial factors stimulating the transitions and developments of rural society.

The Formation of the Old Folks' Association

Since the 1980s, the LRH, an organization that is open to all elderly people, has been set up all over China. "The Committee in Charge of LRH" has been founded at all levels of administration, from the central and municipal levels to county as well as township administrative levels. The LRH committee is fully responsible for all issues regarding elderly people.

Originally founded by prominent elderly people, the LRH has since received recognition from the government, which hopes it will promote support for the government among ordinary people. In the rural areas of southern Fujian province, the LRHs have experienced a rapid growth owing to the support and encouragement of the government. At present, an LRH exists in over 90 percent of all administrative villages and neighborhoods.

Rongqing set up the LRH as early as 1986. In the countryside of southern Fujian where lineage was highly developed historically, people's "memory" of the powerful lineage elders has helped the government-sanctioned LRH to be accepted quickly. The LRH has evoked and reinterpreted "memory" in circumstances of the modern society.

Reaching a certain age is the only requirement for joining the LRH. Different villages have different age criteria, but normally the range is from 55 to 60 years old. All those who meet the age qualification are admitted once an application has been made. In the village of Rongqing, everyone who is over the age of 55, who has made an application and is willing to pay the required annual fee of RMB2.4, is entitled to be a member. By 1995, the Rongqing LRH had more than 400 members. In 1999, Lingshi village alone had more than 200 elderly people of the age of 60 or above who were members of the LRH. They accounted for over 80 percent of all "elderly people" in the village.

In the political framework of modern China, the LRH is officially characterized as "a mass organization under the leadership of the village branch of the Communist Party and the village council."[12] Almost all the LRHs quoted the above-mentioned statement in their regulations. The *Rules of the Rongqing Chief Old Folks' Association in Lingxiu Town of Shishi City* were revised in April 1996. It listed the statement as clause 2 of Chapter I: the General Principles.[13] Apparently, the LRH is distinct from the powerful lineage board of elders that had dominated village politics until state administrative units became deeply involved in local affairs. The LRH works under the leadership of the "two village councils," the local representatives of the state authority.

Although the LRH has accepted the leadership of the state administrative bodies (the government), it does not act as one of the government organs. The "two village councils" (the branch committee of the Communist Party and the council of villagers) and other administrative bodies do not interfere directly in its organizational formation and operations. In Rongqing, the council of the LRH is in charge of its organizational operations. The two village councils do not appoint senior council members, who instead are elders chosen by every *fang* division based on their ability and prestige. The government does not intervene directly in the selection process.

The council members of the LRH are distinct from each other in their backgrounds, experiences, expertise, and capacity. They are, for instance, retired town cadres, former village bosses, retired high school teachers, "peasant enterprisers," fortune-tellers, individuals interested in folk religion, and returned overseas Chinese. Their political backgrounds also show great diversity; some of them are senior members of the Chinese Communist Party, and others are members of the Zhigong Party, including members of the Chinese People's Political Consultative Conference of Shishi City. However, all have one thing in common: they, as the élite of the Rongqing lineage, have represented the interests of different groups and social strata in the village to a certain extent.

Almost all honorary positions of the council are specifically offered to those overseas family members who have the financial capacity. Former local cadres are important for the LRH to communicate with the local governments smoothly, enhancing the authority of the association to a certain extent; overseas Chinese, as prestigious lineage members in their home village, could promote the social status of the association. Furthermore, by inviting overseas Chinese to sit on the council as honorary members, the LRH has also expressed its gratitude to these family members for their powerful support and maintaining close ties with them. The council members of the association are elected every two years for a two-year term, but normally all of them are reelected continually.

Although external factors (such as the local government) play only a small role in the LRH's organizational work, when the association considers council members' qualifications, especially its leading personnel, the complicated interaction of various divisions of the lineage has a remarkable influence on the modern election process. Eventually, the association has to conform its decisions to the different demands of various divisions by combining the modern election with the conventional art of balance. In order to hold one of the leading posts of the LRH, such as director, deputy-director, or secretary-general, a candidate needs to have not only strong ability and high prestige, but also a powerful sublineage for support.

In the case of the Rongqing lineage, the third sublineage has always been the most powerful. As the most populous sublineage, it is known as the "strong" *fang* (*qiang fang*). Furthermore, the "Xiasanluo" *fang* within it, or the so-called "dragon and tiger" *fang* due to its powerful influence, has dominated the third sublineage since it has a large population. Since the

1920s, the elders of the "Xiasanluo" *fang* occupied the post of the Rongqing lineage head. In 1986, when the LRH came into existence, an elder of the same division became the director of the association. The elder was a prestigious country gentleman who had taught in a high school but quit his job and returned to his home village due to poor health. He held the position until 1996, when he died. His successor is an elder of the *fang* as well. He is the recently retired village chief of Lingshi, holding the position until today. The elders of other sublineages hold the other leading posts of the association, such as deputy-director and secretary-general. In each election, all sublineages and *fang* divisions fought each other bitterly, but these open competitions and secret contentions always ended in peace owing to the mediation that operated within the lineage. Obviously, the LRH works in the context of lineage structure.

Without governmental subsidy, the Rongqing LRH raised funds to cover its own operational expenditures. A significant portion of its funds came from donations made by overseas family members and local villagers. The association also ran businesses to support itself financially. For instance, it owned eight shopping lots for rent. These shops, known as "Stores for the Benefits of Aged People," were built with funds from overseas donations. The association also ran markets, mah-jong tables in the recreation room, and funeral facilities, which yield income from fees and rent. It was also entitled to a portion of the village temple's administration fees. The LRH managed to keep a balance between income and expenditure. In addition to covering routine activities, it allocated funds for subsidizing members who were poor, rewarding teachers and pupils of elementary schools, as well as promoting social intercourse with the LRH and lineage groups in neighboring villages.

We may catch a glimpse of the distinct features of the LRH by focusing on its changing organizational structure. According to my follow-up research, which lasted for several years, the organizational structure of the Rongqing LRH adapted itself to the alterations of rural society, continually adjusting and enriching itself in order to play an increasingly significant role in the local social life. Over the six years from 1994 to 2000, the association held four elections to improve its organizational mechanism. The fifth management committee of the Rongqing LRH in Shishi city elected in 1994 is as follows:

the Permanent Honorary Directors (3), the Permanent Honorary Advisors (9), Advisors (8), the Director (1), the Standing Vice-Directors (2), the Vice-

Directors (1 in charge of environmental sanitation, 1 in charge of financial affairs, 1 in charge of conflict mediation, 1 in charge of culture and education, and 1 in charge of liaison), the Secretary-General (1), the Chair of the Cultural Center (1), the Group of Cultural and Educational Affairs (1 head and 1 assistant head), the Group of Financial Affairs (1 head, 1 assistant head, 1 accountant, and 1 cashier), the Group of Mediation (1 head, 2 assistant heads), Council Members (12), Managerial Staff in Charge of Funeral Facilities (3), the Branch Society of Shilin (1 director), the Group of Qiangfang Division (1 division head), the Group of Erfang Division (1 division head), and the Group of Xikeng Division (1 division head).

The organizational mechanism of the Rongqing LRH indicates that it was a multi-village society. Going beyond a single administrative village, it embraced "the eight hamlets and towns of Rongqing," home of the entire Rongqing lineage. The societies in the three natural villages of Qiangfang, Erfang, and Xikeng were named *zu,* or groups, because these villages were a part of the administrative village of Rongqing in 1994. The LRH in Shilin village was referred to as the "branch society" (*fenhui*), since Shilin, a member of "the eight hamlets and towns of Rongqing," has always been an independent administrative village. In addition, the natural village of Yuluo is one of "the eight hamlets and towns of Rongqing," but it has been under the jurisdiction of Tangyuan administrative village since the Liberation. The deputy-director of the LRH in Tangyuan village, an elder of Yuluo, was specifically appointed deputy-director of the Rongqing LRH (in charge of liaison).

In May 1996, the Rongqing LRH, taking advantage of reelection, renamed itself "the Rongqing Chief LRH" to be in line with the administrative change — the administrative village of Rongqing was broken down into three villages. The organization still supervised all the LRHs in the three villages. Meanwhile, the association also revised its regulations. In Chapter III, entitled *Membership*, of the newly updated *Rules of the Rongqing Chief LRH in Lingxiu Town of Shishi City*, clause 10 states that "the society follows the group membership system, which means that all the LRHs located within the Rongqing area may join the association as institutional members."

Thus, the Rongqing LRH actually retained its full authority over all members living in the region formerly known as the administrative village of Rongqing. In other words, the Rongqing Chief LRH (Rongqing Laorenzonghui), as the successor of the Rongqing LRH, functioned as the organizational leader of all the LRHs located in "the eight hamlets and towns of Rongqing" that were under the jurisdiction of the five administrative villages. There were two elections in 1998 and 2000, but the organizational structure remained unchanged.

The LRH, as mentioned earlier, must work under the leadership of the two village councils, which means that it should be an organization set up in line with administrative villages. The Rongqing LRH and its successor, the Rongqing Chief LRH, nevertheless have been based on the Rongqing lineage. The Rongqing Chief LRH, therefore, did not copy the officially designed model entirely from the very beginning. The traditional factors of lineage prevailing in southern Fujian played a part in its organizational formation while the association endorsed the official principles.

Over the past years, the council members of the Rongqing LRH have increased with each election. There were only 58 members in 1994, and in 1996 there were 76 members. In 1998, the number of the council members increased to 132 and grew slightly to 138 in 2000. The council, apparently, has continuously strengthened itself by drawing people with talent from lineage members. In March 1998, the council set up an executive committee. The council members normally held a meeting every six months, but the executive committee met each month or even more frequently, if necessary, to discuss various internal as well as external affairs of the village and the lineage. The LRH obviously handled its routine work in the democratic manner of a modern society.

As the council members increased, the association added a number of subcommittees to be in charge of daily routines. There were merely five subcommittees in 1995. In 1996, the association formed eight new subcommittees: "the Secretariat Committee," "the Financial Affairs Committee," "the Education Committee," "the Management of Cultural and Historical Resources Committee," "the Public Welfare Committee," "the Liaison Committee," "the Culture, Sports, and Publicity Committee," and "the Social Traditions and Conflicts Management Committee." Nine new subcommittees — "the Religion and Popular Customs Committee," "the Lineage Affairs Committee," "the Civil Mediation Committee," "the Welfare and Health Care Committee," "the Friendship Committee of Middle-aged and Young People," "the Women's Liaison Committee," "the Caring for the New Generation Committee," "the Rongqing Old Folks' School Committee," and "the Cultural and Physical Activity Center Committee" — were founded in 1998. Thus there were 22 LRH subcommittees. "The Lineage Affairs Committee" became "the Committee of Lineage Affairs and Popular Customs" in 2000. Meanwhile, four subcommittees — "the

Managerial Committee of the Ancestral Temple," "the Market Managerial Committee," "the Managerial Committee of Lineage Estate," and "the Managerial Committee of the Jinxiang Bodhisattva Temple" — were formed. Thus there were altogether 26 subcommittees. Apparently, in order to deal with various problems in rural society more effectively, the LRH established more and more subcommittees.

The LRH has experienced transformation over the past years. It not only provides recreational service to enrich elderly people's daily life, but also plays an indisputable role in maintaining the stability and development of the village. Although it keeps close ties with lineage groups, the association has grown into a huge organization that assumes such "modern features" as selecting council members by democratic election and settling crucial matters through discussion and consultation. The LRH is, however, not a lineage group.

Affiliated Organizations of the Old Folks' Association

The government expects elderly people to endorse its guidelines and policies actively and to assist the authority in building a stable rural society by giving full play to their influence. It thus lays great emphasis on the rural LRH. The regulations of all the LRHs, accordingly, give clear indications that the association "works under the leadership of the two village councils," "advocates the Communist Party and loves socialism," and "spreads the Communist Party's guidelines and policies." Although the LRH is not a "mass organization" of the village administrative organ, it is required in principle to endorse the leadership of the two village councils, functioning as their aid.[14]

In the rural areas of southern Fujian where lineage was highly developed and Confucianism had powerful influence historically, lineage elders were prestigious figures enjoying a high social status. The "politics of elders" prevailing in the patriarchal society of Chinese history has revived in the new guise of the LRH, taking advantage of favorable government policies. The lineage revival meets the social demands caused by the great political, economic as well as social transitions that have occurred since the 1980s.[15] In the rapid growth of the LRHs and their increasingly deep involvement in local social life, we witness lineage elders returning to today's rural political arena.

The LRHs used their legitimate status to help revive lineage activities. They did so by first establishing lineage-based organizations and then promoting lineage activities through these organizations. For example, the Rongqing LRH set up a lineage-based organization, "the Rongqing School Board of Trustees," very soon after its own formation. Then it gradually established other lineage organizations by focusing on a series of activities to reconstruct the ancestral temple. In this way, the LRH contributed to lineage revival via these organizations. During the entire process, the LRH formed increasingly intimate links with the lineage, helping to bring into existence modern lineage elders.

The LRH founded "the Rongqing School Board of Trustees" in response to the government call to "run schools by local society" in 1988. Six of the seven members of the standing committee, the leading body of the school board, were council members of the LRH. The school board, an organization of villagers, was established primarily to secure financial resources necessary for running the Rongqing Elementary School. The board appealed to villagers' lineage identity, mobilizing overseas and local lineage members to donate to an educational fund.

Under the management and arrangement of the board, the fund was used for issuing "teaching prizes" and "scholarships" to the teachers and pupils of the Rongqing School on New Year's Day, Teachers' Day, and

6. The committee members of the Old Folks' Association are also lineage elders (photograph by Pan Hongli).

Children's Day. The board was responsible for supervising teaching as well as making the final decision regarding the appointment of the school principal. Before the Liberation, as mentioned earlier, "the Rongqing School Board of Trustees" acted as the board of Rongqing lineage elders. Thus the role of the Board of Trustees evoked villagers' "memory" of past lineage elders. Since the board contributed to the management of the village school, the LRH established a good reputation in local society. As these board members functioned as lineage elders to a certain extent, we may regard "the Rongqing School Board of Trustees" as a quasi-lineage organization.

In the early 1990s, under the sponsorship of the LRH, both the higher-order lineage and sublineages established several lineage organizational bodies, such as the "Reconstruction Committees" and "Managerial Committees," which were responsible for rebuilding and running the ancestral temple and ancestral halls.[16] The third sublineage completed rebuilding its ancestral hall in November 1993, and the second sublineage completed its hall later, in September 1994. The first sublineage could not complete its project until 1997 because of the location of its ancestral hall. Since it is located behind the ancestral temple, villagers believed that the first sublineage could not start reconstruction until a new ancestral temple had been built; otherwise, the *fengshui* (geomancy) of the whole lineage would be undermined. Each sublineage formed its own "Reconstruction Committee of the Ancestral Hall" prior to the reconstruction. Afterwards it was transformed into the "Managerial Committee of the Ancestral Hall."

The "Trustee Board and Supervisory Board of Rebuilding the Rongqing Ancestral Temple of the Cais" came into existence in August 1994 and was renamed "Managerial Committee of the Rongqing Ancestral Temple of the Cais" after the temple was completed in January 1996. The LRH initiated these boards and committees, so their members were mainly the backbone of the association. For instance, 11 council members of the LRH held crucial positions on the reconstruction committee of the third sublineage that comprised 16 core members.

These reconstruction or managerial committees carried out numerous lineage activities through their reconstruction and management of ancestral halls. Thus they set the organizational functions of the lineage in motion. To compile genealogies, for instance, the reconstruction committees designed survey forms and distributed them to all families. Traditional genealogical ties, such as the family members' division, subdivision as well as generational ranks, which had vanished long ago, were highlighted when these families

7. Some members of the Old Folks' Association discussing the worship of the local guardian deity Shangdi Gong (photograph by Pan Hongli).

began to fill in these forms. On the occasion of "enshrining the spirit tablets of ancestors," the reconstruction committee "combined the conventional style with modern content," having elaborated a whole set of rules to guide the ancestor worship ritual. Villagers were required to follow these rules closely.

Later, in order to standardize villagers' activities, the managerial committee of the ancestral temple formulated meticulous rules to direct the higher-order lineage and sublineages holding the collective sacrificial rites. These ancestor worship rituals have been institutionalized as new customs during these years. While recreating lineage traditions, these committee members have also become de facto lineage elders gradually, giving significant or even dominant influence upon the local society. Meanwhile, since the director of the LRH was in charge of these committees, he handled a wide range of complicated lineage affairs in a direct and general manner. Local villagers have gradually looked up to him as the de facto lineage head, who became a prominent figure enjoying high esteem.

In conclusion, lineage organizations have been formed gradually, owing to the promotion and overall participation of the LRH. The Rongqing lineage, through rebuilding family halls, ancestral halls and ancestral temples, have amassed the lineage estate, recompiled, updated, as well as extended family genealogies, widely revived as well as developed the ancestral cult, strengthened kinship ties, and reconfirmed the rights as well as the obligations of lineage members.

It is worth noting that in the late 1990s, the LRH, which has close links to the lineage, has also reinforced its ties with the authority. For instance, it set up several important internal organizations in response to the call of the government. These included the Rongqing Old Folks' School, the Association Caring for the Younger Generation, and the Cultural and Physical Activity Center. The center was established specially for enriching the elderly people's recreational activities. The aim of the Association Caring for the Younger Generation was to provide support for the Rongqing Elementary School, in order to better educate the descendants of the Rongqing lineage.

The Rongqing Old Folks' School located in the ancestral temple was set up in November 1996, and it had been very active. On the 2nd and 16th

8. The headquarters of Rongqing Old Folks' Association housed in the lineage temple (photograph by Pan Hongli).

days of each lunar month, it offered lectures on health care, popular science, current politics, and so on. The audience consisted of council members as well as ordinary society members. The school invited retired local teachers or teachers from Shishi to give lectures. Also, in the afternoon of every Tuesday, Thursday, and Saturday, retired Rongqing teachers functioned as storytellers, recounting historical novels, such as *Romance of the Three Kingdoms*, to an audience. This kind of storytelling is called *jianggu* (giving talks on antiquity). Such activities attracted a large number of elderly people. In August 1999, the Rongqing Old Folks' School won a prize at the experience-exchange conference attended by all old folks' schools in the prefecture of Quanzhou.

Originally, the LRH established the above-mentioned organizational bodies to answer the call of the government. These organizations grew smoothly due to the strong support of the LRH, as they were seen as beneficial to the village social life. The government apparently attempted to enrich old people's lives through these organizational bodies, and it intended to influence the elderly people more effectively via these organizations.

Interestingly, one of the organizations affiliated to the Rongqing LRH is the "Rongqing Youth Association of Shishi Municipality." The Rongqing Chief LRH sponsored the association to unite the young people who lived in the urban district of Shishi and to strengthen the communication and exchange between the local young lineage members and those who lived abroad. The regulations of the association stated that it worked under the "guidance" of the LRH.[17] It actually acted as a critical link to bridge the gap between the Rongqing lineage elders and young lineage members. These lineage elders obviously wished to influence or even control young family members via the association.

The LRH founded the above-mentioned organizations because of the interaction of the state and the society. These affiliated organizations have further reinforced the ties between the LRH and the state as well as between the society and the lineage. The backbone of the LRH, as discussed above, holds key positions in these organizations, playing a dual role. Thus they are able to play different roles on various occasions. They act in the name of the LRH while dealing with the government, and they function on behalf of the lineage authority while handling issues relating to the lineage. For instance, lineage elders help local governments solve village conflicts in the name of the LRH.

While the LRH has facilitated the formation of these affiliated organizations and played a crucial part in their operations, these organizations, as firm supporters of the LRH, have vigorously enhanced its prominence. The LRH and its attached organizations headed by the lineage group work in tandem, having noticeably helped each other forward. These affiliated organizational bodies therefore have reinforced the social foundation of the LRH, expanded its action space, as well as increasingly enhanced its impact upon the rural society.

The Old Folks' Association: An Intermediary between the State and the Society

In Rongqing, like everywhere else in China, elderly people sit together, playing mah-jong or chatting joyfully in recreation rooms of various LRHs each day. The most obvious purpose of the LRH appears to provide older villagers with entertainment, enabling them to spend their remaining years happily. In fact, the LRH plays a far more significant social role in the rural society of today. If we focus on the relationship between the state and the society, we may view the LRH as a link between them. As a necessary intermediate and communication channel, the LRH has contributed to the stability and development of the rural society.

We may draw a conceptual chart to illuminate how the LRH has bridged the gap between the state and the society by specifying its position as well as its significance. If we define the "two village councils" as the "state," and characterize the lineage, the traditional social unit, as the local society, we can position the LRH between the two. It keeps a close relationship with both of them. The LRH works under the leadership of the village councils, supporting and assisting the village councils. In this respect, the LRH is authorized by the state. Also, the LRH has promoted lineage revival, and the lineage elders constitute the backbone of the LRH. Thus, the LRH is also strongly supported by the traditional force in the society. We should consider it neither a real administrative organ of the state nor a full lineage group. However, we can view the LRH as the intermediate between the administrative organ of the modern state and traditional lineage in the rural society.

To this day, the state has not yet recognized the lineage openly. Thus, the state and the lineage group cannot communicate with each other directly. However, the lineage group has not only already recovered, increasingly it also has significant influence upon the rural society. Under these circumstances, the village councils cannot easily keep the village under their firm control or smooth administration if the lineage refuses to cooperate. The local authority, including the village councils, thus expects to reinforce its control by relying on the LRH. However, the lineage leaders also wish to keep contact with administrative bodies, especially to exert influence on the village councils, through the channel of the LRH. Only in this way can the lineage take good care of its own interests. The leaders of the LRH in fact skillfully take advantage of their unique position, handling various issues regarding the state and the society in their villages successfully. In the countryside of southern Fujian, because the LRH plays a very remarkable role of intermediary, the state and the society are able to coexist harmoniously; a wide range of social problems, therefore, have been solved smoothly, and the local economy as well as the cultural life have developed with great speed. In Rongqing, the village councils and lineage have helped and supported each other, forming a cooperative relationship relying on the mediation of the LRH. The LRH, as a result, has become a powerful institution in the village.

A deeper analysis of the LRH indicates that it does not always take a halfway stand between the two extremes of the state and the society. Looking at its record over the past decade, one can see that the LRH has gradually moved toward the direction of a traditional social organization, having built increasingly close ties with the lineage. In order to restrict its movement, the government took a series of measures. For instance, as discussed earlier, the government issued officially formulated regulations, such as the *Rules of the Old Folks' Association of Greater Quanzhou*, and distributed them to all the LRHs located in various cities and counties, with the aim of standardizing their regulations. These model regulations laid emphasis on the leadership of the Communist Party and highlighted the role of the LRHs to support as well as cooperate with the government. Also, the government continually urged as well as helped the LRHs to establish schools for elderly people, which offer lectures on current affairs and provide political education.

After July 1999, when the Falun Gong incident occurred, it became publicly known that many elderly people were involved in the "evil cult." The government realized the political significance of elderly people and therefore intervened in the activities of the association more vigorously. In the rural areas of the southern Fujian, Falun Gong had hardly any converts. Nevertheless, the local governments reinforced political education and propaganda among elderly people. In August 2000, for instance, the senior committee in the municipality of Shishi selected key members of the local

LRHs to form a lecture group that toured the countryside to advocate the Party's newly publicized theory of the "three representatives" (*sange daibiao*).[18] These lecturers were retired cadres and teachers, and their audience consisted of ordinary members of the various village LRHs, who were mainly non-Party members. The lecture group explained and publicized the theory of the "three representatives" to enhance the esteem of the political party in power and solidify elderly people's support for the Party and the government.

Consequently, elderly people would obey the directions of the Party and government more willingly, voluntarily assisting the authorities in solving various problems in the rural areas. Although consciously or subconsciously the LRH sometimes tends to lean toward one extreme a little and then move to another extreme, at present it basically maintains a halfway position between the state and the society. The LRH therefore enjoys a vast space of activity, which enables it to freely play a remarkable function in society.

We have already explored how and why the LRH has facilitated the lineage revival. We can now discuss the social functions of the association through an examination of several other issues. We shall focus on the activities of the LRH in Lingshi village, which is affiliated with the Rongqing Chief LRH. Its social functions can be divided into two main categories. First, the Lingshi LRH actively participates in government and political affairs, makes constructive suggestions, and helps village administration with its daily work. The director of the LRH attends meetings held by the village councils. The important members of the LRH attend the "extended meetings" (*kuoganhui*) of the village cadres, offering their opinions on all kinds of work in the village.

The LRH customarily functions "as an advisor of the village administration" (*yi cunzheng dang canmou*). In addition, the LRH earnestly practices what it has advocated, being actively involved in the practical work of the village councils and relying on its influence on villagers and its close ties with overseas family members. For instance, Lingshi village decided to construct an office building, because when the village of Rongqing had been split into two, the newly formed village council of Lingshi had no office space. In May 1998, in order to collect funds for construction, members of the LRH, along with village cadres, made a trip to the Philippines, where there are many people of Rongqing lineage origin. They successfully collected RMB650,000. The recently completed administrative building attracted the attention of local villagers. It symbolizes cooperation between the LRH and the village authority.

In 1999, the village decided to set up a "cooperative clinic" (*hezuo yiliaosuo*) so that villagers could receive convenient medical treatment. The LRH took the lead in collecting donations. It collected RMB300,000 and built the first village cooperative clinic in the town. The LRH, along with the village authority, vigorously mobilized local masses to participate in the cooperative medical service. More than 50 percent of all villagers endorsed cooperative medical care. Consequently, health care has been improved greatly. In addition, the LRH and the village councils worked together to formulate the *Village Rules to Transform Social Traditions*, with the aim of "eliminating harmful local customs and habits." For instance, it made an effort to promote funeral reform (to encourage cremation in place of burial practices and to simplify funeral rituals), carry out birth control policy, repairing rural roads, construct public washrooms, and supervise environmental sanitation. The LRH has played a crucial role in the daily operations of rural administration.

Second, the LRH is indispensable for mediating in disputes within and outside the village, maintaining the stability and harmony of rural society. Conflicts and confrontations have increased sharply in China's countryside, due to the rapid social and political transitions. The local government alone is not able to handle these problems successfully. Since it has an increasingly strong influence upon local society, the LRH can solve disputes smoothly by combining traditional lineage mediation mechanisms with modern legal means. In fact, the LRH helped solve a number of complicated cases, whereas the government failed in settling them properly through legal channels.

Over the past several years, the Lingshi LRH has successfully mediated in many civil disputes, including a case that had dragged on for 50 years. Both parties involved in the case belonged to a powerful lineage; they fought for family properties while living in several countries. Another case was related to a serious traffic accident. The two villages involved could not reach an agreement on the issue of compensation for the dead; the accident therefore, nearly led to an inter-village confrontation. The LRH solved the case skillfully and promptly. In addition, the LRH established an "orphanage fund," helping to raise children who lost their parents due to accidents. It also subsidized poor elderly people with grain and cash on New Year's Day and on Old Folks' Day (Laorenjie). During the summer of 2000, the LRH set up a "recreation room" in the ancestral temple "for elderly people and children to play together." Once a week, elderly people and children of the Rongqing Elementary School played table tennis, indoor basketball, and all kinds of games in the "recreation room," having fun together. In addition, every year the LRH organizes two or three tours to Mount Putuo, offering a chance for elderly people in the village to visit the Buddhist holy land. In order to enrich the life of elderly people, the LRH formed a troupe to play folk music, encouraging the elderly players to entertain themselves. The LRH has therefore won the trust of local villagers, becoming known as the "old folks' government" (*laoren zhengfu*) of the village.

Conclusion

The Rongqing LRH under discussion is merely an example of the organization of elderly people who live in the rural areas of southern Fujian. Nevertheless, an analytical examination of it has unveiled the internal links between the LRH and lineage revival in the areas. It has also shown how the LRH has perpetuated as well as inherited local social traditions, but adapting itself to the political reality of contemporary China. In conclusion, the social functions of the Rongqing LRH have clearly characterized the local features of rural society in southern Fujian within the nationwide social and political order of modern China.

Historically, the lineage was highly developed in the rural areas of southern Fujian. The "reign of lineage elders" was undermined because of strong political campaigns during the chaotic years from the 1950s to the 1970s. Since the 1980s, due to political and economic reforms, the state has been gradually loosening its control. The free market economy has been growing rapidly, and the authorities began to promote and support the "mass organization" of LRHs in the countryside. The traditional "elder politics" (*zhanglao zhengzhi*) first reappeared in the new form of the modern LRHs in the rural areas. It has experienced a fast recovery as well as development within the organizational structure of the LRH.

In southern Fujian province, the rural LRHs have balanced themselves in the interactions of the state and the society, exercising an intermediary function between modern state administration and traditional rural institutions such as lineages. They are backed up by both the state and the society simultaneously, and they keep close ties with both of them. The LRH, therefore, enjoys a triple authority of bureaucracy, tradition, and charisma (Weber 1946).[19] It works under the leadership of local governmental bodies (such as the village councils), helping local governments with their work in the countryside. It is accordingly supported by the administration.

In addition, some members of the association are retired cadres or officials. So, the LRH assumes the authority of bureaucracy, or the so-called "semi-official authority."

Since the formation of the LRH is intimately related to the traditional lineage, largely symbolizing the "reign of lineage elders," it therefore possesses very strong traditional authority. The authority of charisma is also called natural authority, which naturally takes shape owing to unique capabilities and a wholehearted devotion to the people. Although the key members of the LRH, headed by the president, are people from all walks of life, all of them are the élite of the lineage, who have strong abilities and are highly experienced. In addition, they are willing to devote themselves to helping local villagers "selflessly." They are therefore highly prestigious local celebrities.

Other organs of the state and the society, unlike the LRH, do not enjoy the triple authority simultaneously. The administrative institutions of the state, such as the village councils, possess the authority of bureaucracy, since they function within the bureaucratic structure. However, they no longer play a powerful role due to the policy of liberalization. Since the rural collective economy has collapsed, the administrative power of the village councils has been weakened a great deal. The administrative institutions from top to bottom are accordingly losing their authority of bureaucracy. As for the authority of charisma, although recently the village councils have been produced through democratic elections, qualifications like age and educational background for the council members have diminished their natural authority.

The village councils enjoy almost none of their traditional authority. However, organizations of local society — such as the Managerial Committee of the Ancestral Temple, a "pure lineage organizational organ," and "the spiritual committee," a temporary organization holding folk religious activities frequently — enjoy traditional authority. Yet without official approval, they have to a great extent relied on the LRH in order to be involved in local activities and communicate with the state. Because their operations are suppressed or restricted by the state, they cannot fully spread their influence to every corner of the village society. Therefore, they have not secured a natural authority comparable to that of the LRH. In conclusion, the LRH is the most prestigious organization in rural society.

Today, the government refuses to approve certain local social organizations like lineages, which have not only recovered but also have made an increasingly great impact upon the daily operations of the village administration. The state, therefore, needs to communicate with the local society through the channel of the LRH. Similarly, in order to defend its own interests in the prevailing social and political circumstances, the lineage cannot oppose the government; instead, it has to make every effort to avoid conflicts with the authority. In order to accomplish this task, the lineage certainly has to rely on the LRH, the most effective intermediary. The LRH acts as a bridge to fill the gap between the state and the society perfectly.

In the countryside of southern Fujian province, many LRHs are similar to the Rongqing LRH discussed here. They have played a tremendous part in lineage revival.[20] In the rural areas of southern Fujian province, the LRH has distinguished itself by its intimate relations with the traditional lineage. The LRH was deeply involved in the reconstruction of the lineage, having promoted its development. Meanwhile, depending on the LRH, the lineage group is able to keep contact with the state. Since the LRH plays the role of intermediary between the state and the local society, it plays an indispensable part in the development of contemporary Chinese rural society. Overall, the LRHs play an essential part in maintaining the stability and development of modern Chinese society.

Notes

1. Administrative villages are administratively classified, in contrast to *zirancun* or "natural villages," which existed even before official classification.
2. Cai is the most prominent surname in the region of Jinjiang and Shishi. There are 400,000 people surnamed Cai, accounting for over one-third of the local population. The Cais are distributed among 182 villages, of which the overwhelming majority are single-surnamed villages.
3. In 1977, the Cais living in Xiangzhi town of Shishi municipality identified themselves with the Rongqing lineage. The Xiangzhi lineage has 12,000 family members. They moved away from Rongqing in the past. Now the two lineages of the common ancestry have a close relationship, communicating with each other frequently. They support each other in the local society, having grown into a powerful force recently. The town of Xiangzhi is located near the sea, 15 kilometers away from Rongqing. Historically, approximately over 10,000 Rongqing people migrated to Taiwan, Southeast Asia (especially the Philippines), and other parts of mainland China.
4. In addition to the spirit tablets of ancestors of the sublineage, the "long life and bountiful tablets" (*changshengluwei*) of living members of the sublineage are enshrined in the ancestral hall. The grandparents aged 50 or above are entitled

to the honor. "Long life and bountiful tablets" are wooden tablets wrapped with red silk known as "tablet cover." On the front are written the names of the honored couple.

5. Shrines are erected in a hall within the family mansion for installing the spirit tablets of the ancestors of the *fang* division. The hall is a publicly owned place, so the family mansion is also called "family hall" or sometimes "*gongma* hall" (hall of grandparents) because mainly the spirit tablets of close kin, such as those of "grandparents" are enshrined in the hall. Grandparents are locally called *gongma*. *Fang* division members hold weddings, funerals, and other significant life-cycle celebrations in the family mansion. Collective sacrificial rites also take place in the mansion. Generally, after the funeral of the deceased senior of the division, his or her spirit tablet is enshrined in the mansion. Normally, the spirit tablets remain there until a ceremony known as "enshrinement of spirit tablets" (*jinzhu*) is held to move them into the ancestral hall of the sublineage for permanent worship. But a number of spirit tablets stay in the family mansion forever because their owners died unnaturally (a violent or premature death). These tablets are not entitled to be "enshrined" in the ancestral hall of the sublineage. The family mansion symbolizes the *fang* division, the place where the members gather.

6. The "Spring and Autumn Sacrificial Rites" held customarily by the Rongqing higher-order lineage was resumed in 1997, after having been suspended for 50 years. Generally, the members of the Managerial Committee of the Ancestral Temple attended the rites, and women were excluded.

7. In Rongqing, the third sublineage, prior to the others, held the sacrifice in December 1994, because it had completed reconstructing its ancestral hall first. Mainly members of the Managerial Committee of the Ancestral Hall attended the ritual, and women were excluded. A feast known as "eating the public" (*chigong*) as a component of the ritual was held in the ancestral hall in the evening. Those who attended the feast included elected representatives of each *fang* and those locally known as "the newly wedded or joyful couples," meaning that these young couples held their wedding or had their first baby in the current year. The third sublineage stopped holding its "Autumn Sacrificial Rite" for around a century, because a disastrous fire destroyed its ancestral hall by the end of the Qing Dynasty. The other two sublineages had suspended their "Autumn Sacrificial Rite" at least for 50 years before their resumption.

8. Each *fang* division holds eight collective ceremonies to worship its ancestors yearly. They are not pre-planned or well-organized activities but customarily take place on the occasion of the "eight prominent festivals and holidays" (*ba dajie*) prevailing in the local society. In southern Fujian, the "eight prominent festivals and holidays" normally refer to the Lunar New Year, the Lantern Festival (Shangyuan), Qingming (Pure Brightness), the Dragon Boat Festival, Ullambana (Zhongyuan), Mid-Autumn Festival, Winter Solstice Day, and

Niandou (New Year's Eve). Except for the sacrificial rite held on the Lunar New Year, which involves everyone in the lineage, homemakers are generally responsible for all ceremonial activities.

9. The ancestral hall of the third sublineage was destroyed by fire at the end of the Qing Dynasty.

10. When the lineage completed the reconstruction of its ancestral temples and ancestral halls, it simultaneously recompiled the genealogies. When the higher-order lineage and sublineages held "ceremonies to enshrine the spirit tablets of their ancestors," they also held a rite known as "combining the genealogies" (*hepu*), to deposit the updated genealogies inside the recently renovated ancestral temple or ancestral halls. The "general genealogy" (*zongpu*) of the Rongqing lineage was complied personally by such lineage elders as the president and the secretary-general of the LRH. Under the direction of the LRH, all sublineages and some *fang* divisions have recompiled their own genealogies as well.

11. The lineage estate is also called the "lineage property" (*zuchan*), generally including the ancestral temples, ancestral halls, and cash savings. The cash savings were accumulated by the lineage elders sitting on the committees in charge of reconstructing ancestral temples and ancestral halls. They amassed the money by "levying a tax on all males" (*shou dingfen*) (demanding all male members of the lineage to pay a certain amount of cash) and inviting people to give donations. In Rongqing, donations generally accounted for the larger portion of the cash savings, because overseas lineage members donated the most. Over four-fifths of the funds for building ancestral temples and ancestral halls, for instance, came from overseas lineage members. The higher-order lineage and each sublineage have their own lineage property.

12. In China today, a civilian organization not directly controlled by the government is regarded as a "mass organization." Normally a mass organization needs to be approved by the government so as to be legitimate. As elderly people are still influential in China today, the government pays great ttention to the LRH. For instance, the Committee in Charge of Old Folks' Work of Quanzhou City formulated the *Rules of the Old Folks' Associations in Villages and Neighborhoods of Greater Quanzhou* in accordance with the policy issued by the central government. It quoted the statement explicitly in Chapter I, "the General Principles," of the document.

13. The *Rules of the Rongqing Chief Old Folks' Association in Lingxiu Town of Shishi City* comprises five chapters: Chapter I "the General Principles," Chapter II "Tasks," Chapter III "the Membership," Chapter IV "Organizational Structure," and Chapter V "Supplementary Articles". There are altogether 20 clauses in the document. Clause 2 of Chapter I, "the General Principles," clarifies that "the association is a mass organization of elderly people, which works under the direct leadership of the two councils of Lingxiu town and the general branch of the Communist Party of Rongqing village."

14. In 1998, the Committee in Charge of Old Folks' Work of Quanzhou City distributed the *Rules of the Old Folks' Associations in Villages and Neighborhoods of Greater Quanzhou* to the LRHs located in various subordinate cities and counties, in order to standardize their regulations. The "General Principles" of the above-mentioned document clarifies that "the Old Folks' Association, as the bonding agent for the Party and government to unite all aged people, works under the leadership of the Party branch of the village (neighborhood) as well as the village (neighborhood) council. It plays a significant part in stabilizing the society and creating the two civilizations (the material civilization and spiritual civilization)." The measure indicates that the government attempted to further reinforce its guidance and supervision over the LRH.

15. There are numerous reasons for the lineage revival in southern Fujian, several of which are listed here. First, the policy changes of the government have altered the social climate of China and relaxed political control, which led to the resurgence of the lineage. Second, in southern Fujian, the local society is closely connected to the overseas Chinese circles. These overseas lineage members made huge financial contributions, having actively supported the lineage revival in their home villages. Meanwhile, the overseas Chinese have retained and cultivated some traditional aspects of Chinese culture (such as the sacrificial rite to worship their ancestors and compilation of genealogies), which were sent back to China as a kind of "exported goods sold inside the country." These greatly influence the reconstruction of the lineage in their home villages. Third, the lineage structure has been revived in response to the social needs of the local villages, which have experienced tremendous social as well as political transformations. For instance, in order to control and supervise the local society effectively, the village administrative units increasingly need the help and cooperation of the traditional social organizations. Fourth, the climate of opinion in the rural areas of southern Fujian expresses a desire for returning to the traditional culture, which has led to the revival of folk religions and customs. This climate of opinion facilitated the lineage revival as well. Finally, historically, the lineage was highly developed and long-standing in southern Fujian. The tradition promoted the rapid recovery as well as growth of the lineage today.

16. The recently completed genealogies and inscriptions on tablets have recorded the event explicitly. For instance, on the tablet established by the committee in charge of reconstructing the ancestral hall of the Rongqing third sublineage, a *Record of the Third Sublineage to Rebuild its Ancestral Hall* was inscribed: "In the middle of the 12th month of the lunar year 1992, the Qiangfang group of the Rongqing Old Folks' Association proposed to rebuild (the ancestral hall). All lineage members living in China and abroad warmly echoed the call, and they, either giving donations or working hard, cooperated to contribute to

the event. A preparatory committee in charge of the entire reconstruction project was formed...." The tablet was erected in December 1993.

17. The *Rules of the Rongqing Youth Association in Shishi City* comprises 10 clauses. Clause 2 of the document indicates: "The association is a mass organization of the young people, working under the direct leadership of the municipal as well as the neighborhood committees of the Communist Youth League. The association also accepts the guidance of the Rongqing Old Folks' Association."

18. At the beginning of 2000, Jiang Zemin, Secretary-General of the Communist Party, put forward his theory for building the Party in the 21st century: "The Chinese Communist Party always represents the development of the advanced productive forces in China, always represents the progress of the advanced culture in China, and always represents the essential interests of the largest population of China."

19. See Wang (1997: 268–75) as an example of the recently published works on the popular authorities in the rural areas of southern Fujian. The book focuses on the relations between folk religions and the establishment of local popular authorities.

20. Since 1994, in addition to the Rongqing lineage, I have conducted comparative studies on the following lineages: the Cais living in Yujing, Dongshi town of Jingiang city and in Xiangzhi, Guzhai, as well as Dalun of Shishi City; the lineage of Chen living in Xinqiao of Huian county; and the lineage of Zhang in Gangqian. I have found that, like the Rongqing lineage, the LRHs played a direct role in the revival of all above-mentioned lineages.

References

Freedman, Maurice. 1971. *Chinese Lineage and Society: Fukien and Kwangtung.* Second edition. London: Athlone Press. First edition, 1966.

Pan, Hongli. 1997. The Social Organization of the Han Chinese in Southeast China as well as Its Changes: A Study on the Lineage in the Rural Society of Southern Fujian. Ph.D. Thesis. The University of Comprehensive Research College of Japan. (In Japanese)

———. 1999. "The Ceremony to Enshrine Spirit Tablets": An Essential Component of Ritual Symbolism of the Lineage Revival in the Contemporary Rural Areas of Southern Fujian. *China* 21(6): 77–108. (*China*, Japanese edition, 5, a publication of the Society of Modern China Studies, Aichi University.)

Wang, Mingming. 1997. *Cunluo Shiye Zhong de Wenhua yu Quanli: Min Tai San Cun Wu Lun* (Approaching Culture and Power from the Perspectives of Villages: Papers on Three Villages in Fujian and Taiwan). Beijing: Sanlian Shudian.

Weber, Max. 1946. *From Max Weber: Essays in Sociology.* H. H. Gerth and C. Wright Mills, eds. and trans. New York: Oxford University Press.

Glossary

Cai	蔡
chigong	吃公
Chikeng	赤坑
dazong	大宗
Erfang	二房
fangzu	房族
gongye	公業
hepu	合譜
jinzhu	晉主
kuoganhui	擴幹會
Laorenhui	老人會
Lingfeng	靈峰
Lingshan	靈山
Lingshi	靈獅
Lingxiu town	靈秀鎮
Niandou	年兜
Qiangfang	強房
Rongqing	容卿
Rongqing ba xiang	容卿八鄉
Rongqing Laorenzonghui	容卿老人總會
Shanxia	山下
Shilin	仕林
Shishi	石獅
shou dingfen	收丁份
Shuikeng	水坑
Tangyuan	塘園
Xiasanluo	下三落
xiaozong	小宗
Xikeng	西坑
yi cunzheng dang canmou	議村政當參謀
Yulou	玉樓
zongpu	總譜
zucuo	祖厝

4

Chinese Religious Expressions in Post-Mao Yongchun, Fujian

■ Tan Chee-Beng

Introduction[1]

There are a number of significant works on the study of popular religion in China, such as Yang's (1961), Watson's (1985), Feuchtwang's (1991), and Shahar and Weller's (1996a), to name a few. Pas (1989) provides a survey of the works done after 1978, showing the renewed interest in this study. Fujian, the ancestral homeland of many "overseas" Chinese, is obviously an important region to study. However, there are few ethnographic works on Chinese religion in Fujian since de Groot's (1892–1910), although Dean's work (1993) is quite comprehensive. There are some historical works such as Dean's (1998) and Szonyi's (1997, 1998), as well as some works in Chinese (see Tan and Zhang 1999: 71–78), including the publications arising from the Hakka research project headed by John Lagerwey (see, for example, Yang 1997). Overall, anthropological study in Fujian is still rather limited, and most of the studies are about the more prosperous coastal regions.[2]

This paper aims to discuss some features of religious activities in Yongchun as observed in the late 1990s. Yongchun is a county in southern Fujian (Minnan), and the county seat, also called Yongchun, is about a two-hour drive from the port city of Quanzhou. When I began my research there in the summer of 1998, I started by visiting some major temples in the county before taking up residence in a Chen-lineage village in Huyang *zhen* (township) in the eastern part of Yongchun, about 23 kilometers from the county seat. I shall call this village Beautiful Jade. I concentrated my research on its sublineage section that I shall call Half Moon Hill.

Since 1979, there is obviously greater freedom of public religious expression. This is despite the fact that Chinese popular religion — the popular religion of China, which centers on the worship of *shen* (deities) and ancestors as well as the placating of ghosts — is still officially regarded as *mixin* (superstition). Much of this revival is seen in the building or renovation of major temples, and the holding of religious activities that are officially justifiable by their relevance to tourism and to reinforcing relations with Chinese overseas. But what is the situation in places where such religious expressions are otherwise? What is the nature of religious traditions reproduced since 1979? My ethnographic research in Yongchun in 1998 and 1999 may have some answers. By describing the nature of religious expressions in this village and in some of the neighboring villages, we may get a fuller picture of the significance of religion to the family and the community in post-1978 rural Fujian.

Beautiful Jade had 341 Chen-surnamed households in 1998, making up a population of 1,238 persons. The village comprises six sections (*jiao*; corners), each occupied by a lineage branch. This is a case of a *qiaoxiang*, an emigrant village that has received little financial assistance and few visitations from Chinese overseas. Not all *qiaoxiang* have strong transnational links with relatives overseas. If the Chinese overseas do not have close living relatives (*zhiqin*; direct kin links), they generally do not bother about maintaining contact with the ancestral village nor contributing money for the school, infrastructure, or religious activities there. They may pay short visits to see their ancestral village, out of curiosity. This is the case with Beautiful Jade. Most of the emigrants of Beautiful Jade settled in the rural areas of Batu Pahat district in Johor, Malaysia, and few of them have close living relatives in Yongchun. Furthermore, rural settlers are generally less able and so less interested in donating money for the infrastructure development of their ancestral villages, unlike the urban ones who are likely to be more affluent and economically better off. For example, Penglai of Anxi in Jinjiang county, where the temple of Qingshui Zushi (Clear Water Patriarch) is located, is today visited by many relatives from Singapore who participate in the local religious activities (Kuah 2000 and in this book). Similarly, many villages in Huyang township have links with Chinese overseas and are frequently visited by them. Beautiful Jade is not such a place.

This paper provides an ethnographic description of religious "revival" in an "emigrant village," where this "revival" is without any input from Chinese overseas. We can thus see more clearly that the religious "revival" in China is actually the re-establishment of symbolic life that is meaningful to each individual and the local community. The disruption caused by the Cultural Revolution means that the re-establishment of religious life involves both a process of relinking to the past (tradition) and that of relearning, reinterpreting and reinventing. The revival does not just reproduce traditions; it also relates to current life. As Shahar and Weller (1996b: 21) point out, Chinese popular religion is not just a "reflex of Chinese social structure," it is "part of an ongoing dialogue of interpretations." The reproduction of religious activities in Beautiful Jade adjusts to the changing economic and social landscapes after 1978. I classify these activities into family-focused worship and communal worship. I shall also describe a more private practice, the women's worship of the Bedroom Spirit, and argue that its reproduction is reinforced by the one-child policy.

Family-Focused Worship in Beautiful Jade

The worship of the Earth God is particularly important in domestic worship. This is not surprising, as its worship is very important among Chinese masses, and Yang (1961: 98) describes it as "a universal cult found in all villages and towns." In Half Moon Hill, most families no longer live in the common ancestral house but in newly built individual units of their own. However, practical reasons dictate that only a few can afford to install the altar of Earth God and other deities in their new home. A new house is considered ritually officiated with the installation of the Earth God's altar. This shows the importance of the Earth God in the villagers' religious life. Nevertheless, installing the Earth God's altar in a new house is expensive, as it involves hiring a Taoist priest and providing a feast for other villagers of the sublineage section. Since most people do not have the money for this, they have to do without it. When they need to pray to the Earth God, they go to the sublineage ancestral house, where there is an altar of the Earth God beside the ancestral altars. The Earth God features prominently in people's lives. For example, when a person begins to raise a pig, he or she would offer joss sticks and joss papers to the Earth God to ask for blessing. When the pig is sold, the Earth God is offered a portion of a pig's leg in a simple rite of thanks called *sia to-ti* (H),[3] thanking the Earth God. Of course it is also worshipped on its "birthday," on the 2nd day of the 2nd lunar month.

Domestic worship in Beautiful Jade follows the timing of festivals. The grander rituals are during the New Year and Zhongyuan, the latter being the festival for the worship of wandering ghosts during the Chinese 7th month. Festivals have become an integral part of the people's social life, and so their revival is basic to re-establishing a more complete social life. We find that Chinese outside mainland China, especially those in Southeast Asia and Taiwan, cling to similar Chinese festivals. They are inseparable from the Chinese annual cycle of social life. The celebration of festivals is not only social, but is also religious, except for those who have embraced other faiths. Through festivals, Chinese popular religion is diffused into people's social life, making it more prevalent. Chinese festivals regulate people's ritual and social life. In Beautiful Jade, they are also the time when those who have gone to work in the coastal towns return to the village. It is especially important for women to return early, as they play an important role in the preparation of domestic worship. We shall describe the celebration of the Chinese New Year as an important festival in the life of post-1978 Beautiful Jade villagers.

The New Year worship at Half Moon Hill, as observed in February 1999, began at around 9 a.m. on the day before the New Year, when offerings were laid out on the stove to worship the Kitchen God. They comprised both vegetarian and meat dishes as well as three small cups of Chinese tea and five small cups of Chinese rice wine. After worshipping the Kitchen God, the Earth God and other domestic deities were worshipped, followed by worship of the ancestors. Food used for worship of the deities might be used again for worshipping ancestors. Food for worship of the ancestors was cooked, but that for deities also included raw vegetarian food and partly blanched meat. Ancestors were worshipped at the ancestral house: families of brothers and parents worshipped collectively. Those who had installed the altars of the Earth God and other deities worshipped them at home, whereas the others worshipped the Earth God at the ancestral house. At the end of each rite, firecrackers were let off, and the noise added to the atmosphere of celebration. Some of the food offered, such as noodles, was eaten for lunch, but the family New Year reunion feast was in the early evening at around 5.30 p.m. After dinner, at around 6.30 p.m., the villagers collectively made a bonfire in front of the ancestral house, using dry orange branches and bamboo. This is called *chiu he pun* (H), starting the fire basin, and it is a common practice in Huyang. According to the villagers, this is their age-old custom. Depending on who narrates the story, it is said that it originated as a signal for the Han people to kill the Manchu oppressors. Some said that it was a signal to rebel against the Mongols. Obviously the common theme is Han nationalism against non-Han rulers. At midnight, firecrackers and fireworks were let off to welcome the New Year. Because of the good prices of mandarin oranges in 1999, the villagers had more money and were in a happy mood, and so they let off more firecrackers and fireworks than in previous years.

In the morning of the New Year, joss sticks were offered to the Kitchen God. On this day, villagers flocked to the small village temple to worship the deities and ask for blessings for the year. Expecting a crowd, not all villagers rushed to the temple early; but even in the late morning it was still crowded and the interior full of smoke. Joss sticks, in odd number, were first offered to Guanyin (Goddess of Mercy), and two other deities called Xian Gong and Fuyou Dijun at the main altars, and then to the other deities called Sima Shenghou and Jishi. The villagers would then kneel down to pray and shake a bamboo vase containing numbered bamboo sticks to draw a stick (*qian*) that would forecast an outcome to their prayer. When a stick dropped out of the vase, divining blocks were cast to ensure that Xian Gong, the patron deity of the village, had indeed chosen the divination. The number of the stick was matched to one of the verses (*qianwen* or *qian* verses) displayed on a board hung on the wall. If one did not know how to interpret the verse, a temple assistant was at hand to help. If the forecast was not good, one could always draw another *qian* by rephrasing the question or by making an additional vow to the deity. In addition to praying for blessing, this was the occasion for making donations to the temples. An assistant recorded the names of donors and the amount donated. This information would be posted on the temple wall for all to see.

Every evening from the 1st to the 5th day of the New Year, joss sticks and candles were lit at the Kitchen God's altar, followed by burning firecrackers. The burning of firecrackers is a new feature introduced after liberalization. In Beautiful Jade, the first five days of the New Year are days of celebration and rest, and one can return to work on the 6th day. On this day, urine collected in the house for the past few days is taken to the rice field, indicating the return to work.[4] Like Chinese people elsewhere, New Year celebration is observed for 15 days. The 9th day is the "birthday" of Tī-Kong (Tiangong), the God of Heaven, and is celebrated by Minnan people in China, Southeast Asia and Taiwan. In Beautiful Jade, the evening of the 15th day is not celebrated in any particular way, unlike in the city of Quanzhou. This evening, called Yuanxiao in Mandarin, is celebrated on a grand scale. According to my observations, New Year celebrations in Malaysia and in Yongchun are similar, differing only in scale. For instance, in Malaysia there are more items of offering in domestic worship, and firecrackers are not let off at the end of each rite, as it is illegal. Even then, many people in the rural areas still let off firecrackers at midnight on New Year's Eve to welcome the New Year and the God of Wealth. It should be noted that Beautiful Jade is a poor village whose people are only just beginning to reap the benefits of reform. Though simple now, celebrations might become elaborate as wealth increases.

Other major festivals observed in Beautiful Jade include Qingming, when ancestors are worshipped at the grave around 5 April; the Fifth-Moon Festival (Duanwujie) when rice dumplings are made and offered to gods and ancestors; Zhongyuan in the 7th lunar month when the *pusi* rite is performed (see below); and the Winter Solstice Day (Dongzhi), which marks the approaching end of a year and when one visits graves, if this has not been done during Qingming. Birthday celebrations, weddings and funerals also involve religious worship. At other times there is not much religious activity, except the regular incense offering at home for those with altars at home, or visitations to the temple on festival days and the 1st and 15th days of the Chinese calendar.

Within the village, the temple is the site where all sections of the village fully participate. Each village in Yongchun has its own temple and its own patron deity. In Beautiful Jade, the village temple is called Xitou Jing, and Shennong is its patron deity. This patron deity is so identified with this Chen lineage that the local people as well as descendants of migrants in Malaysia refer to it (in relation to the Chen lineage) as Be-Liao Sian Gong (H). Sian Gong, the Immortal God, is the local people's affectionate term for the deity, and Be-Liao is the name of this Chen lineage. The deity provides a ritual identity to the lineage. Each lineage has its own stories and myths to show how its patron deity helped lineage members and protected them in confrontations with another lineage.

Visits to popular temples outside the village are infrequent, as they are generally far away. Visits generally occur when people happen to go to a certain place that is near a temple. On such an occasion, an individual may be requested by the family to pray for certain family members. Thus individual worship at a temple may not be just for oneself but for the family, and in that sense, it is family-focused. Matters prayed for are generally about *yunqi* (fortunes) and *hunyin* (marriage); healing sickness is also much prayed for. Because more individuals are going to coastal towns to look for jobs and work, it is common for one to seek advice and pray for good luck and welfare for emigrant family members, that they be blessed in their endeavors and experience *hou tan-chia* (H), which means good

9. The village temple in Beautiful Jade, Yongchun (photograph by Tan C. B., 1998).

10. The *pusi* worship in front of an ancestral house in Beautiful Jade, Yongchun (photograph by Tan C. B., 1997).

livelihood. The greater opportunities for earning money and the frustration of not earning enough are reflected in the worship practices of Chinese religion.

In Huyang township, in the bazaar part of the town, there is a Mazu temple called Tianfei Miao, but it is not popular and does not function as a communal temple. The closest popular temple is Qingquan Yan, which is located some distance from the town in the hills in Penglai (not to be confused with the one in Jinjiang county). This beautifully renovated temple is now accessible by motorbike and jeep. It is actually the temple of the Huang lineage of Penglai (locally called Ong Lai (H)). This is an example of a lineage village temple becoming a supra-village temple. It is still managed by the Penglai Huang lineage. According to temple records, the original temple was built in 1440 during the Ming Dynasty. It has been renovated several times. The last renovation, in 1995, turned it into a big temple, thanks to donations from overseas Chinese. This is a Buddhist temple. There are statues of 12 Buddhist deities and other deities of Chinese religion as well as three big tablets that honor the Huang ancestors and the monks of the temple.

Outside the temple are a guardian deity (Hujie Gong) shrine, which faces the temple, and a shrine that houses the statues that were damaged during the Cultural Revolution. Each worshipper is told to offer three joss sticks there, too. All the required joss sticks (32 according to the temple keeper) are lighted inside the temple, and are planted into the joss urn in front of the temple as well as at the relevant shrines outside. There is a room for monks. At the main hall, called Daxiong Baodian, there are facilities for worshippers to ask for divine advice by shaking numbered bamboo sticks (*qian*) in a bamboo container. An assistant sits at a desk at one corner of the main hall to help read the divination according to the number selected. Each number is matched with a numbered slip of paper that contains a verse for interpretation. If the worshipper wishes to keep the slip, he or she pays RMB0.5; otherwise the service is free of charge. Usually worshippers only pay for auspicious predictions.

Another temple that some worshippers visit is Daixian Si in Xianyou, which is farther away on the northern border of Huyang. Although the people in Xianyou are not Yongchun people and speak an eastern Fujian (Mindong) dialect, historically the Yongchun people of Huyang had trade relations with the people in Xianyou. My informants in Beautiful Jade mentioned that in the past (meaning before the Cultural Revolution and before 1949), there were villagers from Huyang who walked across the mountains to go to Daixian Si. Nowadays one can go by motorbike to the Xianyou side, park it in the foothills, and walk for an hour up the mountain to reach the temple. It is largely a Buddhist temple, but at the first of the three buildings there, the main targets of worship are the three goddess collectively called San Xian Fei (Three Lady Immortals), and more affectionately known by the Yongchun villagers as Xian Ma (Lady Immortals). The worshippers' interest is really the Xian Ma rather than the Buddhist deities there. My Yongchun informants said that if one slept overnight at the temple, Xian Ma would reveal their blessings through dreams.

Mention should be made about the roadside Buddhist temple Xifeng Si (locally called Sai Pang Si (H)), located some distance from Huyang town in the direction of Yongchun. At the time of research it was under renovation to turn it into a big temple complex for the people of Huyang. Local donors are the various Liu villages in Huyang, but most of the money came from Yongchun people in Hong Kong and some came from Taiwan and Southeast Asia. The main organizer is in fact a retired cadre who has many connections with the Yongchun people in Hong Kong. Claiming to be of Tang Dynasty origin, the rebuilt temple has the blessing of the local government and is designed to attract tourists.

Overall, we see that the villagers have re-established their religious traditions, and because of improvements in the means of transport, they are more easily able to visit popular temples in the region. However, the main religious activities are in the village, at the ancestral house, and at the village temple.

Communal Worship

Chinese popular religion is both family-focused and community-focused. In Beautiful Jade, there are two occasions when communal worship is held annually. The first is the *pusi* worship for wandering ghosts and Pudugong, the deity in charge of the dead. Each lineage section conducts its own worship. The Half Moon Hill section does it on the 20th day of the 7th lunar month at the front yard of the ancestral house. The ritual I observed in 1999 was as follows. At a selected time in the late afternoon, a representative from each family brought some dishes with offerings. These were laid out on the ground. After all the representatives had arrived, an elderly man burnt joss sticks and invited Pudugong and the wandering ghosts of the area to partake in the "feast." He then threw a divining block to ascertain that the invitation had been accepted. After this was ascertained, women and children burnt joss papers, and firecrackers were let off. After some time, the elderly man threw the divining blocks again to see if the meal had been taken. Having received a positive answer, each family representative collected his or her food offerings and took them home to cook for dinner.[5] The simple ritual at Half Moon Hill was both communal-focused and family-focused, and it symbolized the ritual unity of a lineage section rather than the whole Chen lineage in Beautiful Jade.

The occasion when communal worship involves the whole lineage is the worship of the common ancestress. This is observed on the 8th day of the 8th lunar month, when Chinese communities elsewhere observe Mid-Autumn Festival. However, the tomb of the ancestress is at Luntou, a village in a neighboring township. This is thus a clan activity. The Chen of both Beautiful Jade and Luntou can trace their ancestry to the common ancestress. Partly because of the distance, the Chen of the two villages do not have much interaction, but every year they send representatives to perform a collective ritual at the grave of the ancestress, which exists today. Local Chen oral history states that during the course of migration to Yongchun, the ancestor was killed by bandits and it is not known where he was buried. Thus the descendants today use the grave of his wife as the focus of communal worship.

11. Worship at the founding ancestress' grave, Luntou, Yongchun (photograph by Tan C. B., 2001).

Although the worship of the ancestress involves the whole Chen lineage at Beautiful Jade, it is organized at the level of *shengchan zu* (production teams), on an annual rotation basis. The system of production brigades continues to be used in the post-1978 era, for economic and religious activities. The name had been changed from *shengchan dui* (production brigade) to *cunmin zu* (villagers' team), although the villagers generally refer to it as *shengchan zu*. The "team" that one belongs to is indicated in the postal address. More significantly, production teams in Beautiful Jade correspond roughly to lineage sections, and function to organize ritual activities. The villagers belong to four production teams, which coincide generally with the six lineage sections, except for some individuals of a section who belong to a different team. For example, Half Moon Hill belongs to Team 4, which also includes another two lineage sections. Since this team is made up of three lineage sections, it is internally divided into three sub-teams, with Half Moon Hill forming one sub-team.

In 2001, it was Team 4's turn to represent Beautiful Jade at the communal worship of the ancestress in Luntou. Within Team 4 itself, it was Half Moon Hill's turn. Each family, or rather families of brothers in Half Moon Hill, sent at least one representative, and altogether there were 30 persons. Costs were borne by the families in this sub-team. As far as the villagers can remember, the worship of the ancestress has been observed since the past, breaks occurring only during the ultra-leftist periods in 1958–62, and the Cultural Revolution from 1966–76. One difference is that in the past, the journey to Luntou was made on foot but now it is on motorbike.

Lineage-based villages in Huyang township also organize communal religious fairs if finances and cooperation permit. On this occasion, the major deities worshipped in a village temple are taken out for a procession once a year or every few years. Such public religious celebration, the *jinxiang* ceremony, is locally called *chhiā he* (*qinghuo*), inviting incense fire. My informants said that they have a long history of conducting this ceremony, but it ceased during the Communist rule in the 1950s, 1960s and 1970s. This was also true elsewhere in Yongchun. For example, at Kunlun Dong, a temple in Dongping township, a few kilometers east of Yongchun county seat, there is a record of *jinxiang* every year since 1896, but this ceased in 1951. It was revived in 1985 and has been conducted annually ever since.[6] The ceremony, as I had observed in Huyang, involved not only the procession of the village deities but also the bringing in of "incense fire" from outside the village, usually from a selected hill or mountain; hence the name "inviting incense fire." In Huyang, the ceremony is performed

12. Men carrying the "incense fire," Earth Bridge, Yongchun (photograph by Tan C. B., 1999).

during the Chinese New Year period. In February 1999 I observed two such ceremonies, one organized by the Wu lineage of Gaoping Village on the 3rd day of the New Year; and the other by the Li lineage of a village that I shall call Earth Bridge. A Taoist priest was hired to perform the ceremony. For the Gaoping, there were also a few spirit-mediums (*tang-ki*).

In Beautiful Jade, the "inviting incense fire" ceremony is also organized by the production teams which are now regrouped into two bigger groups called *gu*. As there are six lineage sections, each *gu* has three ancestral houses under its charge. An ancestral house is selected to house the statues of the village deities during the few days of ceremony, and the one selected for this purpose is called *he-thau chu* (H, fire-head house). If an ancestral house in the *gu* is selected as the fire-head house, the *gu* as a whole has to sponsor the ceremony. It is an expensive affair, for it involves hiring Taoist priests. In addition, the local government requires a deposit of RMB200, which theoretically is refundable if there is no violation of government regulations. The organizer also has to provide an officially acceptable excuse for holding such a "superstitious" event, and the most convenient excuse is that this is requested by "overseas Chinese." Thus not all villages hold such a religious fair every year. This is so in Beautiful Jade. Villagers say that it is acceptable not to hold an incense fire ceremony every year, as

Taoist rites (*zuo jiao*) are performed at the village temple usually on the 6th and 7th days of the New Year. On such an occasion, each family brings offerings to the temple and takes home some rice and talismanic symbols (*fu*). In 1999, when I was doing research in Beautiful Jade, there was talk of organizing an incense fire ceremony. Some meetings were held but a consensus could not be reached. Apart from some villagers' concern about the cost, there was a lineage section, a small one with few members, that felt it was slighted when it was not informed of the first meeting, so it refused to send representatives to subsequent meetings. There is symbolic politics between lineage sections that is manifested at times like this. It involves the status of a lineage section, and a small lineage section is particularly sensitive that it is not given due respect by the other sections that have more people. Thus my description below is based on those organized by Gaoping and Earth Bridge in the same township. In fact, Earth Bridge is Beautiful Jade's neighbor.

Depending on funds, the celebration is at least a two-day affair. The 1st day involves carrying the statues in sedan chairs in a procession out of the village to an arranged place to receive the incense fire. On the last day there is a final rite to return the deities' statues to the temple. The Earth Bridge celebration took place on 19 February 1999 (the 4th day of the Chinese New Year). Early in the morning of the 1st day, a small party of men climbed the highest mountain in Huyang, Yuzhu Shan (Jade Pole Mountain), to strike the rock at the peak with an axe to obtain the fire to light incense wood pieces. The incense fire (*xianghuo*) was then carried downhill to a pre-arranged place by two men using shoulder poles. Each had a basket of incense fire in the front and another basket containing other things at the back. Meanwhile, the procession from the village temple began at 12.30 p.m., attracting a large crowd from the village, the town, and nearby villages. The noise of firecrackers added to the merry occasion. The procession passed through part of the town and nearby Beautiful Jade to meet the men carrying the incense fire. When the two parties met, noise of gongs and firecrackers exploded, and the Taoist priest performed a simple rite at the site. The procession, now having the "incense fire," returned to the lineage hall in Earth Bridge. However, it took a few hours to reach the village, as the party stopped on the way to perform a Taoist rite called *zou ke'ng* (H) for each family that had requested it. The request was indicated by putting out offerings in front of the home.

At about 4 p.m., the procession reached the Li-lineage hall. The statues were taken from the sedan chairs and carried into the hall of the *he-thau chu*, where they stayed until taken back to the temple a few days later. An elaborate Taoist rite was performed, followed by a puppet show and a Chinese opera for the deities. The villagers got to watch opera shows the following few nights. The number of days of celebration would depend on funds — the cost of hiring the puppet troupe was RMB1,000 a day and double that for the opera show. On the 2nd day, statues of deities were carried in sedan chairs in a procession to the boundary of the village in the four directions of east, south, west and north, where the Taoist priest performed a simple rite at each place. This is called *tin ke'* (H, guarding the place). On the whole, the "inviting incense fire" ceremony not only fulfills the function of divine blessing of the lineage and community; it is also a ritual reaffirmation of the village territory as well as a public display of the lineage community. As Faure (1986: 70) has argued, collective worship serves as a symbol of territorial unity, whether it is centered in an ancestral hall or a temple. Faure further argues, "one type of worship is subordinate to the other." However, our description of the "inviting fire" celebration shows that this may not necessarily be so, as the significance of both the temple and the ancestral hall becomes fused by having the deities residing in the ancestral hall during the communal celebration. The village temple and the ancestral hall actually perform equally important but different functions, the latter representing the lineage organization, whereas it is the deities of the temple who oversee the territory and bless the lineage community.

A Private Rite and the Wish for a Son

In addition to the religious expressions already described, there is a significant rite that is private in that it is performed only by women in the privacy of the bedroom. All the married women of Half Moon Hill observe this rite. This is the Minnan people's custom of worshipping Chuangmu, Bed Guardian Spirit, and in Beautiful Jade it is called Pang-Bu (Fangmu), that is, Bedroom Guardian Spirit. Those who have children usually perform the rite on the Chinese New Year's Eve and on a child's birthday. After the youngest child has reached the age of 16, it is not necessary to observe the rite anymore. This is my observation of the rite on New Year's Eve in Half Moon Hill in 1999. After the ancestors were worshipped, the woman laid out the offerings on the bed in her bedroom. This comprised three bowls of *kiam ke* (H, salty cake), and a bowl of soup containing lily flower buds, lean pork, bean curd, and mushroom. Instead of *kiam ke*, one could offer

13. Propitiating the Bedroom Spirit in Beautiful Jade, Yongchun (photograph by Tan C. B., 1999).

kiam peng (H, salty rice), which is rice cooked with peanuts and bean curd. A small lamp was lit (I had observed that instead of this a lighted red candle was placed on an overturned soft drink container). Holding some joss sticks, the woman knelt down in front of the bed to invite the Pang-Bu to come and partake of the meal and asked for blessings for her child or children. Blessings prayed for usually express the wish to bring up her child or children without any trouble as well as to have a son if one does not have one yet. The wishes are reflected in the recitation of such auspicious sayings as *hou yeo chua* (H, easy to raise), *mi hou kun* (H, sleep well at night), *zit hou tit* (H, play well during the day). After a while, she knelt down again, to divinate by dropping two old imperial coins, to see if the Pang-Bu was satisfied with the worship. If the answer was positive, joss papers were burned in a container in the room and the offerings were then taken away. When not in use, the imperial coins, which were held together with a string through the holes in the center of each coin, were usually hung on the bedpost. No firecrackers were let off at the end of the rite.

The continuing practice of the Pang-Bu rite in Yongchun is striking, as few Yongchun people that I know in Malaysia still perform this rite, although it was still common in the 1950s. Because of better public health care, child mortality and sickness are no longer a threat, and parents are free to have as many children as they like. In the same way, it is extremely rare to see Chinese Malaysians pray to the God of the Well — for very few still depend on wells for water. The better-educated younger people are also not interested in continuing with this rite, which they do not find meaningful anymore. In Yongchun, one can argue that the one-child policy reinforces the continuity of the Pang-Bu tradition, since an only child is extremely precious. Furthermore, in Yongchun, the government allows parents to apply for a permit to have a second child if the first-born is a daughter. Praying to Pang-Bu is thus also a ritual channel for women to express their desire to have a son.

This desire to have a son is also expressed in the posting of a picture of one or more baby boys. This is commonly pasted on the wall in the living room, even on the wall in the central position facing the main entrance, the place where one installs family altars. In fact, I came across a number of families that do not have altars in the living room but instead have a prominent poster of a baby boy or of Guanyin carrying a baby boy. A woman in Half Moon Hill that I know quite well allowed me to observe her performing the Pang-Bu rite in 1999. She had a 5-year-old daughter and desired to have a son. It was thus not surprising to find that she had a big poster of two good-looking baby boys on the wall above her bed (see Plate 13). She was lucky, for by the time of my next visit in February 2001, she had a son. However, the most popular poster is that of Guanyin, the Goddess of Mercy, carrying a small boy; some posters in fact show more than one boys. Called Songzi Guanyin, this depiction is a famous Chinese symbolism for blessed with children. This poster of Guanyin carrying a child is in fact quite commonly seen in different parts of China, including a mixed village of Yi and Han people in Ganluo district in Sichuan, where I visited the family of a Han Chinese man who married a Yi woman. At that house, a poster of Guanyin carrying a boy in her arms with two others standing beside her was displayed prominently on the wall in the living room, together with a Chinese New Year poster, and above them, a poster of Chairman Mao. In the movie *Not One Less,* directed by the famous Zhang Yimou, one scene showed the living room of a poor family that has on the wall a poster of Guangyin carrying a child. In a visit to Baita Shan (White Pagoda Hill) in Lanzhou, Gansu province, China, in July 2001, I noticed a new life-sized statue of Songzi Guanyin in a new temple.

In Yongchun, Guanyin is popularly worshipped for fertility blessings, as is the City God. At the City God Temple in Yongchun county seat, there is a room at the back hall. Called *Zunhou neiqin*, City God's bedroom, it is a furnished bedroom. There is a bed, a cupboard, a desk, a basin, towel, etc. On the bed is a vase containing red and white plastic flowers. The Chinese couplet on each side of the main entrance reads: *bi tianding jincai, you wanjia xingfu*, blessed with children and wealth, blessed with happiness to all families. A woman who desires a child first prays at the large statues of the City God (Fude Zunhou) and his wife (Furen Ma) in the back hall. Then she enters the City God's bedroom nearby, sits on the bed for a short while, and then "buys" a flower, that is, she chooses a flower and leaves a red packet containing some money; how much money is up to her. If she desires to have a boy, she chooses a white flower; otherwise, a red one, which symbolizes a girl. That a white flower symbolizes a baby boy and red flower a baby girl is common knowledge in Chinese symbolism, also important among the Yao people (Tan 1975: 49). The temple attendant told me that very few people choose the red flower. The worshipper brings the flower home and places it under her pillow for seven days. She also has to perform the rite of Pang-Bu.

14. The City God's bedroom at the City God Temple in Yongchun county seat (photograph by Tan C. B., 1999).

Conclusion

The policy of economic and social liberalization since 1979 paves the way for the resurgence and revitalization of Chinese religion. It is really a re-expression of what was once suppressed rather than a revival of what had once disappeared. In this paper, we have seen the basic features of the religious expressions reproduced. Prominent among these are ancestor worship and religious activities in the ancestral house. Family-focused religious activities are basic to this reproduction of tradition. Closely linked to this is the celebration of festivals through which the popular religion is so diffused into people's social life that the reproduction of religious life is a necessary part of re-establishing social life.

The reproduction of religion is important to communal life; and in this study, the village temple and the worship of communal deity play an important part in symbolizing communal unity. There is a lineage hall for the whole Chen lineage in Beautiful Jade, but it sees hardly any activity. Instead, lineage activities are carried out by lineage section, at the ancestral house. Lineage-related religious activities of the lineage are organized at this level. At the same time, we find that the organization of lineage section is incorporated into the official system of production teams. Obviously, this is possible because the original formation of production teams was largely based on lineage sections whose members concentrated on different sections of the village. Anyway, the use of production teams for the perpetuation of tradition is an innovative development that more than makes up for the weak overall lineage organization.

The apparently weak position of the lineage organization is due to a lack of wealth and common property and the support of Chinese overseas. Thus Freedman's argument (1965: 128) about lineage property as holding lineage members together is partially correct. Although a lineage may not be strong and active at the overall level, as represented by the lineage hall and activities (or the lack of it) around it, lineage organizations still function at the section level, as we have seen in the case of Beautiful Jade. Lineage sections unified by an ancestral house are the core of a lineage.

Traditions are reproduced according to changing circumstances rather than transmitted in an unchanged manner. Moving out of the ancestral house and into one's own house is a common feature in post-1978 southern Fujian, as is the case in Beautiful Jade. Following this is a tendency for each family or families of brothers that form a unit to worship separately at the ancestral house, as seen in the case of New Year worship at Half Moon Hill instead of jointly as a lineage section as was in the past. The one-child policy, however, reinforces the need to worship specifically for blessings that concern children, like the rite of Pang-Bu. Economic liberalization eases the way for "incense shops" to proliferate, enabling worshippers to buy joss sticks, joss papers, and other religious goods easily. In fact, the two incense shops in Huyang town are doing very good business, especially during festive seasons and on the 1st and 15th days of a lunar month, when more people visit temples to worship. Shopkeepers occasionally offer advice on what and how much to buy. They also play the role of introducing new religious goods to the local population.

The reproduction of religious traditions takes place naturally, as they are part of the people's social life and are meaningful to the people. Anthropologists have many theories about religion, but for ordinary people, it is both functional and symbolic. For the poor villagers, it is only meaningful and satisfying to ask divine blessing in gaining better *yunqi* (fortunes). This is not merely my functional interpretation, for the wish for *hou tan-chia*, gaining good livelihood, is very strikingly frequent in many prayers. At the same time, the people are very aware of the symbolic nature of beliefs and practices. They are very aware of rites that emphasize the symbolic unity of the community, as we have seen in the case of the incense fire ceremony. To the villagers, tradition as expressed in religious worship is meaningful. And the worship expresses their hope for a better livelihood. They are aware of the symbolic meanings of offerings and rites, and even when they do not know how to interpret certain rites, they still attribute them to having some symbolic meaning.

I received some help in interpretation for part of the "inviting incense fire" ceremony. Among the offerings laid out in the Li-lineage hall were three jars, one containing a small turtle, the second three frogs, and the third a few field eels. All the animals were alive. None of my informants knew the meaning of this. I discussed it with some informants in Beautiful Jade, and one of them finally thought of something very Levi-Straussian. He noted that all the three kinds of animal could survive on land and in water; even the field eels could survive out of water for a short time. He tried to link this coincidence to *yin* and *yang*, land representing *yang* and water *yin*. The others pointed out that these animals are all delicacies and are good for health, and eels, given their number, also symbolize many descendants. To me, these local animals represent the healthy life of the community. The increasing use of chemical fertilizers has been a threat to them. At the end of the ceremony, the three animals are released, thus symbolizing the wish for the community to have continuing good life. After all, the ceremony is to ritually revitalize the community.

I have indicated that the "revival" of religious activities is not really revival in the sense that the people had not given up their religion. They were just barred from practicing it during the ultra-leftist periods. People continued to value their traditions in their minds, and some even carried out some religious activities secretly. Some of my informants mentioned that they continued to worship the Bedroom Guardian Spirit secretly. The idea of *hongsui* (*fengshui*), Chinese geomancy, has remained important, despite the various leftist campaigns. Although rites could not be performed, ideas like *fengshui* could be talked about privately and transmitted. Today, *fengshui* is a very important part of the villagers' discourse, especially when they talk of lineage history and inter-village rivalry. However, the suppression of religious expressions in the past does have its consequences. Young people, for example, have to learn how to worship, and this explains the frequent consultations with temple assistants about the number of joss sticks to light and the sequence of worship. At the same time, new features have emerged. For example, the letting off of firecrackers is a very noisy feature of many religious rites, much more than is observed outside mainland China, and much more than in the past, I was told. In a sense, this highlights the freer atmosphere of religious expression.

Giddens (2001: 62) correctly points out that traditions are "needed, and will always persist, because they give continuity and form to life." The religious expressions of the villagers of Beautiful Jade, and for that matter the people in southern Fujian, serve just that purpose. The religious activities are meaningful now, besides serving as a link to their past even though the past also reminds them of much violence and unhappiness. My informants told me about the destruction of ancestral tablets during the Cultural Revolution. I was told, too, of their vain effort to try to save the old statue of the Earth God at the ancestral house by burying it underground, not knowing that it was made of clay and thus sending it to its destruction. Life has not been easy, even now. People in the coastal cities and towns have benefited economically, but those in inland Fujian where Beautiful Jade is located are frustrated by the lack of opportunities. As they struggle for a better livelihood, many working as migrant workers in coastal cities, they also rely on religion for hope of a better future.

Notes

1. This paper is based on my research in Yongchun under the project "Tradition, Change and Identity: A Study of the Minnan People in China and Southeast Asia," funded by the Hong Kong Research Grants Council, RGC Ref No. CUHK 4025/97H.
2. For recent studies, see the works of Huang (1989), Wang (1997), and Zhuang (1996). Recent doctoral theses include Zhang (1997), Fan (2001), and Friedman (2000).
3. Where Chinese words are transcribed according to the Yongchun/Minnan dialect, this is indicated by H or followed by Putonghua (Mandarin) in parentheses. The vowel /ə/ is indicated by e, /e/ by e', /ɔ/ by o̲, ch is unaspirated, and chh is aspirated.
4. During the period of research, the villagers still did not have modern toilets at home. Urine is collected in a container. When the container is about full, the urine is carried to the paddy field to be used as fertilizer. To defecate, one goes to the few common toilet pits, each owned by related family members. During the first five days of the Chinese New Year, no one works and urine is not carried to the field. The 6th day is the 1st day of work of the New Year.
5. The description of the *pusi* worship is based on my observation in 1999.
6. See *Taiping Wumiao Langai* (Outline Description of Five Temples of Taiping), p. 17.

References

de Groot, J. J. M. 1892–1910. *The Religious System of China: Its Ancient Forms, Evolution, History and Present Aspect, Manners, Customs and Social Institutions Connected Therewith*. New York: Paragon Book Gallery.

Dean, Kenneth. 1993. *Taoist Ritual and Popular Culture in Southeast China*. Princeton, NJ: Princeton University Press.

———. 1998. *Lord of the Three in One: The Spread of a Cult in Southeast China*. Princeton, NJ: Princeton University Press.

Fan, Ke. 2001. Identity Politics in South Fujian Hui Communities. Ph.D. Thesis. University of Washington.

Faure, David. 1986. *The Structure of Chinese Rural Society: Lineage and Village in the Eastern New Territories, Hong Kong*. Hong Kong: Oxford University Press.

Feuchtwang, Stephan. 1991. *The Imperial Metaphor: Popular Religion in China*. London: Routledge.

Freedman, Maurice. 1965. *Lineage Organization in Southeastern China*. Second edition. London: The Athlone Press. First edition, 1958.

Friedman, Sara L. 2000. Reluctant Brides and Prosperity's Daughter: Marriage,

118   *Southern Fujian: Reproduction of Traditions in Post-Mao China*

Labor, and Cultural Change in Southeastern China's Hui'an County. Ph.D. Thesis. Cornell University.

Giddens, Anthony. 2001. *Runaway World: How Globalization is Reshaping Our Lives*. New York: Routledge. Originally published in Great Britain by Profile Press, 1999.

Huang, Shu-min. 1989. *The Spiral Road: Change in a Chinese Village through the Eyes of a Communist Party Leader*. Boulder, CO: Westview Press.

Kuah, Khun Eng. 2000. *Rebuilding the Ancestral Village: Singaporeans in China*. Aldershot, England: Ashgate Publishing.

Pas, Julian F., ed. 1989. *The Turning of the Tide: Religion in China Today*. Hong Kong: Hong Kong Branch of the Royal Asiatic Society in association with Oxford University Press.

Shahar, Meir and Robert P. Weller, eds. 1996a. *Unruly Gods: Divinity and Society in China*. Honolulu: University of Hawaii Press.

Shahar, Meir, and Robert P. Weller. 1996b. Introduction: Gods and Society in China. In Meir Shahar and Robert P. Weller, eds., *Unruly Gods: Divinity and Society in China*, pp. 1–36. Honolulu: University of Hawaii Press.

Szonyi, Michael. 1997. The Illusion of Standardizing the Gods: The Cult of the Five Emperors in Late Imperial China. *The Journal of Asian Studies* 56(1): 113–35.

———. 1998. The Cult of Hu Tianbao and the Eighteenth-Century Discourse of Homosexuality. *Late Imperial China* 19(1): 1–25.

Taiping Religious Affairs Committee, comp. *Taiping Wumiao Langai* (Outline Description of Five Temples of Taiping).

Tan, Chee-Beng. 1975. The Yao Naming System. In Anthony R. Walker, ed., *Farmers in The Hill: Upland Peoples of North Thailand*, pp. 47–53. Penang: Science University of Malaysia Press.

Tan, Chee-Beng and Zhang Xiaojun, comp. 1999. *Bibliography of Studies on Fujian With Special Reference to Minnan*. Hong Kong: Hong Kong Institute of Asia-Pacific Studies, The Chinese University of Hong Kong. (In Chinese and English).

Wang, Mingming. 1997. *Shequ de Licheng: Xicun Hanren Jiazu de Ge'an Yanjiu* (Historical Journey of a Community: A Case Study of the Han Lineage in Xi Village). Tianjin: Tianjin Renmin Chubanshe.

Watson, James L. 1985. Standardizing the Gods: The Promotion of T'ien Hou ("Empress of Heaven") along the South China Coast, 960–1960. In David Johnson, Andrew J. Nathan, and Evelyn S. Rawski, eds., *Popular Culture in Late Imperial China*, pp. 292–324. Berkeley: University of California Press.

Yang, C. K. 1961. *Religion in Chinese Society: A Study of Contemporary Social Functions of Religion and Some of Their Historical Factors*. Berkeley: University of California Press.

Yang, Yanjie. 1997. *Minxi de Chengxiang Miaohui yu Cunluo Wenhua* (Temple

Festivals and Village Culture in Minxi). Hong Kong: International Hakka
    Studies, Overseas Chinese Archives, Ecole Française D'Extreme-Orient.
Zhang, Xiaojun. 1997. Zaizao Zongzu: Fujian Yangcun Zongzu "Fuxing" de Yanjiu
    (Remaking Lineage: "Revival" of Lineage in Yang Village, Fujian). Ph.D.
    Thesis. The Chinese University of Hong Kong.
Zhuang, Kongshao. 1996. *Yinchi: Zhongguo de Difang Shehui yu Wenhua Bianqian*
    (Silver Wing: Local Society and Cultural Change in China). Beijing: Sanlian
    Shudian.

Glossary

Be-Liao (H)	尾寮
bi tianding jincai, you wanjia xingfu	庇添丁進財，佑萬家幸福
Chen	陳
chiu he pun (H)	上火盤
Chuangmu	床母
Daixian Si	岱仙寺
Fangmu	房母
fengshui	風水
Fude Zunhou	輔德尊侯
Furen Ma	夫人媽
Fuyou Dijun	福佑帝君
Ganluo	甘洛
Gaoping	高坪
gu	股
he-thau chu (H)	火頭厝
Huang	黃
Hujie Gong	護界公
Jishi	級使
Jinjiang	晉江
jinxiang	進香
kiam ke (H)	鹹粿
kiam peng (H)	鹹飯
Liu	劉
Luntou	崙頭
Penglai	蓬萊
Pudugong	普渡公
pusi	普祀
qian	籤
qinghuo	請火
Qingquan Yan	清泉岩

Qingshui Zushi	清水祖師
Shennong	神農
Sima Shenghou	司馬聖侯
Songzi Guanyin	送子觀音
Taiping Wumiao Langai	太平五廟覽概
Tianfei Miao	天妃廟
Tiangong	天公
tin ke' (H)	鎮格
Wu	吳
Xian Gong	仙公
Xian Ma	仙媽
Xianyou	仙游
Xitou Jing	溪頭境
Xifeng Si	西峰寺
Yuanxiao	元宵
yunqi	運氣
Yuzhu Shan	玉柱山
Zhongyuan	中元
zuo jiao	作醮
Zunhou neiqin	尊侯內寢

Map of Yongchun

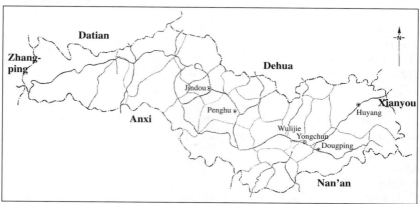

5

The Worship of Qingshui Zushi and Religious Revivalism in South China

■ Kuah-Pearce Khun Eng

Introduction

The 1979 Reform in China brought a strong revival of religious activities in south China, especially among emigrant villages, *qiaoxiang*, where there is a concentration of visitations from overseas Chinese. The term *qiaoxiang* is used both to refer to communities and to larger regions which have many *qiaoxiang* communities. In this paper, *qiaoxiang* refers only to those villages and communities with overseas Chinese connections. Throughout these villages, there are large communal religious fairs and ancestor worship held at regular intervals throughout the year. In this process of religious revivalism, the role of women is extremely important — in recreating ritual practices and in being active participants in all these activities. Women can therefore be regarded as custodial guardians of rituals and religious practices in south China.

This chapter explores the revival of the cult of Qingshui Zushi (Clear Water Patriarch) and ancestor worship and the religious fairs resulting from this revival in Penglai district in Anxi county. It examines the roles of Chinese women in ritual and food reproduction for the religious fairs. It also analyzes the reasons for the support of this revival by the villagers and the official cadres.

The Setting

Anxi county is located in the southeastern part of Fujian and occupies an area of 3,057 square kilometers. In topography, the region is mountainous and numerous ranges rise over 1,600 meters above sea level. It has 186,000 households and a total population of 916,000 people. Of these, 94 percent are engaged in agricultural production — paddy and tea cultivation. The region is most famous for Chinese tea branded under the labels Oolong and Tieguanyin, Iron Goddess of Mercy (Anxi Xian Committee 1994, Vol. 1: 173).

Anxi district has been a home to a sizeable number of migrants to Singapore. It has therefore been an important *qiaoxiang* since the 19th century. During the first half of the 20th century, about 40,000 people migrated from Anxi to Southeast Asia, mostly to Singapore. In the immediate period between World War II and the Communist victory, that is from 1945 to 1949, some 20,000 Anxi villagers migrated to Singapore. Today in Singapore, the number of Chinese from Anxi and of Anxi ancestry is estimated at 186,000, about 10 percent of the Singapore Chinese population (1.87 million) (Anxi Xian Committee 1994, Vol. 2: 854). After 1978, a closer political relationship between China and Southeast Asian governments has resulted in an increasing number of overseas Chinese visiting their ancestral village.[1]

Today, Anxi county is officially listed as an important emigrant region, *qiaoxiang*. Both local and regional government policies are aimed at encouraging overseas Chinese to contribute and assist with village reconstruction in the *qiaoxiang* (SAAY 1994). At the policy level, instrumental considerations take precedence over political ones, and it therefore comes as no surprise that the local and provincial governments would support religious revivalism in exchange for capital investment into the county (Kuah 2000: 104–38).

Traditional Chinese Religion

Traditional Chinese religion consists of two structures, the ritual and the ideological. Each can exist independently of the other. Irrespective of whether it is the rituals or the ideologies that are being considered, the Chinese religious system remains an important aspect of Chinese culture. Chinese religion can be broadly defined as an eclectic mix of three main ideologies — Taoism, Buddhism and Confucianism — interwoven with folk beliefs and animism. This syncretic mix did, and still does, determine the practice of a majority of the Chinese. Various scholars categorize Chinese religious orthodoxy in various ways. Attempts at ideologically "pure" religious practice were confined to a small élite minority — in former times, the state and the literati — who favored institutional forms of religion, either Confucianism or Buddhism, or both. A more diffused ritual-based religion was practiced by the masses (Yang 1961); formerly this meant, for the most part, the peasantry (Granet 1975). As a system of rituals, Chinese religious orthodoxy can be seen as a system of social action, the performance of which required the cooperation of individuals who followed the direction of leaders (La Fontaine 1985: 11). In such ritual practices, rules govern each action and each participant, and there are prescribed sets of actions to be followed in a set of rituals (La Fontaine 1985: 11).

Chinese religion is often practiced as a communal religion by various social groups, such as lineages or surname groups, and occupational groupings. Traditionally, it was common for the whole villages in agrarian Chinese society to engage in communal religious fairs, from celebrating a bountiful harvest to placating the gods and deities in times of natural calamities and epidemics (Hsü 1952). Communal religious fairs were halted and temples destroyed after the Communist victory, as they were considered activities of the bourgeois class, hence enemies of the state.

Individual and communal religious activities were revived only after the 1979 Reform. Since then, temples have been rebuilt and many communal religious fairs organized by different lineages in the emigrant villages to celebrate various occasions ranging from the birthday of the gods and deities to Spring Festival held during the Lunar New Year season. As a result of religious revivalism, many of the rituals and ritual processes that were not practiced for the last half-century have to be painstakingly reproduced and recreated.

Reproduction of Chinese religious practices among the villagers is not a systematic process. Ritual elements changed according to the perceptions and needs of these Chinese through the years. What they remembered as traditions and are familiar with, they reproduced and practiced; in many cases, rituals that served their functional needs are reproduced. These practices are important, as they provided the villagers with cultural familiarity and continuity with traditional Chinese religious culture. Today, these rituals constitute an important part of modern *qiaoxiang* village culture, providing the villagers with a distinct cultural identity in the face of modern challenges.

Centrality of Qingshui Yan and Qingshui Zushi Gong

One of the most important tasks of religious revivalism is the reconstruction of the county temple, Qingshui Yan Temple, and the communal worshipping of the mythical ancestor, Qingshui Zushi Gong. Why is it so important to the villagers and the overseas Chinese? About 90 percent of the overseas Chinese who visited their ancestral village in Anxi county go to Qingshui Yan Temple and make offerings to this mythical ancestor. Since its reconstruction, over 60 percent of the villagers have visited and given offerings to Qingshui Zushi Gong.[2]

This deity is regarded as the founding ancestor of Anxi and provides the villagers and their overseas kin with a shared religious ideology, allowing them to engage in communal religious activities as members of the same ancestral village and native place. The temple complex, Qingshui Yan, is located at the southeastern outskirts of Penglai district. It is 760 meters above sea level and nestled in a hilly area with beautiful greenery. From Penglai market town, it takes about 20 to 30 minutes by car to reach the foot of the temple, and then another 15 to 20 minutes to climb the steps on foot to reach the temple itself. It is an imposing temple complex built in

15. The altar of Qingshui Zushi (central position, third row) at Qingshui Yan Temple in Penglai, Anxi county. Those in front are the guardian gods of different villages in the district, brought here for the occasion of the worship (photograph by K. E. Kuah-Pearce).

traditional Chinese architectural style, with arched roofs. The main building is made of red brick and granite slabs, giving it distinction in the rustic rural landscape. Its position at the top of a peak commands a panoramic view of the villages below it. To the villagers and overseas Chinese, the position of the temple — located in the hills with a river flowing by and overlooking the villages, *beishan wangshui* — is considered to have exceptionally good geomancy, *hao fengshui*.

This temple is dedicated to a Buddhist monk who is popularly known as Qingshui Zushi Gong, the name given to a historical figure who lived during the Song Dynasty and who was renowned for mystical powers that saved the lives of many villagers (see also Dean 1993). There are several versions of both his origin and his mystical power. One version has it that his original name was Chen Puzu and that he was born into a family so poor that he was put into a monastery at a very young age. However, he left the monastery because of harsh conditions, traveled, and eventually reached Anxi. He liked the place, settled there, and lived the life of a recluse, practicing Chan meditation. He was rumored to have attained a high level of spiritual power. He was seen as a compassionate monk who often gave rice to the poor villagers. After his death, the villagers built a temple in his honor.

Another version has it that he was a monk from nearby Yongchun county commonly known as Chen Sengren, who had become a monk at a very young age. His knowledge of dharma, mystical power, and compassion were widely known to the villagers in the region. During the 6th year of Northern Song rule, Qingxi (present-day Anxi) suffered a bad drought. The local inhabitants begged Chen Yin (i.e., Chen Sengren) to perform the rite for rain. After the drought, he stayed behind and lived in the temple at Zhang Yan Shan, known currently as Qingshui Yan. In addition to his life as a monk, he was a practicing physician, who treated the villagers' diseases with herbal medicine, about which he was very knowledgeable. He also helped build bridges and roads. In his spare time and over a period of 18 years, he rebuilt the temple he was living in, afterwards renaming it Qingshui Yan. His efforts, diligence and compassion won the hearts of the villagers. He reportedly arrived at Qingshui Yan in 1101 and died at the age of 55 (Anxi Xian Committee 1994, Vol. 2: 1127–28).

Qingshui Zushi Gong is commonly known as Wumian Zushi Gong because of his black face. One version has it that during his 19 years as a recluse practicing meditation in the cave, he was constantly disturbed by the spirits who, on one occasion, attempted to kill him by blowing on the lamp for seven days and seven nights. He survived the ordeal, but his face was badly burned black.

He is also known as the "Dropping Nose Ancestor," Luobi Zushi Gong, among the Taiwanese today. One story has it that the nose of the statue of Zushi Gong was torn off when part of the roof of the cave where it was housed collapsed. It was later put back in position, but since then, whenever he senses natural calamities, his nose drops off, to be found in front of his chest or buried in his sleeve — a sign for the villagers to prepare for the coming disaster. Another story claims that he disapproved of unclean worshippers making offerings to him and that his nose drops off whenever this occurred (Zhenxiang Zazhi Bianjibu 1987).

After the monk's death, and in commemoration of his contribution to the place, the villagers continued to build various pagodas and to expand Qingshui Yan into an impressive temple. Gradually, the monk assumed transcendental status and was worshipped as a deified ancestor by the villagers. From 1164 to 1210, Qingshui Zushi Gong was posthumously honored by the Southern Song imperial palace four times, each time with two characters having the following respective meanings: "ever-ready," "great wisdom," "ultimate compassion," and "extremely charitable." He was much loved and worshipped by the general population of Anxi county. Today, even though Qingshui Yan is known as a Buddhist temple, the main shrine houses this Wumian Zushi Gong.

Qingshui Yan has undergone two main phases of development, the first being that of the Northern Song and Southern Song eras, when by imperial decree, it was honored as a Buddhist temple. Since then, during the various dynastic epochs, additional honors led to new additions to the main temple, expanding and transforming it into a renowned sacred place.

The second phase of development is the modern period, starting toward the end of the 19th century. In 1899, the main shrine of the temple complex underwent extensive renovation, and two new buildings were added to it. However, in 1933, the complex was destroyed by a heavy rainstorm that caused the walls of the main shrine and those of other buildings to collapse. It was then left in a state of ruin until 1953, when Chinese overseas started to rebuild it. From 1953 to 1976, a group of Chinese overseas collectively renovated and extended the temple complex. It now stands as a complex of three buildings. The main shrine is called the *zushi dian* and is devoted to Qingshui Zushi. In 1978, a temple management committee was formed to manage the complex, and in the following year the complex was modernized to include telephone lines, street lamps, and a surfaced road winding up the slopes to the temple.

Qingshui Zushi Gong has, through the centuries, become the guardian deity of the people of Anxi county, and the villagers of Penglai have regarded it as their ancestral deity. He is also the guardian god among the lineages, who sits in the lineage ancestral houses. His black face is now considered a symbol of good virtue and righteousness. He is widely known for his deeds in helping those in need of assistance, and is a protector of the villagers from natural and human calamities. As he was supposedly a historical figure and not a mythological one, he is called a deified ancestor, Zushi Gong.

To the Anxi Chinese emigrants of the 19th and 20th centuries, Qingshui Zushi Gong was a source of encouragement and moral support, a protector against banditry and the uncertainties of the journey, and the only deity known to all of them prior to emigration. He was also a source of compassion, and the villagers relied on him for blessings and to solve their communal and personal problems, big and small. He was known to answer most requests because of his mystical powers and was thus spiritually powerful, *ling* to these Chinese.

Communal celebration of Qingshui Zushi Gong usually occurred during the Lunar New Year and on his birthday, the 6th day of the 6th lunar month, celebrated as a village religious fair. From the 1980s onwards, religious fairs in connection with Qingshui Zushi Gong are common sights in the *qiaoxiang*, organized to celebrate occasions like the welcoming of the mythical ancestor, *ying* Qingshui Zushi Gong, the worship of Heaven, *bai* Tiangong, "welcoming of god and lighting the fire," *yingshen yinghuo*, and the birthdays of the various buddhas, *fodan*.

For these religious fairs, a local household was selected to be the main organizer and sponsor of each event, the chosen person being known as the Buddha head, *fotou*. Most households in our survey participated in communal religious functions. The religious procession usually starts from one lineage ancestral house, winding its way through the village and ending up either in the Qingshui Yan Temple or the lineage house. The communal religious fairs attracted much attention because of their grandeur, and the atmosphere of excitement has encouraged individuals and households to participate in them. Like the ancestor-worship celebrations, the religious functions add life to an otherwise mundane social environment.

The district-wide *yingshen yinghuo* religious fair was revived only in 1990. The selection of the *fotou* was traditionally based on an annual

16. Religious procession that winds around the village in Penglai, Anxi county
(photograph by K. E. Kuah-Pearce).

rotation cycle among the nine surname groups in the district, and this
procedure was instituted when the fair was revived. Thus, each lineage is
appointed *fotou* once every nine years; and when this occurs it becomes
imperative that the lineage's village and overseas members become involved
in the fair as helpers and participants. In this way, the lineage gains much
"face" and creates a good name for itself and its members, which is
important for maintaining its overall social standing vis-à-vis the other
lineages.

Being a *fotou* is prestigious for the lineage concerned, but it also
involves a huge burden of responsibility — the expenses, the preparation,
the staging of the fair, and the scale is important too. When a lineage is
selected, an ad hoc committee is formed, the majority of whom are lineage
elders. The actual preparatory work — booking the monks and the opera
troupe, arranging the feast and the religious paraphernalia, etc. — is carried
out largely by the villagers, but financial contributions come mainly from
the overseas kin.

Within the lineage, members vie for the position of *fotou*. The selection
procedure is similar to that at the inter-lineage level. Interested individuals

or households are invited to participate in the selection process, which is witnessed by Qingshui Zushi Gong, for it involves the throwing of *mubei*, divining blocks, in front of the deity. The person with the highest number of positive throws becomes *fotou*. A *fotou* is expected to arrange for labor and to provide financial contributions for the fair, so it has now become the norm that the position of *fotou* falls on the shoulders of a lineage member who is relatively wealthy. In the last few years, some village households, with the support of their overseas kin, had successfully vied for the position. The village kin have to carry out the preparatory work in the absence of the *fotou* if he or she resides overseas.

Within a lineage, there is usually a core group comprising both overseas and village members who are most active and interested in its affairs. These are mostly men, but women, ranging from the age of 50 to 80, have emerged in recent years. In most cases, the local members are involved in deciding the details, including recruiting human resources for the jobs that need to be done prior to the actual days of celebration. Usually, younger men from within the lineage are recruited for a variety of tasks, including cleaning and decorating the shrine, erecting the opera stage, and purchasing

17. Offerings by lineage elders in Penglai, Anxi county (photograph by K. E. Kuah-Pearce).

the religious items. These young men are normally available on short notice and are counted on to do odd jobs and to run errands for the celebration.

Religious fairs are usually elaborate and incur substantial costs — some RMB20,000 to 30,000. Some large-scale religious fairs can cost up to RMB100,000 to 200,000. The cost includes: (1) Hiring an opera troupe for about RMB5,000, or a puppet show for about RMB3,000 for several nights of performances. Often both are staged. These performers must also be provided with accommodation and food. This entertainment is one of the two most important and costly items for the celebration. (2) Hiring of Taoist priests or Buddhist monks to lead the religious procession and to perform religious rites. This could amount to another RMB4,000 to 5,000, depending on the number of monks or priests and the duration and intensity of the performance. (3) Religious paraphernalia often cost as much as RMB3,000 to 4,000. (4) A village feast, costing at least RMB10,000.

For a religious fair to be successful, the villagers need to solicit the explicit or implicit endorsement of the authorities at various governmental levels. On such occasions, the celebration is declared a public holiday, and schools are closed so all children can participate. The primary and secondary school pupils perform dances and songs to celebrate the occasion. Each student would be provided with new clothes to wear on the day, drinks, and a small sum of RMB20 to 30 for participating. Many students look forward to these occasions, for they can enjoy themselves, be out of the classrooms, and get new clothes and money.

When a lineage hosts a *fotou* of a communal religious fair, the participation of the lineage members, and especially of the overseas members, becomes extremely important. This symbolizes a visual display of the social solidarity and strength among them and of the overseas members' recognition of their ancestral roots. The participation of village members poses no problem: whenever there is a religious fair, most village households participate in it. However, encouraging the overseas members to visit Anxi and participate in the religious fairs is not so easy, as they need to be convinced of the value of these socioreligious visits. This is especially true for the younger members, who have very little understanding of Chinese tradition and Chinese religious practices. In recent years, however, due largely to the efforts of the older members to persuade their children and grandchildren to accompany them, large groups of overseas Chinese have come to attend these religious fairs. Group travel arrangements have made it easier, and such events now regularly draw a group of 30 or more overseas members.

Upon arrival, they rest and are briefed on preparations for the event. The men gather and discuss final preparations while the women busy themselves instructing their female village counterparts to purchase incense, candles, joss papers, and fruit, and making individual offerings to the gods and ancestors in the ancestral house (*zuzai*) and temples. Over the next few days, the women visit the Qingshui Yan Temple and make offerings to Qingshui Zushi Gong.

The few days leading to the celebration are busy with last-minute preparations, the men looking after the external events while women involving themselves with food preparation and the purchase of ritual items needed for the various rites. The various roles are spelled out for the core participants. Usually, the monks or priests and the *fotou* and the committee lead the procession.

Ancestor Worship

Another aspect of religious revivalism is the resumption of ancestor worship. An important communal ancestor worship ritual is the Rite of Gratification for the Flow of Descendants, *xiezu juanding*. The term *xiezu* means "thanking the ancestors," *juan* means "continuous flow," and *ding* means "descendants." Taken together, *xiezu juanding* is thus the expression of gratification to ancestors for a continuous flow of descendants, that is, for the continuity of the lineage. The ceremony is important to acknowledge the roles of the ancestors in providing the descendants with wealth, good health, and peace. After the 1979 Reform, many lineages in the emigrant villages have restored or reconstructed their lineage ancestral house and performed this ritual (Kuah 1999, 2000: 139–72). The ritual is performed at least once a year during the Lunar New Year season. During this festive season, the doors of the lineage ancestral house are open, and members are expected to participate in both communal and individual worship of the ancestors. Individual households prepare several dishes, bring them to the lineage ancestral house, and offer them to their communal ancestors. In this, the roles of the women are again expressed by their expertise in staging the rituals and their participation brings them out of their private domestic spheres into the public sphere, thus establishing them as bona fide members of the lineage.

On the eve or in the morning of the celebration, women in individual households busied themselves preparing traditional rice cakes, slaughtering poultry, and cooking. In the mid-morning, women and also men, carried tables and the prepared food to the ancestral house, where the tables are arranged in neat rows in front of the ancestral house and foods placed on the tables as offerings to the ancestors. Because of their number, the households were divided into two groups, one of which made offerings in the morning and the other in the late afternoon. A variety of Chinese cakes, dishes of poultry, meat, and fruit were offered to the ancestors; incense was also offered, but on an individual basis. At a stipulated time, priests or monks performed the liturgy and rituals. The sessions lasted about an hour each. After the religious performance, each household burned paper money as offerings to the ancestors. After the session, the women members collected their food, placed it in a basket, picked up their tables, and returned home. The food was then eaten as lunch and dinner.

The ancestral house was packed with lineage members, but other villagers were also present. The master of ceremonies, a local village cadre known for his speaking ability, read aloud a document to inform the community of the achievements of individual members and of their desire to "fragrance" the lineage through these achievements. After this, the Taoist priests conducted various rituals to honor the ancestors. The ceremony took about two hours to complete. Afterwards, firecrackers were lit to mark the joyous occasion, and incense papers were burned for the ancestors and gods.

After this formal ceremony, individual lineage members, including men, women, and children, strolled into the ancestral house and offered their own prayers to the ancestors. The ceremony had also attracted many villagers, who were very curious, and some of them went in to investigate while others watched from outside. In recent years, many overseas members planned their visits to Anxi to coincide with communal ancestor worship. Such occasions provide them with a legitimate excuse to visit the ancestral village. On such occasions, younger members accompanied their elderly parents for a visit. In traditional China, communal ancestor worship was the responsibility of male elders, but this is not so today, and women have become important participants; in fact, female members are often the main participants in communal ancestor worship.

Another important ritual associated with ancestor worship is the "opening of the doors of the ancestral house," *kai zuzai men,* by successful individuals. Individual members with special achievement, such as having attained a doctorate, are often invited to "open the doors of the ancestral house" to honor and give thanks to their ancestors for their achievement and success. This is one way to announce to other lineages one's achievement, thereby to "fragrance the name of the ancestor, family, and lineage." "Opening the doors of the ancestral house" is considered an important act of sharing the achievement and joy with the lineage. In some lineages, this privilege is now extended to female members. Women who have attained great achievements can now open the doors of the ancestral house. So far, there has been one case, considered an accomplishment in the rural setting.

Before one is allowed to "open the doors of the ancestral house," both overseas and village elders must agree on the appropriateness of the occasion. A date is set and arrangements are made for this occasion. Village kin made preparations, bought the necessary religious paraphernalia, had a plaque with the name of the son and his academic achievement prepared, and arranged for a feast. Invitations to all lineage members were issued.

By staging various religious functions, whether *xiezu juanding* or *kai zuzai men*, the lineage is expressing its presence and social dominance vis-à-vis other lineages in Anxi. Through these religious activities, the sense of lineage identity, hidden and buried prior to the reform years, is recreated and articulated openly.

When wealth and success have become part of the social fabric of emigrant villages, then other criteria are needed to measure the social status of these emigrant villages and to differentiate them from one another. The old-fashioned criterion of knowledge, the production of scholar-literati in the Confucian sense, has now become equal to, if not more important than, material wealth. Similarly, becoming an official now has more appeal than before.[3] Such recognition can only elevate the status of one's lineage in competition with others. In the words of one of my informants, "not every emigrant village could produce a *boshi*," a scholar with a doctorate.

Women, Memory and Ritual Practice

Women play an extremely important role in the reproduction of the religious rituals. It is they who "remembered" the types of ritual that are required for domestic and communal religious fairs. It is also they who are primarily involved in the preparation of the food offerings and religious paraphernalia for these occasions. Geary (1994: 51–73) argues that women are active in remembering, preserving, and transmitting the past. Therefore they are significant in the preservation of collective memory of a social group. By actively engaging in the process of reproduction and the performance of daily rituals and rites within the domestic household, women are inevitably drawn into the process of reproducing the religious rituals, rites, and food offerings for both communal religious fairs and ancestor worship. Thus, on such occasions, women are the key players.

In reproducing food offerings for the ancestors during ancestor worship, the types of food offered to the ancestors explain the social relationship and identity of these women in relation to their forebears. In ancestor worship, women gave careful thought to the types of food to be offered to the ancestors. In reproducing food that is offered to the immediate ancestors within home, women often take into consideration the likes and dislikes of the ancestors. Thus, in this category of food offering, apart from the likes and dislikes, the style of cooking, the types of spice and particular local food elements used as well as the presentation are all taken into consideration during the preparation of the food. For example, ancestors who had migrated to Southeast Asia and had acquired local tastes would be offered curry dishes. Likewise, those who had migrated to North America would be offered North American dishes. However, effort was not spared in preparing traditional food for ancestors who had yearned for such food in an overseas environment. For example, among the Fujianese, an important dish served to the ancestors would be the traditional rice cakes, that is made of ground rice flour, and served with a dish of braised pork.

This type of food offering contrasted greatly with that offered to the communal and founding ancestors. The ancestors would be offered only very traditional food, as it is assumed that they were aware of this category of food only. Furthermore, the types and the preparation of them are highly dependent on the extent to which the women members remembered the dishes. There is little attempt to consult any written text on food offering. In most cases, the villagers simply did not have the literacy to explore food offerings found in the early texts. At this level, there were one or two items that vaguely resembled those that were found offered during Chinese antiquity, such as the "ear cakes," which bore no resemblance to modern-day food among the Chinese. Food offered for the communal ancestors was left there for the duration of the celebration and not consumed by the members.

Women are also intimately involved in food presentation and the layout of food on the altar table. Where each type of food should be placed on the table is also a subject of agony for them, as they wrestled with their memory. In offering food to the immediate ancestors at home, three bowls of rice are placed at the front of the altar table, together with three cups of wine and three pairs of chopsticks. In the second row are placed the favorite and special dishes that the ancestors liked. In the third row are the more common dishes. At either the right or the left corner of the table, farthest away from the ancestral tablets, are placed a stack of joss papers that would be burned during the course of ancestor worship. In the communal ancestor worship at the lineage ancestral house, food offerings are arranged according to the types of food, dried food in one row, cakes, biscuits, and buns in another row, fruit in a third row and so on. However, women giving individual household offerings would arrange their food according to its value. At the front of the table are placed chicken, pork, duck, and fish dishes, followed by vegetable dishes, and finally dessert and snacks such as cakes and buns.

Here, we can conclude that food presentation and layout are done according to the following criteria. For the immediate ancestors at home, the layout is according to taste of the ancestors. For communal ancestor worship, it is arranged according to the different categories of food, and for individual offerings to the communal ancestors, it is according to the value of food. Based on food presentation and layout, it is possible to correlate taste with social distance between the members and their ancestors. The closer the social distance and relationship, the more likely it is that the living members know the taste and preference of their dead ancestors and are therefore able to provide food that the ancestors like. For communal ancestor worship, food is laid out according to food categories, reflecting a great social distance between the members and the ancestors where taste and preference do not feature at all in the food offering. Furthermore, the fact that women were trying to remember the traditional food that was served to the early ancestors reflects their ambiguity and uncertainty of the types of food to feed the early ancestors. In the offerings given by individual households during communal ancestor worship, food value becomes important, reflecting the desire of individual households to make an impression on the ancestors. To a large degree, it can be seen as a way the individual members and household attempt to establish a closer *guanxi* (network) with the ancestors in the hope of accruing blessings and protection from the ancestors. By providing expensive food, the members hope to establish a social exchange and reciprocity network between them and the ancestors. In so doing, food becomes a form of cultural capital that opens doors and access to the ancestors and allows members to ask for favors and negotiate for material and non-material things in life.

As well as their role in food preparation and offerings, women busy themselves with all types of arrangement for religious occasions. Women make decisions regarding the types of ritual practice needed for the occasion, religious personnel, food, flowers, and the quantities of incense and joss papers required. They also decide on the types of entertainment, either a Chinese opera troupe or puppet show, and the people, including the cadres and the neighboring villagers, to be invited to the fairs.

On the few days leading to the celebration, women prepare food such as sticky cakes, buns, and fruit. Poultry and meat dishes are prepared on the actual day. The women also prepared a large quantity of joss papers, candles, and other offerings ahead of the celebration. On the actual day, women wake up early and ready themselves for the celebration. They bring their food, joss sticks, incense papers, fruit, and tables and display them to Qingshui Zushi and their ancestors. Others followed the procession that winds around the village. As on most religious occasions, worship is conducted on two levels: the communal offering to Zushi Gong and the individual offerings by the members.

Most members arrive in the morning, and by mid-morning, the crowd gathered in the temple has grown to 100 or more people. Many are elderly women, who generally spend several hours in the temple before returning home. Most stay for a luncheon prepared by the *fotou*'s lineage. There is

18. Offerings of soul houses to the ancestors, Penglai, Anxi county (photograph by K. E. Kuah-Pearce).

also a small number of women in their 20s and 30s, who accompany their mothers or mothers-in-law to the temple and lineage ancestral house. Some of them leave after offering incense to the gods and ancestors whereas others stay behind and join in the socializing among the elderly villagers.

Elderly women are most religious and participate wholeheartedly for they see religious practices as important in satisfying their this-worldly and otherworldly needs, but younger villagers are less enthusiastic and feel ritual practices are less relevant to their lives; some view religion as superstition, not to be encouraged.

Religious fairs also provide an important means of cultural bond among the women. It is possible to identify several groups of women here, from the village, the city and from overseas. Among the village women, it is also possible to identify women of the same lineage and those of other lineage groups. Apart from re-establishing the ritual practices, women are involved in the preparation of food and religious paraphernalia for ancestor worship and other religious fairs. Through cooperation in these activities, the women are brought closer together.

Through ritual practices, they are able to express their sentiments toward their ancestral villages and their village kin. By staging religious fairs and participating in ritual practices, these Chinese are brought together in a physical way to acknowledge their social and kinship ties. These ritual practices serve as cushions against the initial shock of reuniting with village kin, and as an important dialogue platform for the various groups of women. Between the village women and their overseas kinswomen, religious activities provide a ready topic for conversation and thus reduce initial embarrassment of reunions after several decades of separation. This is also the case for the men, as many of them find it difficult to make small talk, so that involvement in some sort of work becomes a desirable aim when they visit the villages. Thus the staging of communal religious fairs becomes a way out, as conversations are directed toward the preparation and the actual ceremony.

The village atmosphere is transformed dramatically with the religious fair. There is intense communication, and visits are made to different households. At night, the men might gather at a particular household, sipping tea, drinking liquor, and discussing the coming events. Likewise, women gather together to talk. The social atmosphere is one of festivity, and the mood increases as the celebration draws nearer. Children, too, are keenly aware of the upcoming celebration and become wildly excited about the event, as the schools announce the holiday. Village routine gives way to festivity and celebration, and most villagers become involved in the celebration one way or another.

Unlike in traditional Chinese society, in which men were responsible for public communal worship, today women are the main participants. By their active participation in the public communal religious sphere, women have not only transformed the religious landscape in rural China but also the gender relationship embedded within the private and public domains. The notion of women being the "inside persons," therefore subjugated to the patriarchal system, has long been repudiated by scholars such as Mann (1997) and Ko (1994). Today, this is even more evident as village women and their overseas counterparts together strive to advance their social visibility through the control and manipulation of rituals and rites within the religious domain in rural China. Overseas Chinese women, through their attainment of wealth, status, and vocal articulation, have provided further impetus to restructure the social relationship between men and women. Together, these women dominate decision making in all aspects of the religious fairs as well as in the economic and social spheres. On religious occasions, they consolidate and display their strength in public.

On this occasion, the social and kinship networks of the members are clearly displayed to everyone. In communal ancestor worship, women, including married and unmarried daughters, are seen as an integral part of the lineage. The majority is related to each other, either sharing surnames or coming from the same ancestral village, and there is a high level of sociability. At the lineage level, women are related to each other through agnatic and affinal ties, and many have known each other for the past three to four decades. These cross-lineage ties of support and friendship have developed into important networks within which the women can draw strength in times of hardship and happiness.

The religious fairs are joyous occasions for all members. On these communal occasions, individual religiosity is consigned to a secondary position, to the individual acts of worship and offering. After their obligatory worship, the women greet one another, gather and socialize in small groups, catching up with one another on a range of issues ranging from the marriages of children and grandchildren, health, recreation, food, fashion and other concerns centering on their families. It is a time to exchange news and to renew kinship and friendship ties as, although most have their own circles of relational kin with whom they regularly interact, this occasion provides opportunities to rekindle relationships with those whom they meet less regularly. After lunch, many make their way home, leaving a handful of them who stay behind.

Men are also involved in religious preparations. Overseas Chinese men provide financial support, whereas village men are involved in the actual preparation for the communal fair. They prepare the stage and the ritual paraphernalia, arrange for a village feast, religious personnel, and lead the procession. They also gather during the night, make offerings of joss incense to the various gods, and engage in conversation. Topics can range from business to politics to events in their home villages in China. Although it is a common sight to see elderly men at the temples, few young men are present.

Religiosity versus Instrumental Needs

In the village world, where religion and overt religious practices have been suppressed for several decades, the revival of communal religious fairs has brought about mixed feelings for some and confusion for others. Overseas Chinese who visit the home village to perform large-scale communal worship expect their village kin to have the same level of religiosity as they do, but this has not generally been the case. I have argued that ritual practices have provided the villagers and overseas Chinese with a shared activity that allows for social bonding to occur. Yet there continued to be differences at the micro-level, at which differences in religious experience, religiosity, and interest have resulted in tensions between them.

Most villagers are supportive and have participated in communal religious functions. They often visit Qingshui Yan Temple individually or with their overseas kin. In addition, some pray to the local village gods. They feel that large-scale religious events provide "noise" and "heat" and brighten the atmosphere of the village. Some view religious revivalism as a way of exercising religious freedom, which had not been possible since the 1960s, so that being able to carry out these activities freely is refreshing. However, they have also expressed their fear that if *qiaoxiang* do not exercise discretion over the scale of the religious celebrations, the government authorities might impose restrictions that would be detrimental to religious freedom. A number of the villagers feel that religious revivalism is a return to superstition.

To the villagers, the significance of religious revivalism and the staging of communal religious fairs is as follows: First, these cultural traditions serve as a bridge between villagers and their overseas kin, helping them to rekindle lost relationships. Second, the activities encourage the Chinese overseas to visit their ancestral home village on a regular basis, which is also instrumental in cementing social and kinship ties with the *qiaoxiang*. Third, these are important social functions that bring the villagers themselves together and help to create social solidarity. Fourth, as significant social events, they create variety to and enliven village life. Fifth, the religious events and the accompanying production of religious paraphernalia and services are important for the local economy, supporting the small cottage industry catering for the dead, the living, and the gods. Women are seen as the main supporters of this cottage industry.

Village, district and county cadres have adopted an instrumental attitude toward religious revivalism, and each group gives varying degrees of support for the religious activities. They see religious revival as a form of cultural capital to lure investment resources to rural China. The village cadres were the most open in their support, and the county level cadres were the least open. The degree of openness is tied closely to the needs of persons in varying official positions to display political correctness in their treatment of social events and activities.

Cadre support for communal religious fairs is rationalized as support for social and cultural activities of the villagers — ancestor worship is seen as part of the moral duty toward the elders, including the dead, and religious fairs as part of the village's social events. Village and district cadres are much more liberal in their interpretation of these communal rites than are county cadres, for two reasons. First, some are genuine believers. Second is the instrumental consideration: they feel that, because of tolerance and support for the ritual activities, they will be able to encourage regular visits by the overseas Chinese. Such visits will eventually lead to contributions and investment into the region, which is in line with the central government's policy of encouraging overseas Chinese investment.

Cadres supported the reconstruction of Qingshui Yan Temple for three reasons. First, they see the temple as having historical value and worthy of preservation, as it is over 800 years old, its history stretching back to the Song Dynasty. The central government has officially named the Qingshui Yan Temple a national historical monument, so obviously the cadres find it necessary to preserve it. Second, the temple is seen as providing for the religious needs of villagers and Chinese from Southeast Asia and Taiwan, who have visited the temple in great numbers in recent years, supported temple reconstruction, and staged massive religious fairs for the deity. Support for the temple and its related functions are thus crucial concessions made to Southeast Asian Chinese to encourage them to invest in the region. Third, the temple is seen as a tourist site and hence significant for the development of tourism in Anxi. The reconstruction has led to an increase in the number of overseas Chinese visiting it, and they have brought substantial revenue to Anxi county but more specifically to Penglai district. Indirect benefits also filter down to the people and to the district and county governments.

However, village and district cadres have expressed the need to maintain a balance in the celebrations, the scale of which must be justified by substantial capital investment and aid to the region. The majority of them do not favor large-scale, ostentatious celebrations, citing waste of resources as the main reason. However, they do not attempt to interfere in the functions. This tolerant attitude can be seen as tacit support. Although most village and district cadres do not participate in the ritual performances, they oblige the organizers and attend the fair and feast, giving the functions legitimacy. Whatever feelings they have regarding these events, they keep to themselves. Some who may feel the events are superstitious nevertheless feel that it would be unwise to stop or boycott them. Others, however, see these as important cultural events that would alleviate the drudgery of village life. Irrespective of the reasons, these cadres want to be seen openly supporting the village cultural and religious activities.

The county cadres are less supportive of religious activities. They feel that such activities are not in line with the ideological orientation of central policies. Their official line of argument is that the functions are superstitious and thus should not be encouraged. They also feel that such activities are a waste of precious resources that could be put to better social and economic use, but they conceded that, given the present socioeconomic situation they could not and would not eliminate them. Some are willing to attend the fair's associated feast, to give face to the overseas Chinese who issued the invitation. Thus they, too, are flexible, wanting to maintain good relationships with the overseas Chinese who have contributed much financially to the development of Anxi county. Some county cadres, too, see religious activity as a part of village cultural tradition that continues to have a profound impact on the life of its adherents, as the communal spirit has increased with the staging of these religious fairs.

When villagers support communal religious celebrations, it is not necessarily a reflection of personal belief or religiosity but is often a means to an end. Irrespective of age group, religion is seen as socioeconomic capital. For example, after the reconstruction of Qingshui Yan Temple, the village economy benefited from an annual income of RMB2 to 3 million from contributions for incense and oil by the Chinese overseas.[4] Part of this income goes to the village treasury and is used for social and economic projects.

Thus, among the cadres at each level of the political bureaucracy, there continues to be tension between support for and disapproval of these communal religious fairs. The main consideration is to maintain a balance between pure social and religious functions and the economic interests of the region where the communal religious fairs are now an entrenched part of the village social landscape.

Conclusion

In traditional Chinese society, religion played a central role in the lives of the villagers. After the 1979 Reform, religion once again dominates the lives of these villagers, as seen from the regular religious fairs that are being held to honor the gods and ancestors. In the process of religious revivalism, women have played an important role in reinventing the ritual practices and food offerings for the gods and ancestors. They have become dominant players, and their skills are essential for the successful functioning of these religious fairs. They are the ones who possess the knowledge and remember the details of the various religious rituals and rites and help reconstruct them for the communal religious activities. They remember the types of rite and ritual, the types and amount of religious paraphernalia that are needed for each ritual practice and the types of religious personnel, Buddhist monks and Taoist priests, needed. They are also involved with the preparation of food as offerings to the gods, deities, and ancestors. In addition, they are the most active in participating in all the religious rituals, both collectively and individually.

Anthropologically, these religious activities fulfill several functions. First, they provide opportunities for the elderly to meet and rekindle their relationships with others. Second, they provide opportunities for younger members to get acquainted with one another. They also allow economic networking among the younger members: of the younger men who visit the temple, many have now taken over the family business; thus, going to the temple allows them to develop *guanxi* and form business partnerships. They enable younger women to be inducted into the wider kinship network and become recognized as daughters-in-law, thereby providing them with a patrilineal identity. By encouraging the participation of younger members, identity with the lineage and ancestral district can be ensured.

Religious revivalism has also brought about much change in the life of the villagers and the *qiaoxiang*. To a certain degree, the communal religious fairs have revitalized the religiosity of the villagers, especially the older ones, whose formerly suppressed religiosity can now come out in the open. Socially, this revivalism has provided overseas Chinese and villagers with a common ideology that allows for a renewal of kinship ties and social networks.

Notes

1. Prior to 1978, all Singapore citizens traveling to China were required to apply for an exit permit from the Singapore Immigration Department. It was a policy that only those 45 years old or above were permitted to visit China.
2. This figure is based on a survey conducted on 200 villagers in the Penglai district in Anxi county.
3. In recent years, those overseas Chinese with high official titles in their adopted countries have been given due acknowledgement by the provincial government. One example here is the restoration of the ancestral grave of the former President of the Philippines, Corazon Aquino, when she visited her home village in Hongjian village, Longhai county, Fujian.
4. This figure is supplied by an official of the Qingshui Yan Temple management committee.

References

Anxi Xian Committee, comp. 1994. *Anxi Xianzhi, 1 and 2 vols.* Anxi: Xinhua Publishing House.

Dean, Kenneth. 1993. *Taoist Ritual and Popular Cults in Southeast China.* Princeton, NJ: Princeton University Press.

Geary, P. J. 1994. *Phantoms of Remembrance.* Princeton, NJ: Princeton University Press.

Granet, Marcel. 1975. *The Religion of the Chinese People.* New York: Harper and Row.

Hsü, Francis L. K. 1952. *Religion, Science and Human Crises.* London: Routledge and Kegan Paul.

Ko, Dorothy. 1994. *Teachers of the Inner Chambers: Women and Culture in Seventeenth Century China.* Stanford: Stanford University Press.

Kuah, Khun Eng. 1999. The Moral Economy of Ancestor Worship in a Chinese Emigrant Village. *Journal of Culture, Medicine and Psychiatry* 23: 99–132. (Special Issue: *The Transformation of Social Experience in Hong Kong, Taiwan and China*, edited by A. Kleinman, J. Kleinman and S. Lee.)

———. 2000. *Rebuilding the Ancestral Village: Singaporeans in China.* Aldershot, England: Ashgate Publishing.

La Fontaine, J. S. 1985. *Initiation: Ritual Drama and Secret Knowledge across the World.* Middlesex: Pelican Books.

Mann, Susan. 1997. *Precious Records: Women in China's Long Eighteenth Century.* Stanford: Stanford University Press.

SAAY. 1994. *Singapore Anxi Association Yearbook.* Singapore: Singapore Anxi Association.

Yang, C. K. 1961. *Religion in Chinese Society.* Berkeley: University of California Press.

Zhenxiang Zazhi Bianjibu. 1987.

Glossary

Anxi	安溪
bai Tiangong	拜天公
beishan wangshui	背山望水
boshi	博士
Chen Puzu	陳普足
Chen Sengren	陳僧人
fodan	佛誕
fotou	佛頭
kai zuzai men	開祖宅門
ling	靈
Luobi Zushi Gong	落鼻祖師公
mubei	木杯
Oolong (Wulong)	烏龍
Penglai	蓬來
qiaoxiang	僑鄉
Qingshui Yan	清水岩
Qingxi	清溪
Qingshui Zushi Gong	清水祖師公
Tieguanyin	鐵觀音
Wumian Zushi Gong	烏面祖師公
xiezu juanding	謝祖涓丁
ying Qingshui Zushi Gong	迎清水祖師公
yingshen yinghuo	迎神迎火
Yongchun county	永春縣
Zhang Yan Shan	張岩山
zushi dian	祖師殿

6

Engendering Minnan Mobility:
Women Sojourners in a Patriarchal World

■ Siumi Maria Tam

Introduction[1]

Minnan (southern Fujian, China) had been exporting male labor to Southeast Asia for centuries, and Minnan women had played a central role in the sustenance of patrilineal families left behind by the men. This chapter examines the interface of gender and migration, as Minnan women struggled to make a living for themselves and their children, as well as simultaneously shouldering the responsibility to support their husbands' patrilineal kin. As they lamented "all Minnan women lead a bitter life" and resigned themselves to a female fate, they practiced self-effacement and self-sacrifice, justifying gender inequality with traditionalism. Indeed, they had helped to construct and maintain the Minnan patriarchal world in which female individuality had no place in face of the good of the patrilineal family. Paradoxically, these same women became successful entrepreneurs, calculating mothers who command domestic resources across generations, and managers of kinship networks — all of them tough survivors in a system of out-migration. Minnan women referred to this quality of theirs as a "strong life force" (*shengmingli qiang*[2]). Although it may be a truism to say that all migrants, and not only Minnan women, manifest a frontier spirit and possess the ability to adjust to a drastically different cultural environment, it must be stressed that these "migrants' qualities" vary in different contexts on how they are selected, combined, and maneuvered to produce intended or unintended consequences.

In this study I argue that the Minnan woman's identification of herself as keeper of her husband's family was the underlying force for her survival.

It was the "life force" that had sustained her in face of fluctuating state policies and economic pressures, as she held on to the hope that someday the family would be complete when reunited with her absentee husband. Also, her responsibility as the breadwinner and her assumption of the dual role of mother and father were important means for her to acquire both domestic and public recognition in a chauvinistic culture. Such women were not just passive recipients of foreign remittances sent home by their husbands. Instead of being dependents, they were more often the central figure that ensured that the migrant family[3] survived and often prospered. But it was also obvious that as they toiled day to day to keep their families afloat, Minnan women reproduced a male-centered culture. Thus, how femininity was interpreted and practiced among Minnan women, whether they stayed behind after their husbands left or if they themselves had moved, sheds light on the dialectics of agency and manifests how these women were simultaneously agents who contributed to and were victims of patriarchal social systems.

This chapter focuses on the personal histories of women from the Jinjiang district (the geo-administrative district in southern Fujian province through which the Jin River flows). They were Minnan women who had constructed a life of migrancy at the interface of three geographical-cultural areas: (1) the Jinjiang district as the place of origin; (2) the Philippines as the destination of mobility; and (3) Hong Kong as the stepping stone between the two. Within this triangular circuit the women experienced mobility, first as the wives of emigrants in China (*fanke shen*), then as ethnic Chinese in the Philippines (*inchik*), and finally as Minnan women immigrants in Hong Kong (*minnan po*). These three categorical ascriptions formed the basis of their subjectivities as wives, mothers, and daughters-in-law, but seldom as women as individuals.

Ethnographic fieldwork was carried out between 1998 and 2000. Data in this paper are drawn from in-depth interviews of 48 Jinjiang women, 30 in Hong Kong and the rest in several villages in the Quanzhou vicinity. Interviewees in Hong Kong aged from the mid-50s to mid-80s at the time of the interview. Those from Quanzhou were between 70 and their early 90s. Most of the interviewees living on the mainland were women whose husbands had migrated to the Philippines, and they were living in a split household. Those in Hong Kong mostly arrived in the British colony in the 1950s as single mothers with young children, except for one who was a teenager when she arrived in Hong Kong with her mother. All of them had lived in Hong Kong for over 40 years. Face-to-face interviews, each lasting between 60 and 120 minutes, were carried out mainly in the homes of interviewees, and a small number were conducted in the interviewees' office, or cafés and *tongxianghui* (hometown associations) offices. While I will generalize the commonalities among the women, I will also illustrate my argument with direct quotes from individual interviewees. These narratives together shed light on Minnan women's life experience as migrant wives and on issues of adjustment as they enacted femininity in mobility.

Reluctant Traverse: Becoming *Fanke Shen*

For centuries, Jinjiang men had participated in the export of male labor to the Philippines, working as traders and laborers in the archipelago even before the Spanish colonization. According to Pan (1999), in 1987 there were 944,500 Jinjiang natives, scattered across 50 countries/territories abroad, mostly in Southeast Asia, with the largest settlement in the Philippines. Around the same time, there were 300,000 Jinjiangese living in Hong Kong, accounting for 6 percent of the colony's population (Hong Kong Jinjiang Tongxiang Association 1986). In 2000, their number was estimated at over 500,000, accounting for 83 percent of the Minnan population and 9 percent of the total population of the Hong Kong Special Administrative Region.[4]

In the long history of male emigration, while their men folk were away, Minnan women played an important role in sustaining the patrilineal families left behind. See Lai Yuk[5], a well-known politician in Hong Kong and native of Chendai, Jinjiang, sums up the conventional view:

> Fujian people are very traditional. The older generation are very traditionally Chinese, that is, very conservative ... and these traditions have implications for women. Traditionally in *huaqiao* (overseas Chinese) families, it's the men who go out to earn a living. The women are to stay behind in the hometown to look after their parents-in-law, to have and care for the children.

See's comment quoted above encapsulates the functions and duties of the migrant man's wife. In this study, we see Minnan women occupying the central position in the reproduction of the *patri*-line. Her centrality lay not only in her bearing of male offspring but more significantly in the daily maintenance of the household into which she was married, and culturally giving her husband the identity of a grown-up man. Without a wife, a man would not be culturally recognized as having achieved his primary life goal — establishing a family and a home (*chengjia lishi*). The implications of taking a wife were that he would then be guaranteed sons and their proper upbringing, a well-maintained household, additional labor and income, and daily care for his aging parents. He would have fulfilled his responsibility toward the generation both above and below him, and hopefully laid the foundation for the care he would need when he himself grew old.

The potential benefits and cultural pressure were powerful enough to propel migrant Minnan men of marriageable age to return to their hometown to take a wife. For a man who was absent from his natal home, marriage ensured proper transfer of these familial responsibilities. He would be a filial son to his parents as well as his ancestors, via the work of his wife. As such, his role in the marriage relationship was relatively simple. As an absentee husband, his spousal responsibility was primarily a financial one — to send remittances home. Hsü (2000: 35) talks about methods of taking money home by overseas Chinese in the United States, similar to those employed in Southeast Asia. The husband might take the money home by himself, or he could send a letter enclosed with money via returning relatives and friends. But this occurred irregularly. He might also hire a courier known as *shuike* (literally "water guest," individuals who participated in the import-export small trade), who would personally deliver and might wait for recipients to write a letter in reply. However, the sender ran the risk of the courier running away with the money. The overseas man could also make use of remittance services offered by private businesses known as Qiaoxin Ju and Minxin Ju.[6] The typical overseas laborer was illiterate or semi-literate, and his letters, often written by professional letter-writers, were usually scarce, sporadic, and brief. Remittances that came with the letters tended to be irregular and often inadequate.

Under these circumstances, women married to *fanke* (literally "foreign guest," meaning a Chinese man who lives in a foreign land) had to work in the fields to create a regular income, as well as attend to housework that was considered the daughter-in-law's primary responsibility. Margery Wolf (1972: 37) has argued with force for the need to adopt "a female focus" in understanding the Chinese family, because only then will "we see the Chinese family not as a continuous line stretching between the vague horizons of past and future, but as a contemporary group that comes into existence out of one woman's need and is held together insofar as she has the strength to do so, or, for that matter, the need to do so."

This "need" to hold the migrant family together, however, was less tangible for the wife than the absentee husband, and so were the benefits of marriage. To all of the elderly women I interviewed, marriage marked the first of a series of reluctant mobilities, responsibilities to be carried out on the husband's behalf, and the elimination of individuality. A woman who married a *fanke* expected a life intertwined with mobility and the lack of control over where she would end up. Indeed, the feeling of helplessness regarding removal from one space to another was the most obvious sentiment that came through in the interviews. Tan Ming Hui was married in Jinjiang when she was 15. She described her wedding:

> It was during the Japanese invasion ... [On the wedding day] the door of the sedan chair was kicked by a rooster ... It was like this at that time. Men couldn't come back [from the Philippines] because of the war. The bride was brought [to the man's family] in a sedan chair. The man wasn't there, so a rooster [symbolizing the groom] was used to kick the sedan. There were four of us [girls] in our *xiang* (rural township) who had weddings like this ... He (my husband) didn't come home until three years later, after the war was over.

The lack of choice and of autonomy over one's life, and the pervasiveness of such practice in those days, led women to accept it as fate, comforted perhaps by the very occasional success stories that the husband would send enough money home to build a mansion of 200 rooms.[7] Women, participating in these movements over their life, resented the arrangement but at the same time they did not choose to resist it. As another interviewee Chua Li Ping said, "Women at that time were all like that ... They were being sacrificed in the old society." Typical of this "old society" was the one found in the Jinjiang area. Livelihoods there were intertwined with livelihoods in the Philippines. In villages like Dalun, for example, if the broadest sense of the word *qiaoshu* (dependents of overseas Chinese) was applied, almost every family in the Jinjiang area would qualify. Families would arrange for their sons, husbands, fathers, and uncles to earn pesos in the Philippines. The lives of females in the rural regions of Jinjiang area thus hinged on remittances from the Philippines. Their male kin ran businesses or were employed in businesses owned by *tongxiang* (people from the same places of origin). They had built up networks that would secure their own livelihood in the Philippines. This same network could only guarantee its own reproduction through marriage with women in China.

Tan Ming Hui was a typical case. Her marriage was arranged by her parents. The only thing she knew about her husband was that he was a *fanke*, and it was the prospect of becoming a *fanke shen* that decided her betrothal. She remembered vividly sitting in the red sedan chair on the wedding day, and on the way she could only worry for herself because she did not even know where she would be taken! Tan's husband had been employed in a timber factory in the Philippines since he was 17. At the age of 20, he was recalled home to marry the Chinese woman selected for him. After the wedding he stayed home for three months. Thereafter he went home twice in all: once two years after the first return, and the other time it was nine years later. During that last return, the Japanese invasion prevented him from leaving China, but as soon as the war was over, he left again. Tan gave birth to two sons. But the remittances she received were small and never enough to support the family. She had to do agricultural work besides caring for her children and parents-in-law. 18 years lapsed before Tan met her husband again, when she was given permission to go to Hong Kong in 1964. Her husband traveled to Hong Kong to see her. By that time he was terminally ill, and was not able to leave for the Philippines again. Tan carried out her last duty as a wife. She took him back to his hometown and cared for him until he died.

A woman's lack of control over her own mobility under the male-centered family institution and state migration policy, and her sense of responsibility toward her husband's family, were typical of all those interviewed in this study. In similar ways, Chiu Yiu Lan began her life as a *fanke shen* at the age of 18. A native of Shishi, she was one of the children of a poor farming family. Her parents believed that the most important thing for a girl was not education but to be married into a good family. She was married to a *fanke* who had a grocery store in the Philippines. He had already married a Filipina over there and had several children. However, his parents did not recognize this non-Chinese daughter-in-law and her children, and ordered him to marry a Chinese wife. Chiu's husband stayed in China for two months after the wedding, and then left for the Philippines. Chiu had no children of her own, but in order to carry on the family line for her husband, she adopted a son. She was given permission by the Chinese government to migrate to Hong Kong in 1974. She did so only because it meant that she could see her husband again. In 1975 she managed to arrange a visit to the Philippines, which was 28 years after her husband left her. This kind of long wait was typical for many other *fanke shen*. For them, like Chiu, life as a female was only meaningful when there was the hope that someday she would see her husband again.

Yao Ching's case shows some variation. As she sat in the sitting room of her family *chu* (H, house) in Hanjiang, she recounted how her life as the wife of a migrant man began, with a certain sweetness in her voice:

When I married [my husband] this house wasn't even built yet. Somebody introduced us ... I was still at school. The marriage was arranged when I was 15. I didn't even know about it ... Both our families worshipped Shangdi (the Christian God), so I was introduced to this [family].

Marriage based on religion was quite uncommon. Yao married her husband when she was 20. And before she married, she received education from a private tutor who taught her English and Tang poetry at home. Yao was undoubtedly a relatively well-off and highly educated woman in her days. She was not accustomed to doing housework, let alone agricultural work. Because of her education, she was able to write letters to her husband herself after he left for the Philippines. She was all smiles when she told me that she even helped other *fanke shen* to write to their husbands:

> [Interviewer: Did you write long letters?] "No. [I wrote] the same things over and over again. So little time ... I had no spare time ... Nothing to talk about. What can a housewife do? [There's] so much work [that you'd] die. So many children in the house. [I] had to help them study, wash the clothes, cook meals, take care of my mother-in-law. What can [I] do?"

Although Yao was satisfied with her husband and her marriage, she lamented about the harsh life that marriage brought her. When I asked whether her husband sent home enough money, she said:

> No, no! I needed to arrange everything carefully, what can [I] do? I could *not* let my mother-in-law starve. But there wasn't enough money, so I had to borrow from other *huaqiao* [in the neighborhood], and I repaid them when the remittance arrived ... I had to pull the cart (of the production unit), fetch water, work in the fields ... I was very famous (for being a good worker), got a lot of merit certificates. I served food to my mother-in-law first, then I would close the door and go out to work ... I raised chickens and ducks ... no pigs — I'm very clean ... I got this award plaque for my cleanliness ... Everybody [in this village] knows where I live; and everybody knows I was very filial and respectful to my mother-in-law.
>
> [Emphasis added]

Yet, life was not easy, and she complained, "My eyes are bad; I can't walk. At the age of 84, I'm ready to go ... I can't do anything any more ... Life in the past was so hard that I wanted to die." Physical labor and the pressures to make ends meet were very difficult adjustments for young women with absentee husbands. Yao was able to survive these difficulties only because "it was the way then." She accepted life and fulfilled familial responsibilities on her husband's behalf. This she did with the "strength" that Wolf (1972) argues that Chinese women had as they struggled to keep their uterine family together. During the Cultural Revolution, life was particularly difficult for Yao and her family because of their status as *qiaoshu*, dependents of overseas Chinese; but she managed to keep her family together and even send her children to university afterwards. She declared proudly:

> I managed to send all my children to university. I have five children, four sons and a daughter, all of them university graduates. My grandchildren will also be university graduates.

Yao was certainly proud of her achievements in fulfilling her familial responsibilities and in establishing herself as a good woman who had successfully contributed to the prosperity of the family. But more obviously she considered herself fortunate to have a husband who, unlike most of the husbands of the women in her village, wrote letters and sent money home very regularly, and who remained loyal to the marriage throughout his life. This was particularly important, as the life of a *fanke shen* was, in the words of Minnan people, equivalent to that of a *huo guafu*, a widow although her husband was still alive. The husband's fidelity and sense of responsibility were essential to the wife's sense of being.

For most other interviewees, it was the sadness of being deserted that made life most intolerable. Many Minnan men did marry Filipinas, sometimes before their marriage in China, but mostly after. This was believed to be a practice necessitated by the Philippines government's restrictions over foreign ownership of business. But the fact that many businessmen and workers did not marry Filipinas shows that the issue was more complicated than one of state policy. The existence of a second household in the Philippines often meant that remittances would be irregular and meager. The backbreaking work of maintaining a household was meaningless without the belief that some day the husband would return to make a Minnan woman's life goal complete.

Hong Ai Zhen was living alone in Dalun during the interview, after spending 20 years in Hong Kong. She had grandchildren living variously in the USA, the Philippines, and Hong Kong, and she sounded very pleased with them. Yet she had not forgiven her husband. She got married when she was 15. Her husband was sent home to marry when he was 20. He stayed home for barely a year before he left for the Philippines again. The next time he came back it was 10 years later. Hong was aggrieved when her husband *zhao fanpo* (literally "find a foreign woman," meaning marrying a Filipina) after his second return to the Philippines. Since then, Hong had not talked to him. She said, "I wasn't angry [with the woman] ... Just let him die, [we] never talked since. He married a *fanpo* [only when he was] in his 40s and we never talked. He didn't care about me, I didn't care about him ... He sent me money for food and to use, but we didn't talk ... [We were only] in our 40s when we stopped talking [to each other]. Just let him, he wanted to marry a foreign woman." The third and last time he returned to China was 22 years later. But they had never talked again.

Life as both a *fanke shen* and also that of a *huo guafu* was doubly difficult. The social responsibility and cultural expectations for a mother, wife and daughter-in-law might have created enough social pressure for them to remain loyal to the family, but, for my interviewees, it was invariably the ultimate life goal, that someday the husband would return and that the family would be complete, that had kept them going. It was ironically the acceptance that the hard work of a *fanke shen* as a normal way of life and the realities of social pressure for chastity that had helped the women to "stick it out." The self-effacement and sacrifices of the women as they maintained the household of the absentee husband thus allowed the reproduction of the patriarchal world that spanned Minnan communities in China, Hong Kong, and the Philippines.

Moving on: Becoming *Minnan Po* and *Inchik*

The proximity of Hong Kong offered an alternative to Minnan women in migrant families to fulfill their domestic duties as members of their husbands' families. For a long time, the lack of diplomatic relations between China and the Philippines made it impossible for *fanke shen* to join their husbands directly. So they went to Hong Kong, using it as a stepping stone, as they made further plans to move to the Philippines to join their husbands. Failing that, their husbands could go to Hong Kong to visit them. Some of the women were able to achieve their life goal, settling in the Philippines, raising their families with their husbands. But most others were not so fortunate and instead found themselves living in Hong Kong for longer periods than they had planned. This was typical of the first wave of emigration immediately after 1949. Many of those women who were "stuck in Hong Kong" were illiterate and could not speak Cantonese, the lingua franca. And because of their mainly rural background, they were unable to go beyond low ranking jobs in factories. More often than not, remittances from their husbands were small and irregular. The PRC's (People's Republic of China) emigration policy required them to leave the eldest child in the hometown, and so most of them brought their younger children. They were thus in effect single-mothers who had to support themselves and their younger children in Hong Kong, and at the same time needed to send remittances to their older children and in-laws, or maybe even other relatives in China. Typically, they lived in poor conditions such as in the squatter areas, or shared a very small room with another Minnan single mother and her children in an old apartment in North Point.

The second wave of Minnan emigration to Hong Kong began in 1962, when the PRC's emigration policy changed. Those with secondary school and college education were eligible to exit, and Ong Li Na was part of this cohort. She married her husband in the early 1940s, at the threat of the arrival of Japanese troops. Her husband stayed for a few months after their wedding and then left for the Philippines where his parents lived. Because of the war it was uncertain when he would return. In 1962, Ong was given permission to leave for Macao, but her only son had to stay behind. She first arrived in Macao and then, like many others who believed that pastures in Hong Kong were greener, entered Hong Kong illegally by boat. She shared a rented room with another Minnan woman in a similar situation, and survived by assembling plastic flowers and embroidering beads on sweaters. With her meager income, she remitted money to her mother who helped to take care of her son. Later, she found a clerical job and moonlighted in a Chinese bank. Her salary helped pay for her son's education, supported her mother and her husband's grandmother back home, and even sponsored the building of her husband's family house in Jinjiang. In contrast, her husband's remittances were little and irregular. In her words, "they were never enough to even make ends meet."

As a new immigrant in Hong Kong, Chua did not speak Cantonese and, believing that Hong Kong was an evil place according to Communist propaganda, she avoided most public places. In addition, she felt that she was looked down upon in public. In the market, for example, where she had to buy her food every day, Cantonese shopkeepers would call her and other Minnan women by the derogatory term *minnan po*. The term literally means "Minnan woman" but it stereotyped Minnan women as stingy customers, ignorant, country bumpkins, and hence not welcome. Like other Minnan women, Chua tried to avoid the discriminatory attitudes of the Cantonese by staying, working, and socializing only with fellow Minnan women. They did not take part in *tongxianghui* activities, partly because they could not afford the fees, but more importantly because those were male domains, and they considered it inappropriate for "proper women" to be seen enjoying themselves outside the home, mingling with men, and thus inviting rumors. Indeed, Minnan women were extremely careful about safeguarding their reputation within the ethnic community, especially since there was no direct supervision and endorsement by mothers-in-law. All interviewees pointed out that rumors spread very quickly. This state of having strong informal sanction within the ethnic community was characterized by an interviewee as "very noisy." So women must try to avoid these "noises" and maintain a *ho-mia-sia* (H, good reputation) by not being seen. They could not go anywhere lest they become *xia-pai* (H, to bring shame to ancestors). Hence, Chua and her female friends could only seek help among themselves. Obviously, to many Minnan migrant women, informal networks were the only resource to alleviate financial, social, psychological, and cultural problems.

In 1965, Chua's husband arranged for her to visit him in the Philippines. It was 18 years after they first met at their wedding. He had an ice-cream factory in the outskirts of Manila. She was full of hope as she imagined her new life as a middle class woman and as the wife of the boss of the factory. She arrived in the Philippines, only to find that he had already married a Filipina and had several children. She realized after staying there for a few months, that as an *inchik* (a term used by Filipinos to refer to ethnic Chinese), she had lower social status than Filipinos. Like many other Chinese men, Chua's husband claimed that he could only set up his business by marrying a local woman who officially owned the factory. The Filipina wife, whom Minnan people called *fanpo* (literally, "foreign woman"), had higher status than her ethnically as well as within her husband's family and business. Thus, instead of arriving in the Philippines to enjoy a better life, Chua found her identity characterized by ambiguity and redundancy, and she was subordinate to the *"fanpo"* who took her husband away. Though disheartened by her experience in the Philippines, Chua did not seek a divorce. She simply returned to Hong Kong.

Chua's son was allowed to migrate to Hong Kong in the early 1970s when he was already in his late 20s and had gotten married. Chua's husband soon traveled to Hong Kong to see his son. He traveled to Hong Kong again when his grandson was born. He had never visited Hong Kong while Chua was living there and struggling to make ends meet. The PRC's open-door policy promulgated in 1978 was another turning point in Chua's life as a sojourner in Hong Kong. She and her son started a trading company, and they began importing small goods from Fujian and exporting them overseas. After merging some operations, in just a few years the company expanded to invest in various manufacturing businesses in another province.

But the success of Chua as an entrepreneur did not compensate for her "bad fate" as a wife. When her husband died in the Philippines in 1979, she refused to go to his funeral. Recounting the decision calmly, she said, "[I] did not cry because there were no more emotions. [I] did not scold [him], because he was already dead." However, she still felt let down. "In my entire life, the total time that I spent with my husband was at most a year or two ... Women were made sacrifices in old society. If you are not strong enough, or do not have something to keep your spirits up, you'll go crazy or jump off the roof." She felt let down by her husband who was unfaithful, did not care about her livelihood, and had not shown any affection to her in the entire time they were married. In short, her effort and sacrifices were misplaced when she waited all her life for a reunion with him and had spent her work life maintaining *his* family both in China and in Hong Kong. To her, all the physical, mental, and emotional hardships were wasted. Her only comfort was that her son showed filial respect to her. But, just like other interviewees, she did not believe that it was the patriarchal system that was to blame. Although she resented her husband for not upholding their marriage contract and not fulfilling his familial responsibilities toward her and her child, she had not complained about his family. She had commented that it was the "feudal, old society" that had sacrificed women, but she fell short of criticizing structural or institutionalized gender inequality. To her and many other interviewees, it was "fate" that had caused their misfortune in life.

Shengmingli: Female Life Force in a Patriarchal System

"*Minnan nüren hao ku de*" (literally, Minnan women's life is very bitter) was the very first thing Lim Sui Mei said to me when we met on an excursion sponsored by the Hong Kong Quanzhou Tongxianghui. She was in her mid-50s and worked as a volunteer deputy head of the women's section of the association. Although she was a rather successful businesswoman and happily married, Lim was full of grievances for the hardships caused by "chauvinistic Minnan men" that all Minnan women had to endure. She considered herself very lucky though. She recounted how her family was never really materially deprived even during the

Cultural Revolution, because her aunt in Indonesia kept remitting money and sending them household needs. She went to Hong Kong in the 1970s during the third wave of emigration from Fujian. An estimated 10 percent of this cohort left for the Philippines, and Lim, like the majority, stayed in Hong Kong to make it their new home. Typical of this group, her father relied on relatives and other fellow *tongxiang* to accumulate enough capital to start a small trading business. And, like other children of migrant families, Lim started to work when she was an adolescent. She went to school in the morning, and gave three sessions of private tutoring to primary school children after school. On her way home she bought food from the market and then cooked dinner for the family. After graduating from high school, she had a full-time job in a stockbrokerage but kept up with tutoring work. She handed the entire paycheck to her father until she got married.

This "hardworking, no-complaints, family-oriented" attitude, in Lim's words, was characteristic of Minnan females. She talked about Minnan women in Hong Kong this way:

> I know these girls, many of whom came [to Hong Kong] with no money. They just stuck it out, until they had [enough] money to build a house on the mainland, and *then* they would get married. [They worked] from scratch, from nothing to something. It's true … Their life force is so strong … They could do two jobs a day … Say they collected garbage for people, and [as a sideline] they collected people's discarded food, put it in a huge bucket to sell as pig feed. So they carried another bucket with them … It's [hard work but it's] one way to make good money.

> [Emphasis added]

After Lim got married, according to Minnan convention she became a full-time homemaker. Her main responsibility was to serve her ailing mother-in-law. It was a few years later when she decided that her husband was not a good businessman, that she decided to "come out" to help him with his manufacturing business. At the time of the interview, she had to travel weekly to Shunde, Guangdong province, where her husband's factory was located. She told me she was responsible for negotiating prices, getting new contracts, and maintaining customer relations. Her husband, whom she described as too straightforward and shy, took care of the engineering part of the business. Lim enjoyed the work but she felt it was backbreaking. To her, it was for her family that she was living a hard life (*hao xinku*).

But the hardest part of her life experience was not in running the family business and taking it through economic crises. It was in the household. The cause of the problem, she believed, was her mother-in-law. "She was very good to everybody. But when she was with her daughter-in-law, she had a totally different face." Lim was not entirely happy with her husband's patrilineal family, but she was ready to forgive. She added quickly, "Well now it's all right. She idolizes her son and loves her grandchildren. In a word, she is very traditional." I asked her what she meant by "traditional." She illustrated her point this way:

> We Minnan women have a low status ... [We] are very diligent ... [We] do so many things ... Maybe we bring this upon ourselves. First, many traditions are like this. When I was young I was like this. Like ... if I bought RMB0.5 worth of barbecued pork, I would save it for my younger brother ... He was very young, and he was so skinny and did not have a good appetite. Even his head was small. I thought I should let him eat. [I] adored him. And I saw my mother save food for my father and would not eat it herself ... Yes she was a role model [for me], so it's a tradition.

And so in her husband's family, the practice was carried on:

> ... it's the tradition. Why? Well, like my mother-in-law, she just treats my husband like treasure, so much so that to this day he can't spit out the bones when he eats fish. It has to be boneless. He is always given meat without bones. He's used to it. So I eat the parts [with bones]; I can do it very well. And he can't shell a crab, so I take off the shell for him. He just gets spoiled ... And he doesn't do any housework. If he ever does, my mother-in-law would say that he's helping me. So I have to do everything myself. This avoids quarrels. You understand?

She adds:

> I have lived with my mother-in-law for over 20 years ... For 20 years I have done this: get up early in the morning, sweep the floor ... I go off work, go to the market, buy food, cook dinner, even when I was pregnant. I also clean the house, and he doesn't do a thing. It's a habit [in the family].

I asked whether her husband ever offered to help. She answered:

> No! In a nutshell, he comes home from work and reads the newspaper, that's the "right" thing to do.... If he helps? His mother will be angry. And when she returns to their hometown, she'll spread rumors about me ... Hey, I go to work too. But women in the past didn't. *They* only took care of children. But *we* are

different; *we* come home from work and still have to work. Sometimes *we* do housework until 11 or 12 before *we* can go to bed. Once I was so tired, oh dear! I fell asleep. [My mother-in-law] woke me immediately, saying, you haven't washed the clothes; why are you sleeping? I said, oh, sure. I'm not sleeping. I just took a nap ... You can't scold her, right?

[Emphasis added]

So, being "traditional" amounted to being relegated to a lower status and deprived of privileges and respect even though the woman may bring in an income. This applies especially to daughters-in-law living in their husbands' family. Note that Lim changed her way of identification with Minnan women. She started saying "they" and "them" to make a class distinction regarding economic activities. But a sense of camaraderie came through when she switched to "we" and "us" while speaking of women's domestic responsibilities. Her affiliation with Minnan daughters-in-law as a social group was obvious, as they all shared the same bitterness in life.

But "tradition" also demanded that daughters-in-law should accept the household imbalance of power without complaint. Lim believed she had fulfilled this expectation, as she explained her situation, with a sense of pride:

Just take it as *yingchou*. When everybody told me they found me awesome [for living with my mother-in-law for such a long time], I said "no problem." You can't say no, right? ... Now it's OK; she now thinks that I'm good to them.

The word *yingchou* refers to unnecessary but unavoidable entertainment with people whom you do not like, especially among relatives and business connections. The fact that Lim used this term to describe her filial behavior toward her mother-in-law projected the sense of reluctance and helplessness that characterized Minnan women's situation in the husband's family. Their work as daughters-in-law was never recognized but taken for granted. They were not supposed to be rewarded but instead were expected to practice self-effacement. They should do it for the sake of the family and should be proud of it. Lim justified inequality with traditionalism and resigned herself to her female fate.

Conclusion: Gendered Mobility

Minnan women whose husbands were migrants lamented that they had lived a bitter life, but their action as keepers of their husband's family paradoxically made them successful entrepreneurs, breadwinners who commanded domestic resources across generations, and managers of kinship and *tongxiang* networks. In the process they made themselves tough survivors. This was referred to as a "strong life force" (*shengmingli qiang*) that all Minnan women possessed. Growing up in an essentially female household would have given Minnan women the opportunity to learn to organize daily life, make decisions, and plan for the future. Whether this was under training and supervision by mothers-in-law or as independent female heads of households, their social and financial skills should be recognized. Like the rural Chinese women who successfully applied their survival skills in a newly established socialist state as described by Wolf (1974), Minnan women would be greatly adept individuals as they struggled to survive in such foreign spaces as in their husband's family, in Hong Kong as immigrants, or in the Philippines as an ethnic minority. Whether as entrepreneurs, employed workers, or homemakers, they were intricately involved in the management of the household — their husband's household. In fulfilling the demands of roles as daughters, wives, and mothers, Minnan women helped to concretize the multi-site patriarchal system of which they are part.

Notes

1. This study was funded by the Research Grants Council as part of the study, "Tradition, Change and Identity: A Study on the Minnan People in China and Southeast Asia" (CUHK 4025/97H). Parts of this chapter were presented earlier as "Sustaining 'Power of Life' in Immigration: Minnan Women and Their Patriarchal World" at the annual meeting of the Association for Asian Studies, 9–12 March 2000. I wish to thank Ding Yuling, Wang Lianmao and the staff of Quanzhou Maritime Museum, and the government officials in Quanzhou and Shishi for their support during my fieldwork in the Jinjiang area. Fieldwork in Hong Kong was ably assisted by Wu Sui Chu and Ng Yuk Yung. My gratitude also goes to all the elderly Minnan men and women who shared their personal histories with me.
2. Transliterations are mainly based on pinyin. Hokkien terms are marked H.
3. In this paper I have used the term "migrant family" to mean the migrant man's nuclear and extended family. The term covers the various situations resulting from the man's mobility, including the family that stays in China after the man leaves for the Philippines, when the whole family has settled in the Philippines, and when the wife herself has moved to Hong Kong with the children.
4. Interview with Shao Shengduan, Secretary of the Hong Kong Quanzhou Tongxianghui (8 August 2000), and see Zhengxie JC Committee's anthology (1998).

5. Unless otherwise stated, pseudonyms are used for all informants and institutions to assure anonymity. See was interviewed at her office in December 1998.
6. Before the establishment and popularization of banks and post offices, letters and remittances sent from Southeast Asian countries were mainly handled by the "overseas Chinese letters industry," *qiaoxin ye*, or "overseas Chinese remittance industry," *qiaopi ye* (Ding Yuling, personal communication 2002). These were private businesses offering letter writing and remittance services, and according to Hsü (2000: 198, note 86), they were variously known as Minxin Ju, Pixin Ju, Pi Ju, Huidiao Ju, and Xin Ju. The industry had prospered due to the number of overseas Chinese abroad. During the 1920s and 1930s, Western style banks and postal service emerged to take over this role. These included foreign banks and Chinese banks like the Bank of China, the Bank of Canton, and the Communications Bank (Hsü 2000: 198, note 84). After 1949, the PRC tried to maintain control over letters and remittances that flowed between the *qiaoxiang* and overseas Chinese. This was done through the Overseas Chinese Affairs Commission that either encouraged letter writing by *qiaojuan*, dependents of overseas Chinese, to solicit remittances, or to influence the content of the letters to the favor of the PRC government (Fitzgerald 1972: 38–41). During the Cultural Revolution, overseas relations caused discriminatory treatment for *qiaojuan*, and remittances were sometimes not claimed by the recipients for fear of political consequences.
7. Cai Qian was one of these success stories. His business prospered so much that he kept sending money home to build a housing complex for his extended family, which numbered over 200 rooms. Not only was his family the envy of the village, his achievement was officially recognized, and the housing complex is now designated as a heritage for conservation.

References

Fitzgerald, Stephen. 1972. *China and the Overseas Chinese: A Study of Peking's Changing Policy 1949–1970*. Cambridge: Cambridge University Press.
Hong Kong Jinjiang Tongxiang Association. 1986. Xianggang yu zai Xianggang de Jinjiang Ren (Jinjiang People in Hong Kong). In *Jinjiang: Jinian Xianggang Jinjiang Tongxianghui Chengli Yizhounian* (Jinjiang: In Commemoration of the First Anniversary of the Establishment of the Hong Kong Jinjiang Tongxiang Association). Hong Kong: Hong Kong Jinjiang Tongxiang Association.
Hsü, Madeline Yuan-yi. 2000. *Dreaming of Gold, Dreaming of Home: Transnationalism and Migration between the United States and South China 1882–1943*. Stanford: Stanford University Press.
Pan, Lynn. 1999. *The Encyclopedia of the Chinese Overseas*. Surrey: Curzon.
Wolf, Margery 1972. *Women and the Family in Rural Taiwan*. Stanford: Stanford University Press.

———. 1974. Chinese Women: Old Skills in a New Context. In Michelle Zimbalist Rosaldo and Louise Lamphere, eds., *Woman, Culture and Society*, pp. 157–72. Stanford: Stanford University Press.

Zhengxie Jinjiang City 8th Committee Literary and Historical Materials Committee. 1998. *Jinjiang Wenshi Ziliao Xuanji: Jinjiang Ren Zai Xianggang* (Anthology of Jinjiang Literary and Historical Material: Jinjiang People in Hong Kong). Issue no. 20. Jinjiang: Zhongguo Renmin Zhengzhi Xieshang Huiyi Fujian Jinjiangshi Weiyuanhui Wenshi Ziliao Weiyuanhui.

Glossary

Chendai	陳埭
chengjia lishi	成家立室
chu (H)	厝
Dalun	大侖
fanke	番客
fanke shen	番客嬸
fanpo	番婆
Hanjiang	蚶江
hao xinku	好辛苦
huaqiao	華僑
huo guafu	活寡婦
Jinjiang	晉江
Minnan	閩南
minnan po	閩南婆
Minxin Ju	民信局
qiaojuan	僑眷
qiaoshu	僑屬
Qiaoxin Ju	僑信局
Quanzhou	泉州
Shangdi	上帝
shengmingli qiang	生命力強
Shishi	石獅
shuike	水客
Shunde	順德
tongxianghui	同鄉會
yingchou	應酬
zhao fanpo	找番婆

7

Economic Activities and the Construction of Gender Status among the Xunpu Women in Fujian

■ Ding Yuling

Introduction

In popular view, women in feudal China were seen as submissive and oppressed by patriarchal culture. However, anthropologists nowadays are able to see how, within the orthodox framework of traditional Chinese culture, women were able to develop a set of indirect and informal methods to safeguard their interests and wield influence (Wolf 1972). They also managed to set up a network of support through their natal homes (Judd 1989). They resorted to marriage resistance or were unwilling to go to their husband's house, to avoid his authority (Topley 1975; Stockard 1989; Li 1994). These studies represent an anthropological breakthrough in women and gender research. They highlight the change in the image of Chinese women from being passive to active, and show the tenacity of women in adapting to changing circumstances. Women, after all, have their own roles and functions to play in history.

The study of women in China generally locates women in the Chinese patriarchal structure, over which they have minimal influence, and certainly not in reforming it. Indeed, this phenomenon is widespread among Han people in China and influences our view of Chinese gender relations. This paper describes economic activities and the construction of gender status among the Chinese women in Xunpu, a fishing village in southern Fujian. There is no strong lineage organization in this village. Because of ecological reasons, the sexual division of labor in the village enables women to participate directly in the market economy. As a result, women attain economic independence. This paper describes women's strategies in constructing a favorable status that is different from that generally perceived of them in Chinese society.

Giddens (1984: 25) regards social system and its agents as interactive, not antagonistic, to each other. This principle guides us to understand gender relations in traditional Chinese society in two ways. First, it emphasizes the interaction between the social system and the unlimited individual agency. Second, social structure is not a certain "pattern" of relations or phenomena, as is understood by structural functionalism, but is a series of rules and resources involved in the process of social reproduction, or a series of changes of relations. In the vast territory of China, many different social customs and lifestyles are found. Their social structure is not confined to a fixed pattern; what it manifests is a continuous realignment and transformation of various rules and resources. Gender relations are thus not confined to a fixed pattern.

By discussing Xunpu women's economic activities in different time periods, this paper shows how they have negotiated cultural rules and used local resources and opportunities to construct a gender identity that differs from the usual Chinese pattern. Field research in Xunpu was conducted in July and August of 1999.

A Brief Account of Xunpu Fishing Village

In southern Fujian, a group of women still wear the traditional attire of blouses with buttons on the left side, and wide trousers. They have their hair combed into a bun and decorated with chains of fresh flowers. In the years when the Han Chinese women practiced foot binding, these women did not. Instead, they were always barefooted and were able to carry heavy loads on their strong bodies, peddling marine products through streets and alleys. Now most have switched to a more sedentary style of running stalls in wet markets, still attired in their distinctive style of dressing.

These are the women of Xunpu village, on the shore of southeastern Fujian, southwest of Quanzhou Bay. Xunpu village is under the jurisdiction of the ancient city of Quanzhou, 5 kilometers away, and it lies to the north of Zhegu Hill. The Xunpu women have for long been engaged in marine activities, a trademark activity glorified by the Qing poet Chen Yi. His poem reads:

> Living on the Zhegu seashore,
> Ladies selling seafood from young.
> In beautiful clothes with bamboo hats and scarves,
> Even without flowers, they look so fresh and pretty.

> [My translation]

19. A Xunpu woman showing her hairdo (photograph by Ding Yuling).

There is an obvious division of labor between the sexes for a livelihood based on the sea. According to the 1999 census, out of a population of 6,002 people, 2,990 are male, and 3,012 are female. Over 90 percent are engaged in deep-sea fishing, sea farming, seafood processing, and seafood sales and trading. As shown in Table 1 (according to the record of the

Table 1. Social Division of Labor of Xunpu Village

Occupation	Number of Laborers	Percentage (%)	Sex
Sea fishing	2,181	53.16	Male (outer-sea), Female (inner-sea)
Sea farming	890	21.69	Female (oyster breeding)
Aquatic product processing	98	2.39	Male and Female
Industry	90	2.19	Male and Female
Handicrafts	14	0.34	Male and Female
Transportation	90	2.19	Male
Commerce	530	12.92	Female
Others	210	5.12	Male and Female
Total	4,103	100	

Xunpu Village Committee of 1999), the women are responsible for sea farming and seafood trading, whereas the men do deep-sea fishing. Together, they are equally responsible for the economic welfare of the family and the village.

Xunpu village had a population of 6,000, according to the village government's census in 1997. 70 percent of Xunpu villagers have the surname Huang, the rest bearing the other 10 surnames. Before 1950, marriage was prohibited among those of the same surname. There were intricate and complex relationships through marriage among people of different surnames, and it is still so today. The bond thus formed among families has brought harmony to the community.

Women play an equally important role in communal activities, particularly in the religious activities of the village. They are the planners, organizers, and leaders of various activities. In Fujian and southern China, it is normal that women share the responsibility of family welfare. Like men, women have to work in the rice fields. However, they seldom hold prominent positions in communal activities. How, then, could the women of Xunpu break away from the threads of traditional Chinese culture and the orthodox cultural construct? They are able to do so because, together with changing circumstances, they are willing to shoulder much hardship in return for economic rewards, which in turn have brought social and political recognition from the family, the village and the local society.

My research is largely dependent on oral history and participant observation, as there are few records on the history of Xunpu village, other than those mentioning its geographical location. From these oral reports of people of different age groups, we can at least grasp Xunpu people's working and living circumstances in the 20th century and the process in which the women took advantage of rules and resources to construct their gender status.

Many defining events took place in China in the 20th century, which brought about tremendous changes to its modern politics, cultural practices and traditions, and its social structure. These events and the accompanying changes can be analyzed in three distinct periods: before the Liberation in 1949, the period 1949–78 when there were many experiments with various production programs, and the period 1979 and thereafter, a period of Liberalization of the Chinese economy. All the changes had direct influence on the productive organizations and economic systems of Xunpu, which affected gender relations.

Economic Activities

Strictly speaking, Xunpu faces a bay, not the sea. There are many big shoals in its waters. Many shoals of mud sediment are also found in the Jinjiang River. Shoals are suitable grounds for breeding oysters. The shallow waters are rich in small fish and shrimp, as well as crabs and clams. These aquatic creatures provide opportunity for plentiful catches; and because of the shallowness of the water, work here has been the domain of the women.

Breeding rocks for oysters are prepared in the traditional way, whereby four or five rocks are put together leaning against one another with a solid support in the center to prevent the rocks from falling. This solid support comprises sacks filled with grass and broken shells. Incoming tides bring in oyster seedlings, which become attached to the rocks where they grow year round. Sometimes these rocks can fall with the ebb of the tide, which is why the women have to check them every few days. If left unattended for some time, the fallen rocks could be buried in the mud and become "dead" rocks. Oysters are harvested year round, so the women are kept busy throughout the year.

Oyster farming is muddy and slippery work, as the oyster beds are as muddy and even more slippery than the rice fields of southern China. Just walking on them is difficult, as one's feet get stuck in the mud. However, Xunpu women have mastered the art of walking on them so that using shoulder poles, they can carry bags of broken shells on their shoulders.

The time of work on these farms depends on the ebb of the tides. When the tide falls, the women go out and return after about four or five hours when the tide rises. Each day, the time to go ashore is about 40 minutes later than the previous day. Work on the oyster beds means ensuring that the rocks are upright, by banking them up with earth. The women can be so busy that they do not have time to even rest for a few minutes. In fact, there is no place for them to take a rest, as everywhere is so muddy. Work is year round, and harvesting season is from October to December. A woman of the age of 70 describes her work in the past as follows:

> Even in cold winter we went out barefooted and in shorts. At that time we were so poor that we could not afford to wear long trousers. Sometimes I cut my feet stepping on a "dead oyster rock," and sometimes my hands were cut by shells. Look at my hands and see how rough they are. Nowadays, people wear gloves to protect their hands, and foot covers to protect their feet. Foot covers are made from old trouser legs that are stitched up to form a kind of socks. But

at that time how could we make foot covers? We did not even have enough trousers to wear. How could we have surplus trousers?

Summer was also difficult for us. The burning sun refracted hot air from the earth's surface. This made us breathless when we bent down to put the rocks upright. When it rained, we had no shelter. We all wore bamboo hats. The hats protected us from the rain and the sun. All Xunpu women did the work in this way. We were accustomed to it.

Xunpu women regard oyster farming as their "main occupation," but their income is supplemented by catching other aquatic creatures that abound in the shallow waters and areas around it. Although the majority of workers are women, a few men and boys also work there.

The main occupations of Xunpu men are sea fishing and shipping, that is, engaging in sea transportation. Almost all young men go out to sea together with their elders to learn the skills of navigation and fishing. Usually, men go out to sea at about the age of 14. A fisherman of the age of 84 related his first experience to me, as follows:

I was 14 years old then. I can still remember that morning when my mother prepared a bowl of vermicelli noodles and two eggs for me. Neighbors, relatives, and friends also presented me with vermicelli noodles and eggs. It is our custom that when a boy goes out to sea for the first time, his relatives and friends give him the gifts of noodles and eggs, to express congratulations. I went with my father and other villagers. I do not remember where we went. Anyway, we came back after two or three days. At that time, we used a wooden sailing boat that belonged to some other villagers. It was the biggest boat in the village then. But compared with the boats today, it was not big. That boat could only carry a load of 20 to 30 *dan* (1 *dan* = 50 kilograms) of fish....

Before the Liberation, the village had only a few boats: three or five big boats, a dozen medium-sized boats, and some sampans. At that time, it was dangerous to go out to sea for there was no navigation device, only a compass on board. We did the sailing based on our experience. In bad and stormy weather, disasters happened. Whenever there was one, the villagers were overcome with sadness. Then, seafood was very cheap. Even though we worked all year round, we were very poor.

The fishermen had worked hard and lived frugally to save up to buy a boat, either on their own or in partnership with other villagers. Either way, a fisherman would be a boat-owner but few could afford to buy one, let alone a big one. Owning a boat did not necessarily make one rich, for I did not see any mention of such a person in the old records from Xunpu. According to the custom of Xunpu village, 30 percent of the catch went to the boat-owner, the rest equally divided among the workers.

Besides deep-sea fishing, services in the shipping industry were and still are other important lines of occupation. Before 1949, it was estimated that 50 percent of the men were involved in deep-sea fishing and the other 50 percent in shipping. They provided the human resources for the transport companies based in Quanzhou.

Likewise, ownership of sampans is an individual or a partnership business. Sampans are used to get to the oyster farms. If a family owns a sampan, it is usual for the husband and wife to go out to work together.

As elsewhere in southern Fujian, there was emigration from Xunpu to Southeast Asia in the past. Surabaya of Indonesia was where the overseas Xunpu people congregated. Although some settled down permanently to do business, most were sojourners for a few years and shuttled between their hometown and Southeast Asia. Most chose to go back to their hometown to spend their old age. An old lady in her 80s sadly told me her life story:

> I was married at the age of 14. At that time I was very young and knew nothing about life. My parents arranged the marriage for me. Not long into the marriage, my husband went abroad to Southeast Asia. When I was 16, my father-in-law died and my husband came back to show his respect. The next year when I was pregnant with my first child, he went abroad again. This time, his travel fee was from the sales of my oyster rocks. When I was 21, he came back. Not long after I got pregnant with the second child, he went to Surabaya again. Soon afterwards, the Second World War broke out. He did not come back. Neither did I get any message from him. People said that he had an Indonesian woman in Surabaya. I farmed oysters and planted peanuts, potatoes, barley, and wheat to support my children. My father and brother were engaged in shipping, usually to Taiwan. They often gave me money secretly. So, my life was not bad. After the war, my husband sent me a letter asking me to take my children to Surabaya. I did not answer him. Since he had a foreign woman, I would not go to him. Later he asked somebody to bring me some material and dresses. Again he wanted us to go to him. He could not come to bring us over, because of his business. I still did not reply to him. After the Liberation it was impossible to go abroad. He was so sad that he died not long afterwards, at the early age of 44.

As most Xunpu men were engaged in either deep-sea fishing or shipping or had simply emigrated, they led a wandering life. Because they were away from home, the responsibilities of the family fell on the shoulders of the women. Deep-sea fishing did not bring in a steady income, as the catch and weather were unpredictable. In contrast, women's income from oyster farming and the catching of other aquatic creatures was steady, though less. Again women had proven their worth by being able to help provide for the family, too. With much tenacity, they were able to supplement their income by planting peanuts, potatoes, barley, and wheat on the hills.

It follows that after the oysters are harvested and the fish caught, they are sold. Thus to be engaged in selling them is the other activity of the Xunpu women. From the Qing Dynasty poems, we know that they had done this throughout history. It was the women who carried the baskets of seafood on their shoulder with a bamboo pole to the rural centers where they hawked their goods. At times, they peddled them along streets and alleys. Mrs. Huang, in her 80s, could not help laughing when she told us what she did long ago:

> At that time we went to the urban centers on foot, not by bus like now. And, we were all barefooted. We were accustomed to being barefooted. Every day we left home at 2 or 3.00 a.m. I had been to Jinjiang and Quanzhou. If the places were farther, we had to leave earlier. I am afraid that you'll laugh at me, but I'll tell you the truth anyway. In those days we did not have enough clothes, only one or two sets at any one time. So, we were afraid that our clothes might become worn-out quickly by the bamboo pole. To preserve their durability, we walked topless in the morning darkness. Only on approaching the city and as it was beginning to dawn did we put on our blouses. We peddled our goods along streets and alleys, and each of us had our own territory to cover. I sold seafood in the southern part of the town. I knew the residents there. At that time, the price of seafood was very low. We did not earn much money, and it was only enough to cover family expenses. The fish and shrimp I sold in town were either caught by my husband or bought from other villagers. Each day I managed to sell two baskets of seafood by noontime.

Obviously, the Xunpu women participated widely in economic activities during this period. Although women in other Minnan farming regions also took part in economic production, Xunpu women played even more important roles in the family. They were financially independent and had to manage all family matters, ranging from daily expenditure, children's education and marriage, to ritual ceremonies and construction of houses. The reason was that fishing at sea took Xunpu men away from home frequently, often for an extended period. Nevertheless, women's influence was confined to the domestic sphere and men were still in control of the village administration. The idea of "men managing the public sphere, and women managing the domestic sphere" reflected the tradition in Xunpu.

Socialization and Institutionalization of Women's Roles: 1949–78

After 1949, political changes in China brought about many changes to society. The state policy of collectivization was implemented throughout the country. This had the drastic effect of changing communal organizations, economic structure, and regulations on production and distribution. The policy was also implemented in Xunpu village. Individual family activities were replaced by collectivization. Collectivization in other parts of rural China began with land reform; in Xunpu it began with the boats and oyster beds. In 1954, the system of rural mutual-aid groups comprising a dozen households in the same neighborhood was institutionalized, whereby privately owned boats and oyster beds were surrendered for common production. In forming the mutual-aid groups, Xunpu village authorities had the power to determine the class status of each villager. Then, there were three boats and 10 medium-sized boats; the rest were sampans. The owners of the boats and sampans were designated as "boat-owners," "rich fishermen," and "fishermen" respectively. The few persons who were classified as "boat-owners" fell into one of the four classifications of "bad elements." Their boats were "sold" to the mutual-aid group, but they never received any payment.

An old man showed me the house where he lived when he was classified as a "rich fisherman." It was built in the typical local style, with a low roof and two walls of white oyster shells. It is next to his present house, which he built 10 years ago. He said:

> My father had a very hard life in the old society. You know how hard fishing was. My parents lived frugally and saved hard to buy a boat. Soon after Liberation they were classified as "rich fishermen" and our boat was sold to the mutual-aid group and was taken over by the People's Commune. Although a price was assessed, the money was never paid to us. Who dared ask for payment? Though we were not publicly accused or denounced, my younger brother wanted to join the army but he was rejected because of his bad family status. You can see that my former house was as bad as those of the other people. In fact we were very poor then.

In 1955 in Xunpu, the elementary agricultural producers' cooperative (*chuji she*) was established based on the mutual-aid principle. Six such cooperatives were formed. In the following year, the advanced level cooperative (*gaoji she*) was established. Now the whole village of Xunpu became an advanced agricultural producers' cooperative. In 1958, the People's Commune System was established, and again the change in the production program transformed Xunpu into a production brigade under the Donghai People's Commune.

Xunpu Production Brigade comprised both the fishery and oyster brigade units. Each unit comprised different teams. Under the fishery brigade unit (*yuye dadui*) were the outer-sea fishing team, net-fishing team, and transportation team. Under the oyster brigade unit (*haoye dadui*) were the inner-sea fishing team, the fishing-tools factory team, and a tree-planting team. The traditional division of labor was continued here, the different sexes put in different units. The males were in the fishery brigade unit; the females were in the oyster brigade unit. The Aquatic Company of the Quanzhou City held a monopoly on the purchase and sale of the produce of the Xunpu fishermen. The fishermen received a monthly wage of RMB15 each from the fishery brigade unit.

The inner-sea team of the oyster brigade unit was responsible for oyster farming and catching other aquatic creatures. The female members were mobilized into six groups. Each group was led by a female leader and a female deputy leader under the supervision of the female brigade head. Work points (a unit indicating the quantity and quality of labor performed) were fixed according to age and the number of hours worked. The rate of payment was very low, as an average yearly wage was only RMB20. This was much less than that earned by the men, who received an average monthly wage of RMB15. Still, they worked with full vigor for the Commune.

A former head of the oyster brigade unit (1975–79), Huang Xuezhen, was still in good health when I did my research in 1999. She was then 80 years old. In 1954, she became a member of the Communist Party of China and had held the posts of Director of the Village Women's Organization and Head of the Elementary and Advanced Agricultural Producers' Cooperatives. As she was young and full of energy, she responded to the call of the Party with much enthusiasm and she managed and led all the production teams eagerly. As head of the brigade, she led the villagers to build dykes to reclaim land from the sea for paddy fields, only to find out later that the water and soil were not suitable for paddy.

Under Huang Xuezhen's leadership, collective work went full steam.

Those who engaged in trading had to pay work points to the brigade. She was a leader but still did her share of labor. She criticized cadres of today as not qualified and working for their own projects. She said, "Now the cadres ask for an allowance when doing something for the village. In those days, we cadres did not do this. I was a cadre of the brigade but still worked alongside the team. If I didn't, I received no work points. As I had to solve many problems in the village, I often missed my farm work. I did more work than others but received less pay." Huang's views were confirmed by my interviews with members of the oyster brigade unit, who respected the village cadres of this period.

All fish and aquatic catches of the two brigades went to the Marine Products Bureau, as it held the state monopoly on all purchases and sales. However, 20 percent of the catch was kept to be distributed equally among the workers. This portion was known as "privately owned." The fishermen could keep their share for their own consumption or sell the catch, but personal dealing in sales was considered "capitalist"; thus it was illegal. The merchandise then could be seized and confiscated by the Urban Management Administration. Despite the risk of being caught, Xunpu women, who handled the sale, risked it, as they could get an average price that was six times higher than the state price.

Other opportunities of work for women could be found at the two factories responsible for maintaining fishing gear and nets. Comparatively speaking, oyster farming is much more toilsome than factory work. So, working in the two factories was the women's common wish. The criteria of selection by the brigade leaders were the poverty level and health condition of the women. Class status was also a reference point. Few people with bad social status were allocated to the factories.

During the period between 1949 and 1978, China experienced serious economic hardships. There was a shortage of material goods, and people's purchasing power was low. The Xunpu fishing economy conducted under the state's central planning became worse off. However, the restructuring of the production system brought unexpected rewards to Xunpu women. The bureaucratic system of economic production facilitated women's political participation and affirmed their political status. During this period, state power penetrated the rural society. The production brigades were the most basic grassroots organization recognized by the state. In fact, they replaced all traditional village organizations, including lineage and religious organizations. The production brigades in Xunpu, as elsewhere, had autonomous power to administer and allocate human resources as well as redistribute economic gains. Unlike the men's fishery brigades, the women's oyster brigades took up the additional role of settling conflicts within the family and in the village.

In fact, men earned much more than women during this period. But the social status of women improved due to their active participation in all spheres of social life, taking an active part in the running of the collective system. Although the women could not forget the economic hardships of the time, they were satisfied with their position. They told me about organizing collective activities, including tours. Other than factories whose recruitment was strictly controlled, the women were free to choose joining men's fishery brigades or women's oyster brigades. I have talked to some Xunpu women aged around 40 to 50 about their life in the past:

> Woman A : We were very poor at that time. When I was 8 or 9 years old, I had to dig for *gongdai* [a kind of shells] at the seashore.
>
> Woman B : How could you be so poor? At that time you were in the marine tools factory. The work there was much easier than ours, farming in the sea.
>
> Woman A : Not easy at all. We worked the whole day, but earned only a few work points.
>
> Woman B : You didn't have to endure the hardships of cold winter and hot summer. Despite that, we earned almost the same number of work points as you did.
>
> Woman C : My work was the hardest. I did deep-sea fishing.
>
> Researcher: Did women do that?
>
> Woman C : Yes. Like the men, I went out fishing in the sea. I did the same work as them.
>
> Researcher: What did you do on the boat?
>
> Woman C : I did a man's work. I could do what a man did. The work was hard, but I felt free. I was a work point recorder. I earned the same wage as a male worker. At that time, few women chose to do that. There were only four of us. Other women worked in the factories or farmed oysters.
>
> Researcher: Were the men willing to go with you?
>
> Woman C : Why not? They laughed at my great strength.

Local superstition of fishing communities prohibits women from boarding a boat, much less going out to sea. Xunpu women knew of this taboo, but as the sea was their only source of livelihood, it was conveniently overlooked by all. Moreover, even if they did not go out to sea with the men, they still had to go on a boat to get to the oyster farms. In other words, they could not survive without a boat. They could do anything on a boat, except to cross over its bow during menstruation.

The experiences of working in the various production organizations for many women and of leadership for some taught them about collective power. They learned to use their newfound power to deal with external pressure. In the 1950s and 1960s, there were several incidents involving calls for giving up the traditional style of dressing. Local cadres (government officials), including those in the villages, regarded the traditional attire as an expression of feudalism, so wearing such a style was regarded as backward and not in line with modern times. Thus, the proponents demanded that women undo their hair-buns and cut their hair short. As the community was then under the Commune system, the people of the whole village shared food in one common canteen (*da shitang*). It was even proposed that those women who did not agree to the change would be barred from going into the canteen. As cooking of food at home was forbidden, this threat was really harsh.

Despite the harsh threat, Xunpu women banded together to resist the call to change and came up with the following strategy. Some old women were chosen to "open up a pathway" to the canteen as young cadres dared not stop them because of their age and the respect they commanded. The other women followed immediately behind them and were thus able to enter the canteen. They explained their opposition, "We neither liked nor agreed to the change, as the style suited us in our work. How could we work with our hair hanging down?" This statement had two meanings. One is the pride in being different in their identity. The other is the suitability of sporting such styles to work. They needed the broad-brimmed bamboo hats as shelter from the sun and the rain. The small stick horizontally inserted in the bun prevented the hat from being blown away by the wind. With such resolute opposition, the women were able to sway opinion to their side. Except for a small number of young women, few responded to the change. Public interests in this issue died a natural death.

Compared to the pre-1949 period, Xunpu women were no longer limited to the domestic sphere during this time. Instead, they participated widely in village administration. They had their own production brigades and enjoyed the same political status as the men in the village.

The Rise of Women's Economic Power after 1978

Fundamental changes occurred again in the Chinese rural economic system after 1978. Production units suffered repeated reorganization and disintegration, as experiments with them failed to bear fruit. In Xunpu, as various collective production units began to disintegrate one after another, it was decided to return to the individual household as the basic production unit. As such, the aim of every family was to build a house and buy a boat; these were the status symbols of the rich and successful. Under the cooperative system, several people teamed up to buy a boat. The co-boat-owners were brothers, relatives, neighbors, and friends. However, the nature of ownership kept changing, as each strived to be the sole owner. At the time of my research, Xunpu village had 78 big boats, each with a 250+ horsepower engine, and about 400 small boats. All the boats used diesel engines. Huang Cong was the admiration of everyone in the village, because he had a big boat of his own. He was quite content with his career. He said:

> My father was an experienced boatman. I went out to sea when I was a teenager. At the time, I was in the oyster brigade unit of the People's Commune. The price of seafood was very low then; of course it is quite different now. Because of the Reform, many people were able to buy their boats, and I bought my boat for RMB300,000. That was more than 10 years ago. The money came from our savings and sale of some property, and a loan from our friends. Now my wife has her own oyster beds and her income is quite good. We have paid off the loan. Going out to sea is safer now, as navigation equipment is much better than before. Our US-made equipment, which cost RMB10,000, was bought by a friend in Hong Kong. It is very useful, as we can see the location of the boat on the screen. Besides, the weather forecast is more reliable.
>
> Our boat is also equipped with a walkie-talkie, so I can keep contact with my family. You see, yesterday evening when my ship was about to enter the port, I was able to tell them of my return. My wife then sent a car to pick me up at the port, so that the catch could be taken to the market immediately. I sell my fish to another villager. He does not have to pay me on the spot, as the accounts can be settled when I cannot go out to sea. Perhaps you do not believe me, but on my last trip out to sea, I did not close my eyes for five days and nights. Yesterday after I came back home, I was so busy that I did not get to sleep. This morning I have to buy boat supplies and mend my fish net. If the weather is fine in the afternoon, I shall go out to sea again. I sell all the fish that I catch; I do not take fish at will. When I want some, I will pay for them. I am the boss, so I have to set a good example.

In Xunpu village, it was the women who experienced the biggest changes and reaped the biggest reward from them. After 1978, the oyster brigade unit was disbanded and oyster beds were redistributed to each production unit, that is, the individual household. Brigade leaders had absolute authority on this redistribution. One way of redistribution is based on the number of people working on the oyster farms. No matter which way was followed, the number of oyster beds allotted to each family was not the same. It was here that the change was seen. In each household, only one female was left to farm the oyster beds; the other females were more interested and willing to sell in the market. Oyster farming yielded revenue not only from the sale of oysters but also that of small fish, shrimp, crabs, and clams that were found in abundance in the shallow waters. At the time of my research in 1999, the price of seafood was 10 times more than that in 1979. Xunpu villagers regard their location on the shore as godsend, a "treasure," from where they can easily reap money. The wife of the village head also does oyster farming, and she is quick to point to her important contribution to the family's income:

> I often tell him [her husband] that our whole family would starve if we rely only on his monthly salary of RMB450. That amount of money I can earn

20. A Xunpu woman catching crabs (photograph by Ding Yuling).

21. A Xunpu woman making the breeding rocks for oyster (photograph by Ding Yuling).

from working just four or five days. He looks very smart sitting in the office of the Village Committee but he earns little money. He always laughs when I say so. Now my eldest daughter also works, selling aquatic produce in the market, and she can earn several dozen dollars a day. During the oyster harvest time, I can earn more than RMB100 a day. At first I had about 1,000 piles of rocks for oyster breeding; now I have more than 2,000. The rocks must be turned over three or four times a year. Therefore, I have to turn over about 200 rocks a day, yet I feel good because I can make money. He keeps his salary for his own use; he never gives it to me for family expenses.

Other village cadres also frankly told me that their salaries were far less than their wives' income. Sometimes the salary was not enough even for their expenses, and they had to borrow from their wives. While talking about their earning power, Xunpu women were confident and conceited. They admitted that working on the seashore is very laborious, but they are accustomed to hardship. Even in the cold winter, they go to the water barefooted in shorts.

It is during the past 20 years of reform that the Chinese coastal areas have enjoyed the most rapid growth. The consumption level of the people has risen rapidly, and the ensuing increase in demand for food has interested more Xunpu women, especially the younger ones, in selling at the market. Running the stalls is easy and lucrative. At present, no women under the age of 30 work on the oyster farms in the sea; this is left to their elders. Many younger women say: "I like to work in the markets. I am more independent there." Most of the girls do not like to go to school but prefer to work in the market. They think Xunpu women are born to do business.

Without the help of male family members, Xunpu women have accumulated a lot of experience in wholesale and retail sales. Wholesale transaction is carried out at the Quanzhou Aquatic Produce Wholesale Market, which was established after economic liberalization. This is the collection and distribution center that caters to other Chinese and foreign ports. The market starts to get busy by about 1 or 2 a.m. each day, when traders and their transport vehicles begin arriving there. The Xunpu women are ready and waiting for them. By about 4 a.m., unsold produce is rushed to other wet markets to be sold there.

At present, Xunpu women monopolize almost all the wet markets in various districts of Quanzhou. At the beginning of the economic liberalization, they were found only in urban central markets. With the development of market economy, small-sized wet markets sprang up in many urban residence districts, and Xunpu women rapidly moved in. To them, it is more attractive to sell in smaller markets because it is easier to establish good relationships with the residents in the neighborhood where taxation is lighter. With the aid of motorized transport, they have expanded and moved their business to various cities of southern Fujian province.

There is a very good cooperation among the Xunpu women sellers. They know they have to band together to avoid discrimination. Together they have been able to drive out sellers from other places. They often ridicule the non-locals for using calculators during sales transactions, because they can do mental arithmetic and are faster at it. They also take great delight in being able to trick their buyers. A woman at about the age of 20 said: "Sometimes people want to bargain down the price. Even then I can make a good sale for, in the blink of an eye, I can substitute the produce. They cannot spot my trick even with four pairs of eyes."

During my fieldwork, I accompanied some Xunpu women to their muddy oyster beds and to the wet markets in the early morning. I experienced their hardships firsthand. What do they do with the income they have earned from such hard work? Women of various ages assume different attitudes. The younger women tend to emphasize their own consumption or keep the income to themselves. Their families usually do not ask for the money. However, when money is needed to build the family house or for other good reasons, they will voluntarily give their contribution. The savings of a young woman are kept for her dowry, which embodies her self-worth and capability.

Middle-aged women, in contrast, are very thrifty and contribute their income to the family to buy boats, build houses, and feed the family. Generally speaking, the old women of Xunpu are relatively independent; the majority have their own savings. Although they do not work actively by the time they are 60, they can still man the stalls in nearby markets. There are some elders who do not need to work at all, thus turning their energies to organizing lineage and religious activities. Temples were repaired under their leadership. No matter what age group they are in, all share the same opinion about their arduous labor. They say: "We work hard and experience all kinds of hardships. In the past, we did all kinds of physical labor, on land and at sea, and still we never had enough to eat. Now, life is easier and more carefree. With more money in our hands, we can do anything we wish." This is the attitude of many Xunpu women. They do not regard hard work as suffering, for it has given them financial and personal freedom, a freedom they have achieved on their own.

Compared to policies in the pre-1978 period, the policy of economic liberalization has enabled Xunpu women to expand their economic activities. They have become more involved in village affairs as their economic roles became influential. For example, they formed a "Buddhist Society" to organize religious activities within the village. The Buddhist Society is a local non-governmental organization and is as influential as the male-dominated village government. The women raised funds to build and renovate temples in the village, and organized large-scale religious celebrations. Having their own income makes it easy for the women to raise funds and organize activities. They can decide how much to donate to sponsor village activities. Besides managing the religious affairs of the village, the women leaders of the Buddhist Society help to settle disputes within the village as well as disputes involving neighboring villages. When official interventions fail, the village government invariably seeks help from the Buddhist Society to settle the disputes through this non-governmental channel. Obviously, Xunpu women have made use of their favorable economic status to construct their gender status actively, making themselves distinct from those of other rural Minnan women.

Conclusion

This paper explores the relationship between the female gender and Chinese social structure in the face of a series of eventful episodes in the recent history of China. Eventful episodes in the 20th century have enabled us to divide the century into three distinct periods for analyzing how changes to Chinese society have affected women.

As we have seen, state policies inevitably played a prominent role in enhancing women's status. Policies are rules and resources that Xunpu women used to their maximum advantage. After the founding of New China in 1949, the state's policies broke down the production units based on households and replaced them with collective production based on communes. During this period, Xunpu women adapted to these circumstances while maintaining the original family and kinship system. They went out to work and took part in village and local political affairs. After 1978 and the collapse of the collective program, Xunpu women continued to make full use of the past practices and were able to expand their market network to cover a wide area. This economic activity within the fabric of family and village life reflects the interplay between structure and dynamic forces. According to the theory of structuration, structure is not a fixed social system but one that generates varied social systems that are reproduced by an agent's use of rules and resources. The village structure of Xunpu is still in the patriarchal family system, yet this structure is both restrictive and active. The dynamic role of the Xunpu women displayed after liberalization has given them a new status in their community. Their involvement and achievement in the economic sphere have contributed greatly to raising their social status.

Many scholars have explained that the Chinese patriarchal family system caused the submissive nature and position of women. Has their position really changed since the socialist revolution of China? Some scholars argue that it did not really liberate the women, pointing out that more laborious work was given to women under the disguise of letting them go into society to work (Diamond 1975; Stacey 1983; Wolf 1985), and women submissively accepted this due to the patriarchal system. The fact is that the Xunpu women have not tried to change the patriarchal system, for the practice of patrilineal inheritance still prevails. The woman's new right in decision-making is not gained in her natal family but in her husband's family. They are regarded as "full members" in their husband's families. They have to do their duty as "full members" when an ancestral temple or village temple is to be built. However, they enjoy the same rights as other male "full members." The opportunities for equal participation in leadership and economy during the 1949 to 1978 period, and the opportunities for commercial achievement in the post-1978 period, in the absence of competition from men, have enabled Xunpu women to exert their influence in the local community and redefine their gender status.

References

Diamond, Norma. 1975. Collectivization, Kinship, and the Status of Woman in Rural China. In Rayna R. Reiter, ed., *Toward an Anthropology of Women*, pp. 372–95. New York: Monthly Review Press.

Giddens, Anthony. 1984. *The Constitution of Society: Outline of the Theory of Structuration.* Oxford: Polity Press.

Judd, Ellen R. 1989. Niangjia: Chinese Women and Their Natal Families. *The Journal of Asian Studies* 48(3): 525–44.

Li, Yongji. 1994. Kanghun yu Zhencao Guanlian: Guangdong Zishunü he Buluofujia de Ge'an Fenxi (Marriage Resistance and Women's Virtue: Case Study of Zishunü and Buluofujia in Guangdong). In Ma Jianzhao, Qiao Jian, and Du Ruile, eds., *Hua'nan Hunyin Zhidu yu Funü Diwei* (Marriage System in South China and Women's Status). Nanning: Guangxi Minzu Chubanshe.

Stacey, Judith. 1983. *Patriarchy and Socialist Revolution in China.* Berkeley: University of California Press.

Stockard, Janice E. 1989. *Daughters of the Canton Delta: Marriage Patterns and Economic Strategies in South China, 1860–1930.* Stanford: Stanford University Press.

Topley, Marjorie. 1975. Marriage Resistance in Rural Kwangtung. In Margery Wolf and Roxane Witke, eds., *Women in Chinese Society,* pp. 67–88. Stanford: Stanford University Press.

Wolf, Margery. 1972. *Women and the Family in Rural Taiwan.* Stanford: Stanford University Press.

———. 1985. *Revolution Postponed: Women in Contemporary China.* Stanford: Stanford University Press.

Glossary

Chen Yi	陳翊
chuji she	初級社
dan	擔
Donghai People's Commune	東海公社

gaoji she	高級社
gongdai	公玳
haoye dadui	蠔業大隊
Xunpu	潯埔
yuye dadui	漁業大隊
Zhegu	鷓鴣

List of Contributors

Dr. DING Yuling is the Deputy Curator of the Quanzhou Maritime Museum in Quanzhou, Fujian. Her research interests are on Minnan communities in Fujian and the Chinese in Southeast Asia. Her e-mail address is <ding_yuling@yahoo.com.cn>.

Dr. FAN Ke is the Director of the Institute of Anthropology, Nanjing University. His research interests include ethnicity and nationalism, history and anthropology, cultural diversity in southern Fujian, and Muslim communities in south China. His most recent project is on social change in Yangzhou and Nanjing Muslim communities. His e-mail address is <fanke11@netscape.com>.

Dr. KUAH-PEARCE Khun Eng teaches anthropology at the Department of Sociology, The University of Hong Kong. Her research interests include the transnational relationship between Chinese overseas and the Fujianese emigrant villages of south China, popular religion and ancestor worship of the Chinese, and religion and politics in Singapore. Her most recent books are *State, Society and Religious Engineering: Reformist Buddhism in Singapore* (2003) and *Chinese Women and Their Cultural and Network Capitals* (edited, 2004). Her e-mail address is <kekuah@hkucc.hku.hk>.

Dr. PAN Hongli teaches at the Department of International Communication, Faculty of Human Sociology, Heian Jogakuin University in Japan. His research interests in southeast China include social organization and transformation, Chinese popular religion, and minority peoples, as well as the sociocultural interaction between the Chinese overseas and their hometowns in southeast Fujian. His recent book is *Gendai tonan chugoku no kanzuku shaki: Minnan nosonn no souzokusoshiki to sono henyou*

(Contemporary Han Society in Southeast China: Lineage Organization and Transformation in Rural Minnan) (2002). His e-mail address is <hongli@galaxy.ocn.ne.jp>.

Dr. Siumi Maria TAM has joined the Department of Anthropology, The Chinese University of Hong Kong since 1989. Her research interests include issues of cultural identity particularly in relation to migration, gender, work and the family. Her recent projects focus on the global and local identities among former Hong Kong emigrants, and the cultural construction of the Chinese family today, especially through examining relations among wives, mistresses, and husbands across the Hong Kong-China border. Her e-mail address is <siumitam@cuhk.edu.hk>.

Dr. TAN Chee-Beng teaches at the Department of Anthropology, The Chinese University of Hong Kong. His research interests include Chinese overseas, southern Fujian and Chinese in Southeast Asia, Chinese popular religion, cultural change and identity, and ethnicity and ethnic relations. His most recent book is *Chinese Overseas: Comparative Cultural Issues* (2004). His e-mail address is <cbtan@cuhk.edu.hk>.

Dr. WANG Mingming teaches anthropology in the Institute of Sociology and Anthropology, Peking University. He has done field research in Fujian, Taiwan, Yunnan, and France. His research interests include Chinese popular religion, historical anthropology, and comparative culture. His most recent publication is *Zou Zai Xiangtu Shang: Lishi Renleixue Zhaji* (Beyond Rural China: Essays toward an Anthropology of History) (2003). His e-mail address is <wangmingming@263.net>.

Index

fang, 71–73, 75–76, 92n5n7n8,
   93n10
Fangmu (Pang-Bu), *see* Bedroom
   (Guardian) Spirit
fanke, 148–150, 162
fanke shen, 146, 149–153, 162
fengshui, 81, 116, 119, 125
festivals: Chinese New Year, xi, 57,
   80, 88, 92n8, 99–102, 108–110,
   112, 115, 117n4, 123, 127, 131;
   Lantern Festival, xi, 12, 63n16,
   92n8; Qingming, 58, 62n9, 72,
   92n8, 102; Fifth-Moon Festival,
   102; Mid-Autumn Festival, xi,
   12, 92, 106; Universal Salvation
   Festival, xi, 12, 15, 18; Winter
   Solstice Day (Dongzhi), 92,
   102
fishery brigade unit (*yuye dadui*),
   172, 174, 183
folk religion, *see* Chinese religion
food offerings, 100–101, 105–106,
   110–111, 133–135, 142
fotou, 127–131, 136, 144

gender relations: desire for sons, xiv,
   112–113; division of labor, 166–
   175; marriage, 148–152; red
   flower (boy), 113; white flower
   (girl), 113
Guandi Miao (Quanzhou), 10
Guanyin (Goddess of Mercy), 101,
   112, 120

Hinduism, 5
Hong Kong, xv, 12, 105, 146–147,
   150, 152–157, 160, 176
huaqiao, 8, 147, 151, 162; *see also*
   overseas Chinese
Hui: identity, 36–37, 40–41, 46, 49–
   54, 58–60; official status, 42, 46,
   56, 60

inchik, 146, 153, 155
Indonesia, 157, 169
Islam, 40, 50, 62n10n11

Jiang Zemin, 95n18
jianggu (giving talks on antiquity), 84
Jinjiang, xv, 37, 44, 46, 52, 69, 91n2,
   98, 104, 119, 146–147, 149, 154,
   160n1, 162
jinxiang ceremony, 107–108, 110, 115,
   119
jinzhu, 71, 92n5, 96

Kitchen God, 100–101
KMT (Kuomintang), 8

Lanzhou, 112
Laorenhui (LRH), *see* Old Folks'
   Association
lineage: *chigong*, 92, 96; lineage estate,
   73, 83, 93n11; lineage revival, 73,
   80, 85, 89, 91, 94
Lingshan (ancestral grave of the Ding),
   xiii, 58

Macao, 12, 154
mah-jong, 76, 85
Malaysia, ix, 98, 101–102, 111–112
Manichaest temple, 6, 10
Mao Zedong, 2, 25, 112
Mazu temple,104
Middle East, xiii, 4
migrant family (defined), 160n3
minzu, xii, xvi, 46–47, 49–50, 52, 56,
   60, 62n10
mosques, 6, 10, 39, 62n11
Museum of Fujian and Taiwan
   Relations, xi, 10–11
Museum of Overseas Chinese History
   (Quanzhou), 10
Muslim, xii–xiii, 6, 37, 39–42, 47, 50,
   58, 61n5